Six
Ingredients
or Less ®

Also by Carlean Johnson

Six Ingredients or Less Chicken Cookbook

Six Ingredients or Less Cooking Light & Healthy

Six Ingredients or Less Pasta & Casseroles

Six Ingredients or Less®

Carlean Johnson

CJ
Books
Washington

Six Ingredients or Less®

Cover Design by Judy Petry
Illustrations by Judy Perkins and Arttoday.com
Typography and production design by Linda Hazen and Katie Church

Library of Congress Catalog Card Number: 2001118386
ISBN: 0-942878-05-1

_____

CJ Books
PO Box 922
Gig Harbor, WA 98335
1-800-423-7184
www.sixingredientsorless.com

Dedication

This book is dedicated to all the people in my life who have so generously given of their love and time in the writing and promoting of my cookbooks: To my children and grandchildren who never seem to get bored with what Mom and Gramma are doing. To my Mother, my brothers and my friends, who have stood by me and encouraged me over the years. And to Genie Smith, Betty Karr, and Cindy Adams, dear friends and coworkers, who continue to inspire me to write more books.

Acknowledgments

There are many parts to a cookbook and eventually they all start to fall into place. Authors are given the credit, but none of this is possible without the talent and devotion of so many other talented people.

I would like to thank my family for being willing to try so many "unfamiliar" dishes. When invited to dinner, they never know what they will be served. Lots of testing is involved in writing a cookbook, but thankfully, there are a lot of willing tasters.

I have been fortunate to have my daughter Linda Hazen with me again on this book. Her typography and production design is outstanding. Thank you Linda for being such a big part of my life and for your love and support in all of my endeavors. Linda is also the director of our Cooking School; with a husband and 3 children she wears many hats.

Another big thank you to Judy Petry for the cover design. She has designed all the Six Ingredients or Less cookbooks and thankfully, was willing to do yet another one. Judy is a very talented designer and so dedicated to her work. Thank you, Judy.

Judy Perkins took time out from her busy schedule to do some of the illustrations for us. Judy has been a life-long friend and I appreciate all the work she has done for us. Thank you, Judy, for your time and devotion to our cookbooks.

My granddaughter Paulina Hazen has contributed a new "Kids Corner" section to this edition. I want to thank her for the many hours she spent in the kitchen testing new recipes. There were times when she perhaps would have preferred doing something else, but she hung in there until the job was completed.

I want to offer a big thank you to Katie Church. Katie came on board rather late in the production of this book, but pitched right in and worked diligently to help bring it to completion. A thank you also to Katie's family for their patience and understanding during the long hours and weekends devoted to keeping us on schedule.

Table of Contents

Basic Recipe For Using This Book

- Always read through the recipe first. Then assemble and measure the ingredients before starting. These two simple steps will save you a lot of time. Also, check to see if you have the necessary pans and baking dishes. Then, prepare ingredients for the recipe, such as cooking bacon or rice, chopping nuts, grating cheese, chopping onions, etc.

- If necessary, remove eggs, butter and cream cheese from the refrigerator and allow time to soften. This is always necessary when creaming the ingredients.

- Eggs are easier to separate when cold, but the whites should be beaten at room temperature.

- Organization is the key to less stress-filled days and better meals on the table. If you have the ingredients in the house you are less likely to order out or go through the fast food window.

- Keep a well-stocked pantry for last minute entertaining. It doesn't always have to be fancy, but it does have to be good.

- A meat thermometer should always be used when cooking ground beef patties, meatloaf, roast, poultry and candies or any recipes where accuracy is important for safety as well as taste.

- Recipes and information not contained in former editions are highlighted in color.

Ingredients

Eggs - Eggs are large unless otherwise specified. Because the salmonella bacteria is occasionally found in raw eggs, any recipes using raw eggs have been eliminated from this edition. The risk remains extremely low, but could be a danger, particularly for very young children, pregnant women, the elderly, and those with a compromised immune system.

Butter - Butter is specified in all the recipes, but that doesn't necessarily mean you can't use margarine. Just make sure you know what you are buying. Margarine-like products are higher in water content and lower in fat. Make sure that your product contains at least 80% fat, which is usually in the form of vegetable oil. Also, if you are suddenly having problems with some of your recipes using butter (especially baked goods and candies) try a different brand until you get the results you want.

Cream Cheese - Cream cheese is another product that isn't necessarily what it used to be. Have you noticed how soft some of the cream cheese is, even chilled? Some of the companies are either adding something new or leaving something out, but they no longer work in some recipes.

Whipping Cream - See information on page 235.

Dry Ingredients/Liquid Ingredients - Individual cups are used to measure dry ingredients and should be measured by running a knife or spatula across the top. Cups with spouts are used for liquid ingredients; check measurement at eye level.

Vegetable Cooking Spray - Use for spraying baking dishes and pans to prevent sticking.

Process Cheese Spread - See information on page 263.

Cheese - 1 cup equals 4-ounces cheese.

Chocolate Chips - 2 cups equals one 12-ounce bag.

Flour - Measure by stirring the flour so it is less compact, then lightly spoon into measuring cup.

Servings - Means servings, not necessarily people.

Introduction

This is the cookbook for the cook who never has enough time. Time or lack of it, is a problem for many of us. Yet there is a concern about feeding our family well and selecting foods that are quick and nutritious as well as pleasing to everyone. This is a collection of recipes designed for the busy person who wants to serve tasty dishes with a minimum of time and effort. Included are basic recipes for everyday cooking as well as those for special occasions and holiday entertaining. Not only will you save time, but hopefully money as well.

With our ever-changing lifestyles, we do not have time to spend long hours in the kitchen planning meals from lengthy and complicated recipes. I saw a real need for a different type of cookbook; one that would get you in and out of the kitchen fast and yet could be a gourmet's delight or just a simple Sunday dinner. People I interviewed wanted to use basic types of foods they normally have on hand. They didn't have a lot of time to spend in the kitchen and many wanted to be able to share cooking responsibilities. Thus was born SIX INGREDIENTS OR LESS, a one of a kind cookbook that you will enjoy even if you are not in a hurry.

The time is right to revise and redesign SIX INGREDIENTS OR LESS. Recipes have been updated. Favorite time-tested recipes have remained and new recipes have been added. Every kitchen needs a book that belongs out on the counter where it can become worn with frequent use. This is that type of cookbook. It was written to be used daily for most of your cooking needs. Add your own personal touches and who would guess you hadn't spent all day in the kitchen. Cooking needn't be a chore and can be fun. Let others help in the preparation and time in the kitchen can be kept to a minimum.

These recipes are enjoyed in my kitchen and they can be enjoyed in yours.

Happy Cooking!

Carlean Johnson
Gig Harbor, Washington

Appetizers & Beverages

Apricot Almond Brie

1   wedge (8 to 10-ounces) Brie cheese
½   cup apricot preserves
1   tablespoon Grand Marnier liqueur
1   tablespoon toasted sliced almonds

1. Remove top rind from cheese. Place cheese on serving plate.

2. In a small saucepan, combine preserves and liqueur and heat until hot, but do not boil. Spoon some of the sauce over cheese (save remainder for later). Sprinkle almonds over top. Serve with butter crackers.

Probably my favorite appetizer, and definitely the one I use most often. Serve with a glass of white wine and your guests will never know it took you less than 10 minutes to put together.

Pineapple Cheese Balls

2   packages (8-ounces each) cream cheese, softened
1   can (8-ounces) crushed pineapple, drained
2   cups finely chopped pecans or walnuts, divided
¼   cup finely chopped green pepper
2   tablespoons finely chopped onion
1   tablespoon seasoned salt

1. In mixer bowl, beat cream cheese until smooth. Add crushed pineapple, 1 cup of the nuts, green pepper, onion and salt; mix well. Cover and chill.

2. Divide mixture in half; shape into balls and roll in nuts. Cover and chill several hours or overnight. Serve with crackers. This is especially good with Wheat Thins®. Makes 2 cheese balls.

Serve this most requested recipe to friends the next time you feel like entertaining. If desired, you can place the mixture in a small serving dish rather than rolling in the nuts. This eliminates the second cup of nuts, making the recipe somewhat less expensive.

Hot Artichoke Dip

1   can (9-ounces) artichoke hearts, drained, coarsely chopped
1   can (4-ounces) chopped green chilies
1   cup mayonnaise
1   cup grated Parmesan cheese

1. Combine ingredients in medium saucepan; heat through. Serve warm with chips, crackers or bread cubes.

*Variation: Add 1 cup smoked salmon, crab, bacon or chopped water chestnuts.
A 4th of July must for our family and friends.*

Dill Dip

⅔   cup mayonnaise
⅔   cup sour cream
1   teaspoon dry minced onion
1   teaspoon dill weed
1   teaspoon Beau Monde seasoning

1. Combine ingredients until well mixed. Cover and chill several hours or overnight to blend flavors. Remove from refrigerator just prior to serving. Makes 1⅓ cups.

An oldie, but still a favorite. Serve with chilled fresh vegetables such as carrot sticks, cherry tomatoes, raw cauliflower, celery, cucumber rounds, and green pepper.

Heavenly Fruit Dip

1   package (3.4-ounces) instant vanilla pudding mix
2½ cups half and half
1   tablespoon sugar
½   teaspoon rum extract
½   teaspoon vanilla extract

1. Combine ingredients in small mixing bowl; beat with rotary beater or lowest speed of mixer for about 2 minutes. Cover and chill several hours or overnight. Makes about 3 cups.

It takes about 3 minutes to mix this and have it chilling in the refrigerator. Serve as a dip with fresh fruit or as a dressing over fruit salad. Yum!

Linda's Guacamole

  2   ripe avocados
  1   clove garlic, minced
  Juice of ½ lime
  Dash hot pepper sauce
  1   small tomato, diced
  Salt and pepper to taste

1. Peel and slice avocados.

2. In a small bowl, combine avocado slices, garlic, lime juice, and pepper sauce; mash with fork until blended. Add tomato, salt and pepper to taste. Makes about 2 cups.

To prevent mixture from turning brown, cover with a layer of mayonnaise, spreading completely to the edge. Cover and store in refrigerator. When ready to serve , simply stir in the mayonnaise. Serve with nachos, quesadillas or fajitas.

Quesadillas   Oven 400°F

  8   (8-inch) flour tortillas
  3   cups (12-ounces) Monterey Jack cheese, shredded
  2   cups (8-ounces) Cheddar cheese, shredded
  Sliced black olives
  Chopped green onion
  Diced tomatoes

1. Place tortillas on ungreased baking sheet and bake 1½ minutes.

2. Remove from oven and sprinkle four tortillas with cheese and remaining ingredients. Top with remaining tortillas. Return to oven and bake until cheese is melted, 3 to 4 minutes. Cut into wedges and serve with salsa or guacamole.

Cucumber Sandwiches

Spread party-size slices of pumpernickel or rye bread with mayonnaise flavored with dill weed; top with thin cucumber slices and sprinkle lightly with freshly ground black pepper or with finely chopped tomatoes.

Camembert

You will need an 8-ounce box of Camembert cheese. Remove cheese and unwrap; return to box and replace cover. Remove any labels on box. Place on baking sheet and bake at 350°F for 25 to 30 minutes or until cheese is soft. Carefully remove top rind from cheese, keeping cheese in the box. Serve with bread chunks, breadsticks, or crackers.

These stuffed peppers make a colorful side dish with assorted menus and pasta dishes. It also makes a nice addition to a vegetable tray served with a salad and your favorite hot bread. Simply make the amount you desire.

Sausage Stuffed Mushrooms   Oven 350°F

ALLOW 2 TO 3 MUSHROOMS PER PERSON:

Large mushrooms
Italian sausage
Grated Parmesan cheese

1. Wipe mushrooms with damp cloth or clean with mushroom brush. Remove stems and center, making room for sausage.

2. Fill each mushroom with sausage until mounded and rather compact. Place on baking sheet and sprinkle lightly with Parmesan cheese. Bake 25 to 30 minutes or until sausage is cooked through. Serve hot.

Stuffed Pepper Shells   Oven 375°F

Small red peppers, halved and seeded
Mozzarella cheese, shredded
Pesto

1. Fill each pepper half with cheese. You will want to mound slightly because the cheese will compact as it melts. Drizzle with 1 to 2 teaspoons pesto. Place on a baking sheet and bake 10 to 12 minutes or until cheese is melted. Serve hot.

Variation: Use firm, but ripe, plum tomatoes. Cut tomatoes in half and remove flesh and seeds to form a bowl. Continue as above. You can omit the pesto and substitute Monterey Jack cheese with peppers for the Mozzarella cheese.

Microwave: Place on microwave dish and cook 1½ to 2 minutes or just until cheese has melted.

Sweet and Sour Wrap-Ups

Oven 375°F

- 1 pound lean bacon
- 2 cans (8-ounces each) water chestnuts
- 1½ cups ketchup
- ⅔ cup sugar
- ¼ cup fresh lemon juice

1. Cut bacon crosswise into thirds. Cut small water chestnuts in half or larger ones into thirds. Wrap 1 piece of bacon around each water chestnut. Secure with wooden toothpicks. Place in 13x9-inch baking dish and bake 30 minutes or until bacon is crisp. Drain off fat.

2. Combine remaining ingredients; pour over bacon. Reduce heat to 325° and bake 20 to 30 minutes, basting once or twice. Serve hot. Makes about 4 dozen.

These go fast. You can prepare the bacon and water chestnuts ahead; cover and refrigerate. Mix sauce, cover, and set aside.

Canned water chestnuts seem to be getting smaller. You may want to open the cans ahead and check, especially if you are serving a crowd.

Herbed Tomato Appetizers

Oven 350°F

- 1 French bread baguette
- ¼ cup herb or other flavored olive oil
- ½ teaspoon minced fresh garlic
- 18 thin slices Mozzarella cheese (to fit bread)
- 4 medium Plum tomatoes, thinly sliced

Chopped parsley or fresh basil leaves

1. Cut bread diagonally into ½-inch slices; place on baking sheet. Combine oil and garlic. Brush on bread slices. Bake 6 to 8 minutes or until lightly toasted.

2. Top each with a cheese slice, then a tomato slice. Lightly brush with remaining oil. Sprinkle with parsley or basil. Return to oven for just a minute to slightly soften the cheese. Makes 18 appetizers.

A richly glazed appetizer that can also be served as a main dish. To make life even easier, I like to marinate meat and poultry in a large zip-type bag. This way, you simply flip the bag over a few times instead of having to turn each piece.

Teriyaki Chicken Wings

Oven 350°F

16   chicken drumettes (meaty leg portion)
¼   cup light soy sauce
¾   cup firmly packed light brown sugar
1   tablespoon honey
4   thin slices fresh ginger
2   green onions, cut into 1-inch pieces

1. Rinse drummettes and pat dry. In a medium bowl, combine remaining ingredients, stirring to dissolve the sugar. Add chicken; cover and chill at least 3 hours, turning occasionally.

2. Place chicken in a foil-lined shallow baking pan. Bake 30 to 35 minutes, or until cooked through, basting frequently. Makes 8 servings of 2 each.

Water Chestnut Appetizers

Oven 400°F

1   can (8-ounces) water chestnuts
¼   cup light soy sauce
¼   cup sugar
1   pound lean bacon

1. If water chestnuts are large, cut in half. Combine soy sauce and sugar in a small dish; add water chestnuts and marinate 30 minutes, stirring occasionally.

2. Cut bacon slices in half crosswise and lengthwise. Wrap each water chestnut with 2 strips of bacon; secure with wooden toothpick. Arrange on rack in shallow baking pan and bake 20 to 30 minutes or until bacon is crisp. Drain on paper towels. Makes 3 to 4 dozen.

Sweet~Sour Meatballs

❖ ❖ ❖

Combine purchased meatballs with a sweet-sour sauce (Yoshida's® is very good) and heat through. If desired, add cubed pineapple. Place in a slow cooker to keep hot.

Dorothy's Coconut Chips

Oven 350°F

1 fresh coconut
1½ teaspoons butter, melted
Salt

1. Pierce eyes and drain coconut. Bake 30 minutes. Reduce heat to 250°.

2. Break coconut open with hammer. Trim off brown skin. Shave coconut into thin strips with vegetable peeler.

3. Spread coconut on large baking sheet. Bake 1 to 1½ hours or until lightly toasted. Coconut should be very light in color with just a touch of brown around the edges. Drizzle with melted butter, sprinkle lightly with salt and toss to coat. Makes 1½ cups.

A great snack for kids, or place on the coffee table for snacking during a cocktail party.

Caramel Corn

Oven 200°F

2 cups firmly packed light brown sugar
1 cup butter
1 teaspoon salt
½ cup light corn syrup
1 teaspoon baking soda
6 quarts popped popcorn

1. Combine first 4 ingredients in heavy saucepan. Bring to a boil and cook 5 minutes, stirring occasionally. Remove from heat and stir in baking soda.

2. Pour over popcorn; stir until coated. Spread in a large roasting pan. Bake 60 minutes, stirring every 15 minutes. Remove from oven and let cool. Makes 6 quarts.

Tip: My daughter likes to use microwaved popcorn. It usually takes 3 to 4 bags to get 6 quarts popped.

This may seem like a lot of caramel corn, but it really isn't. It goes very fast. If desired, add peanuts, pecans, walnuts, cashews or a mixture of nuts to popcorn before mixing with syrup mixture.

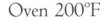

Holiday Glazed Nuts

Oven 200°F

This tasty treat has become a Christmas tradition in our family. Best if not made on a rainy day.

6	cups mixed nuts
1	cup sugar
½	cup light corn syrup
½	cup butter
1	teaspoon vanilla extract
1	teaspoon baking soda

1. Arrange nuts evenly in a 15x10-inch jelly roll pan.

2. Combine sugar, corn syrup and butter in a heavy medium saucepan. Cook over medium heat, until sugar melts, stirring frequently. Bring to a boil and cook, but do not stir, 5 minutes. Remove from heat. Carefully stir in vanilla extract and baking soda.

3. Pour mixture over nuts and stir well to coat. Separate nuts as best you can. Bake 60 minutes, stirring every 15 minutes. Carefully spread on foil. Using two forks, quickly separate the nuts and let cool. Makes about 6 cups.

Sugar Coated Peanut Snacks

Oven 200°F

Loved by all ages, these peanuts don't stay around very long. Very easy to make and can be frozen.

2	cups sugar
1	tablespoon packed light brown sugar
1½	teaspoons vanilla extract
4	cups raw peanuts

1. Combine both sugars and vanilla in a large heavy saucepan along with 1 cup water. Stir until well mixed and cook over medium heat until most of the sugar has dissolved. Add peanuts. Bring mixture to a boil and cook, stirring frequently, until syrup has cooked away and peanuts are coated. This happens very quickly at the end, so watch carefully.

2. Spread on a sprayed 15x10-inch jelly roll pan. Bake 60 minutes, stirring every 15 minutes. Makes about 4½ cups.

Holiday Eggnog Punch

2 quarts purchased eggnog
1 quart vanilla ice cream, softened
1 bottle (2-liters) lemon-lime soda pop, chilled

1. Combine eggnog and ice cream in a large punch bowl. Gently stir in the pop. Makes about 4 quarts.

This is a large recipe that will serve at least 12 to 14 people. If you have a small group, make half the recipe. The punch doesn't keep~so enjoy it all!

Easy Party Punch

1 package (.14-ounces) cherry Kool-Aid®
1 package (.14-ounces) raspberry Kool-Aid®
2 cups sugar
2 quarts water
1 can (46-ounces) unsweetened pineapple juice
2 quarts ginger ale (or to taste)

1. Combine first 5 ingredients, chill.

2. When ready to serve, stir in ginger ale. Makes 50 punch cup servings.

Kind to your budget. Great for picnics, wedding, showers, parties, etc.

Cranberry Punch

2 cans (46-ounces each) unsweetened pineapple juice
½ cup fresh lemon juice
2 cups cranberry juice
1 cup sugar
2 quarts ginger ale

1. Combine first 4 ingredients and chill.

2. When ready to serve, stir in ginger ale. Makes 40 punch cup servings.

Cappuccino

At home, Cappuccino can be made by pouring hot milk and hot espresso into a blender and processing until frothy. Sprinkle with nutmeg or cinnamon. Or, top with sweetened whipped cream and chocolate sprinkles.

This is a delicious nonalco-holic drink to serve with appe-tizers or as a beverage before dinner. It can be made in a pitcher using equal quantities or to taste.

This recipe makes a colorful punch for weddings, St. Patrick's Day, Christmas or any special occasion. For a White Wedding Punch, use va-nilla ice cream.

A refreshing party drink on a hot summer day or evening. The crushed pineapple adds that extra something special.

White Grape Juice Spritzer

PER DRINK:

 ¾   cup white grape juice, chilled
 ¾   cup lemon-lime soda pop, chilled
    Lime slices, cut in half

1. Combine ingredients. Pour into an attractive serving glass with ice. Add a lime slice and serve. Makes 1 serving.

Sherbet Punch

 2   quarts lime or raspberry sherbet
 3   quarts lemon-lime soda pop, chilled

1. Spoon sherbet into a large punch bowl; pour in pop to taste. Stir care-fully until most of the sherbet has dissolved. Makes 36 punch cup serv-ings.

Diablo Drink

 1   can (12-ounces) limeade concentrate
 1   juice can white rum
 1   bottle (2-liters) lemon-lime soda pop, chilled
    Crushed pineapple, drained
    Ice cubes

1. In pitcher, combine limeade concentrate and rum. Add pop to taste.

2. To each glass, add a little pineapple and ice cubes. Pour limeade mixture over top.

Strawberry Smoothie

1   can (6-ounces) frozen lemon juice concentrate
2   cups sliced strawberries
1   cup milk
½   cup sugar
6   ice cubes

1. Place ingredients in blender along with 1 cup water and blend until thoroughly mixed and ice is crushed. Serve right away. Makes 3 to 4 servings.

Linda's Orange Julius

1   can (6-ounces) frozen orange juice concentrate
1   teaspoon vanilla extract
1   cup milk
1   cup water
½   cup sugar
6   ice cubes

1. Place ingredients in blender and blend until thoroughly mixed and ice is crushed. Serve right away. Makes 3 to 4 servings.

Fresh Sunshine

1   quart freshly squeezed orange juice, chilled
1   bottle champagne, chilled

1. Combine orange juice and champagne and pour into stemmed glasses. Makes 8 to 10 servings.

Fruit Spritzer

Combine equal amounts of fruit juice (apple, cranberry, orange, etc.) with ginger ale.

Easy & Elegant

Place 3 or 4 raspberries, blackberries or peach slices in champagne flutes. Slowly fill with champange.

An elegant "wake up" drink for a brunch.
Variation: Add half orange juice and half peach nectar.

25

Can you believe our sweeping passion for flavored coffees? Mocha seems to be quite popular, but my vote is for white chocolate. For a richer drink, use equal amounts of whole milk and half and half.

Tip: *The amount of batter and rum used depends on the size of cups and individual tastes. Experiment to find what you like. This recipe makes a lot. It also makes a nice Christmas or hostess gift.*

White Hot Chocolate

4	ounces good quality white chocolate
⅔	cup brewed coffee
1	teaspoon vanilla or almond extract
3	cups whole milk

1. Coarsely chop white chocolate. Melt in heavy saucepan over very low heat or in top of a double boiler. Add coffee, extract and milk; mix until smooth. Increase heat and bring to a simmer, but not a boil. Carefully pour into blender and blend until frothy. Pour into cups and serve.

Hot Buttered Rum

1	pound light brown sugar
1	pound butter, room temperature (do not substitute)
1	quart vanilla ice cream (quality brand), softened
	Dry white rum

1. Combine brown sugar and butter in a large mixer bowl; beat until smooth. Add ice cream; beat until well mixed. Store in covered container in freezer.

2. Remove from freezer when ready to serve. For each cup desired, add 1 heaping tablespoon batter to cup; fill with hot water and add 2 teaspoons rum (or to taste). Stir to melt batter. Serve hot.

Hot Spiced Coffee

4	cups coffee
1	stick cinnamon
1	teaspoon whole allspice
2	small packages sweetener or 1 tablespoon sugar
	Dash nutmeg

1. Heat coffee; add remaining ingredients and simmer 2 to 3 minutes.

Breads

English Muffin Bread

Oven 350°F

1 package dry yeast
1 teaspoon salt
1 tablespoon sugar
1½ teaspoons oil
5 cups flour
Yellow cornmeal

English Muffin bread is very good for sandwiches, but it is especially good for making toast. Just top with butter and your favorite jam.

1. In a large bowl, combine all the ingredients except the cornmeal. Stir in 2 cups hot tap water and mix thoroughly. Tightly cover bowl and let stand at room temperature at least 6 hours or overnight. Dough may double and fall, but that is okay.

2. Butter two 7x3-inch loaf pans. Sprinkle lightly with cornmeal, turning to coat evenly. Shake out excess.

3. Punch down dough; divide in half. Shape into 2 loaves, as best as you can (dough will be sticky) and place in pans. Cover and let rise until doubled, about 1½ hours.

4. Bake 60 minutes or until golden brown and bread tests done. Remove from pans and cool on rack. Makes 2 loaves.

Yeast ❖ Yeast ❖ Yeast ❖ Yeast ❖ Yeast ❖ Yeast

Yeast is a living substance that causes the bread to rise. Granulated yeast is probably the most popular form of yeast used and is readily available and can be purchased in small ¼-ounce packages, in 4-ounce jars and sometimes in bulk packages. Yeast will expire so be sure to check the date on the package.

Active dry yeast can be regular yeast or the rapid rise. Both must be activated with a warm liquid. For best results, rapid rise yeast should be used in recipes calling for that particular type of yeast.

There are also special yeasts for Bread Machines. Experiment and see what works best for you.

Batter Bread

Oven 375°F

This is exceptionally easy if using a food processor.

1	package dry yeast
1¼	cups water (105° to 115°F)
2	tablespoons honey
2	tablespoons butter
1	teaspoons salt
3	cups flour

1. Combine yeast, water and honey in small bowl; stir slightly. Let stand until doubled in size, about 10 minutes.

2. In large bowl, combine yeast mixture, butter, salt and 2 cups of the flour. If using mixer, beat on low speed until blended. Beat at medium speed for about 1 minute. Stir in remaining flour with wooden spoon. Cover and let rise in warm place, about 1 hour or until doubled.

3. Stir batter down; spoon into a sprayed 9x5-inch loaf pan. Cover and let rise in warm place, about 45 minutes or until doubled. Bake 35 to 45 minutes or until browned and bottom of loaf sounds hollow when tapped. Remove from pan and cool on rack. Makes 1 loaf.

Variations

Rye: Combine ingredients with 2 cups white flour, then add ½ cup white flour and 1 cup rye flour.

Whole Wheat: Combine with 1½ cups white flour and ½ cup whole wheat flour, then add an additional cup of whole wheat flour.

Egg: Use only ½ cup water with yeast. Add 3 large eggs along with the first 2 cups of flour.

Cheese: Add 1 cup (4-ounces) shredded Cheddar cheese along with the remaining 1 cup flour.

Breads

Today's busy lifestyles prevent us from making fresh homemade bread like our Mothers or Grandmothers used to make, but what a way to welcome your family home. The aroma is heavenly. It doesn't always have to be fancy, but it should be good.

Focaccia

Oven 425°F

1 package dry yeast
2 to 2½ cups flour
1 teaspoon sugar
½ teaspoon salt
1 tablespoon, plus 1 teaspoon olive oil
Garlic salt or grated Parmesan cheese

1. In a large mixer bowl, combine yeast, 1½ cups of the flour, sugar and salt. Add ¾ cup hot tap water and the 1 tablespoon olive oil. Beat until smooth. By hand, stir in enough of the remaining flour to make a soft, but not sticky dough. Place on a lightly floured surface and knead about 5 minutes. Place in a lightly greased bowl. Cover and set in warm place until doubled, about 60 minutes.

2. Lightly spray a 12-inch pizza pan or large baking sheet with nonstick spray. With fingers, flatten dough into an 11-inch circle. Prick surface of dough with a fork. Brush with remaining 1 teaspoon olive oil. Sprinkle lightly with garlic salt or Parmesan cheese. Let rise in warm place 30 minutes. Bake 18 to 20 minutes or until golden. Best served warm. Makes 10 servings.

Sit back and enjoy the compliments when you serve your own, hot from the oven Focaccia. Makes delicious bread for sandwiches and a good base for a pizza. This recipe works well in my bread machine using the dough cycle.

Variation: *Brush with oil. Top with ⅔ cup narrow strips of red and green peppers. Sprinkle with ¼ cup (1-ounce) Mozzarella cheese, shredded. Or omit oil and spread lightly with 2 to 3 tablespoons pesto. Top with ¼ cup chopped oil-packed sun-dried tomatoes.*

Testing for Doneness
❉ ❉ ❉

Always check breads just before the minimum baking time. Yeast type breads should be nicely browned. Carefully turn out bread and tap the bottom with your fingers. If it sounds hollow, it should be done. If not, return to pan and bake a few minutes longer. Quick breads should be dry when a tester inserted in center comes out clean.

My mother told me about this recipe. Different, delicious and very easy to prepare. My daughter likes to add 1½ teaspoons of fresh orange peel for a delicious citrus flavor.

Easy Dinner Rolls

Oven 400°F

1   box (8½-ounces) yellow or white cake mix
1   package dry yeast
½   teaspoon salt
1¼   cups hot tap water
2½   to 3 cups flour

1. Combine cake mix, yeast and salt. Add water and flour to make a soft dough. (Dough will be quite sticky.) Cover; let rise until double, 1 to 1 ½ hours.

2. Stir down dough; spoon onto a well-floured surface. Gently turn dough a couple times to lightly coat with flour. Shape into desired size rolls and place on sprayed baking sheets. Or shape into balls and place in sprayed muffin tins. Cover and let rise until double, about 1 hour. Bake 10 to 15 minutes or until golden. Makes 15 to 18 rolls.

Refrigerator Rolls

Oven 400°F

2   packages dry yeast
3   large eggs, beaten
½   cup shortening
½   cup sugar
1½   teaspoons salt
4½   cups flour

1. Dissolve yeast in ¼ cup water (105° to 115°F). Set aside for 10 minutes.

2. Combine yeast mixture, eggs, shortening, sugar, salt and 2½ cups flour with 1 cup water. Beat by hand or with mixer until smooth. Add enough remaining flour to make a soft dough. Cover; let rise until doubled, about 1 to 1½ hours.

3. Punch dough down. (At this point you can shape into rolls, let rise and then bake or you can refrigerate dough.) If refrigerated, remove about 3 hours before baking. Shape into desired size rolls. Place on baking sheet and let rise until doubled, about 2 hours. Bake 12 to 15 minutes or until lightly browned. Makes about 18 to 20 rolls.

Easy Cheese Rolls

Bread Machine
Oven 400°F

1½	cups milk
1	cup (4-ounces) Cheddar cheese, shredded
1	tablespoon sugar
1	teaspoon salt
4	cups flour
1	package dry yeast

1. Combine ingredients in pan in order given or as directed for your bread machine. Start dough cycle and mix thoroughly, adding a small amount of water or flour if needed to make a nice dough that isn't sticky or dry.

2. When cycle is completed, remove from pan and punch down. Divide into 15 pieces (about golf ball size). Form each into a smooth ball and place in greased muffin cups. Cover with towel or waxed paper and let rise until doubled in size, about 45 to 60 minutes.

3. Bake 12 to 14 minutes or until golden. Remove and serve or let cool. Makes 15 rolls.

A rather sharp tangy flavor of Cheddar cheese is enclosed in one of the lightest rolls ever. The dough cycle of the bread machine makes this recipe a dream for the busy cook. These also freeze beautifully. Don't use this recipe unless your machine will hold 4 cups flour on the dough cycle — the dough will rise quite high and could overflow the machine.

Tip: *If shiny tops are desired, brush hot rolls with a little melted butter.*

Pizza Dough

Bread Machine
Oven 425°F

1½	cups water
3¼	to 4 cups flour
½	teaspoon salt
1	package dry yeast

1. Combine ingredients in pan in order given or as directed for your bread machine. Start dough cycle and mix thoroughly, adding a small amount of water or flour if needed to make a smooth dough.

2. When cycle is completed, remove from pan and punch down. Press dough into desired pans, add toppings and bake until cooked through and cheese is melted.

   Tip: **Thin crust:** two 16-inch pizzas

   Thick crust: two 12-inch pizzas

   Individual: five 9-inch pizzas

Pizza dough mixed in a bread machine is a breeze to make and so much better and economical than purchased crusts. Your bread machine must be able to hold 4 cups flour on the dough cycle. This recipe has an added bonus of being very low in fat, only 4 grams for the entire recipe.

An old favorite. Serve hot with plenty of honey and butter.

Banana Bread

Oven 350°F

1	cup butter, softened
1¾	cups sugar
2	cups mashed very ripe bananas
4	large eggs, well beaten
2	teaspoons baking soda
2¼	cups flour

1. In a large mixer bowl, cream butter and sugar. Add bananas and eggs. Combine baking soda and flour. Add to banana mixture; stirring by hand, until flour is moistened.

2. Pour batter into two sprayed 9x5x3-inch loaf pans. Bake 50 to 55 minutes or until tester inserted in center comes out clean. Run knife around edge and turn out immediately. Cool on rack. Makes 2 loaves.

Muffins
❀ ❀ ❀

Muffins are wonderful breads to make when you don't have a lot of time to cook, but you still want something hot from the oven. They are easy to make, but you do need to follow a few simple rules.

Mix batter only until the ingredients are moistened. The batter should appear lumpy, otherwise you will have tough muffins full of holes. Remove muffins from the tin immediately after baking and serve warm. Muffins are rarely that good reheated, so enjoy!

Cornbread Muffins

Oven 400°F

1	cup yellow cornmeal
½	teaspoon salt
2	tablespoons sugar
2	tablespoons flour
2	tablespoons shortening
2	large eggs, separated

1. In mixing bowl, combine first 4 ingredients. Add 1 cup boiling water. Add shortening and stir until mixture is moistened and no lumps remain.

2. Let cool in refrigerator while beating egg whites. Beat egg whites until stiff, but not dry. Remove mixture from refrigerator; stir in the egg yolks to blend. Fold in the egg whites. Pour into greased muffin cups, filling ¾ full. Bake 15 to 20 minutes or until golden and tester inserted in center comes out clean. Makes 6 to 8 muffins.

Cheesy Muffins

Oven 425°F

2 cups flour
1 tablespoon, plus 1 teaspoon baking powder
¾ teaspoon salt
2 tablespoons butter, chilled
1 cup (4-ounces) sharp Cheddar cheese, shredded
1 cup milk

1. Combine flour, baking powder and salt in medium mixing bowl. Cut in butter with a fork or pastry blender. Stir in cheese until coated with flour mixture. Add milk and stir just until flour mixture is moistened.

2. Spoon into 12 sprayed muffin cups. Bake 12 to 15 minutes or until tester inserted in center comes out clean. Makes 12 muffins.

A biscuit-like muffin with crunchy sides on top. Best eaten hot from the oven. If using a dark pan, reduce heat to 400°.

Bran Muffins

Oven 375°F

2 cups milk
2 cups All-Bran® cereal
¼ cup butter, softened
2 large eggs
5 teaspoons baking powder
2 cups flour

1. Pour milk over cereal. Let stand until soft (about 5 minutes).

2. Cream butter in mixer bowl. Add eggs and beat until smooth. Add bran mixture. Combine baking powder and flour. Add to bran mixture, stirring just enough to moisten the flour. Spoon into sprayed muffin cups, filling almost full. Bake 25 to 30 minutes or until tester inserted in center comes out clean. Makes 12 large muffins.

Note: Recipe does not require sugar.

A wonderfully light and not too sweet muffin.

Sally Lunn Muffins

Oven 400°F

½ cup butter, softened
⅓ cup sugar
1 large egg
3 teaspoons baking powder
1½ cups flour
¾ cup milk

1. In mixer bowl, cream butter and sugar until thoroughly blended. Add egg and mix well. Combine baking powder and flour. Add to the creamed mixture alternately with the milk, starting and ending with flour.

2. Spoon into sprayed muffin cups, filling ¾ full. Bake 18 to 20 minutes or until tester inserted in center comes out clean. Remove and place on rack. Best served right away. Makes 12 large muffins.

Muffin Tips

If you want to be really organized, you can mix the dry ingredients and the liquid ingredients ahead, but do not combine. Lightly spray muffin tin and set aside.

Tip: *To prevent muffin tins from warping, fill any empty cups with water.*

Whole Wheat Muffins

Oven 375°F

2 cups whole wheat flour
½ cup sugar
3½ teaspoons baking powder
1 large egg, lightly beaten
3 tablespoons butter, melted
1½ cups milk

1. In large mixing bowl, combine first 3 ingredients. Combine remaining ingredients and add to dry mixture stirring just until flour is moistened. Spoon into sprayed muffin cups, filling ¾ full. Bake 25 to 30 minutes or until tester inserted in center comes out clean. Makes 12 muffins.

Popovers

Oven 425°F

    1   cup flour
    ½   teaspoon salt
    1   cup milk
    2   large eggs

1. Combine ingredients in small bowl; mix with hand mixer just until smooth. Pour into sprayed muffin cups or custard cups. Bake 35 to 40 minutes or until golden. Serve immediately. Makes 8 popovers.

Kristina Kringler

Oven 350°F

    1   cup chilled butter, plus 2 tablespoons melted
    2   cups flour, divided
    2   teaspoons almond extract, divided
    3   large eggs
    1½   cups sifted powdered sugar
         Chopped walnuts or pecans

1. With 2 knives or a pastry blender, cut ½ cup of the butter into 1 cup of the flour. Sprinkle 2 tablespoons water over mixture; lightly mix with a fork. Form into a ball; divide in half. On ungreased baking sheet pat each half into a strip 12x3-inches, allowing about 3 inches between the strips.

2. In medium saucepan, bring ½ cup butter and 1 cup water to a full boil. Remove from heat; quickly stir in 1 teaspoon almond extract and the remaining 1 cup flour. Return pan, over low heat, and stir until mixture forms a ball; this takes about a minute. Remove from heat. Add eggs; beat vigorously until smooth. Spread half of mixture evenly over each strip completely covering the dough. Bake 35 to 45 minutes or until lightly browned. Remove from baking sheet and cool on rack.

3. Combine remaining 2 tablespoons butter with powdered sugar, 1 teaspoon almond extract and 1 tablespoon water. Beat until smooth. It may be necessary to add more powdered sugar or water to make a nice consistency for spreading. Spread strips with frosting and sprinkle with nuts. Makes about 12 servings.

Variation: Add ¼ cup shredded sharp Cheddar cheese or 2 tablespoons finely chopped pecans and 1 teaspoon lemon zest.

Have some friends over and serve fresh fruit with Heavenly Fruit Dip and Kristina Kringler. They'll love it and you won't have spent all day in the kitchen.

This versatile crepe is good for many things, such as pancakes, main dishes, and desserts. The best thing about crepes is that they can be made ahead and frozen.

Basic Crepes

3 large eggs, well beaten
1 cup milk
1 tablespoon sugar
¼ teaspoon salt
¾ cup flour

1. Beat together the eggs and milk in a mixer bowl. Add remaining ingredients and beat with mixer until smooth.

2. Pour about 2 tablespoons batter into a buttered 8-inch skillet that has been preheated. Working quickly, rotate pan to spread batter evenly over the bottom. When cooked (this takes just a minute) turn crepe and cook other side.

3. Turn out on dish and leave flat or roll up. Repeat, lightly buttering pan for each crepe. Makes about 16 crepes.

Cream Puffs   Oven 400°F

½ cup butter
1 cup water
1 cup flour
4 large eggs

Leave cream puffs whole and frost with powdered sugar glaze. Or fill with whipped cream, pudding or ice cream. Tiny cream puffs can also be filled with assorted meat fillings and served as appetizers.

1. In medium saucepan, bring butter and water to a rolling boil. Add flour and stir vigorously over low heat until mixture forms a ball, about 1 minute. Remove from heat.

2. Add eggs, one at a time, beating thoroughly. Drop from spoon onto ungreased baking sheet, about 3-inches apart, making desired size cream puffs. Bake 45 to 50 minutes for large and 30 minutes for small cream puffs, or until lightly browned and dry. Allow to cool. Cut off tops; remove soft dough and fill with desired filling. Makes 10 to 12 large or 35 to 40 small cream puffs.

Breads .....in a Jif

Supper Cheese Bread
Oven 400°F

- 1½ cups baking mix
- 1 large egg
- ¼ cup milk
- 1 cup (4-ounces) Cheddar cheese, shredded, divided
- 1 teaspoon poppy seeds
- 2 tablespoons butter, melted

1. Combine baking mix, egg, milk and ½ cup of the cheese; stir just until moistened. The dough will be stiff but sticky. Pat dough evenly onto bottom of a sprayed 9-inch pie pan. Sprinkle with cheese and poppy seeds; pour butter over top. Bake 20 to 25 minutes or until lightly browned. Cut into wedges and serve hot. Makes 6 servings.

A definite cheese flavor. Best served fresh from the oven, but can be reheated.

Herb-Cheese Bread
Oven 350°F

- 1 loaf French bread, halved lengthwise
- ⅓ cup olive oil
- ½ teaspoon dried oregano, crushed
- 2 teaspoons dried basil, crushed
- 1 cup (4-ounces) Monterey Jack cheese, shredded
- 1 cup (4-ounces) Cheddar cheese, shredded

1. Combine oil, oregano and basil. Spread on cut sides of bread. Combine cheese and sprinkle on bottom half of bread, using all the cheese. Top with second half of bread. Press slightly; making sure cheese is inside the bread. Wrap in foil. Bake 10 to 15 minutes or until hot. Cut into 1½-inch slices. Makes 10 to 12 servings.

This bread packs an impressive amount of flavor. Serve with Barbecue Ribs or Grilled Chicken. Add potato salad and corn on the cob and you have a full meal everyone will enjoy.

I wouldn't plan on leftovers with this recipe. You can reheat bread in the oven, but it doesn't work well in the microwave.

Poppy Seed French Bread

Oven 400°F

1	large loaf unsliced French bread
¾	cup butter, melted
1	teaspoon poppy seeds
¼	teaspoon garlic powder
½	teaspoon paprika

1. Remove crust from top and sides of loaf. Slice lengthwise down the center, being careful to cut down to the bottom crust, but not through it. Then cut bread in ½-inch slices, again being careful not to cut through the bottom crust.

2. Combine remaining ingredients. Brush mixture over top and sides of bread and between the slices (you may not need all of the mixture, depending on the size of the bread). Wrap bread in foil and set aside until just before serving.

3. When ready to bake, fold foil down on all sides; place on baking sheet. Bake 12 to 15 minutes or until golden brown. Serve on plate or in basket and have guests pull off pieces of bread to eat.

Quick Pecan Rolls

Oven 450°F

Occasionally we just have to have something to satisfy our sweet tooth. I like to make these on a lazy Saturday morning when I can linger over a cup of hot coffee and enjoy a roll or two.

½	cup firmly packed brown sugar
½	cup butter, melted
36	to 48 pecan halves, depending on size
	Cinnamon
2	cups baking mix

1. In muffin tin, place 2 teaspoons brown sugar and 2 teaspoons melted butter in each of the 12 cups; stir to blend. Place 3 to 4 pecan halves in each cup. Sprinkle lightly with cinnamon.

2. Combine baking mix and ½ cup water until a soft dough forms; beat about 20 strokes. Spoon into muffin cups. Bake 8 to 10 minutes; watch carefully so they don't burn. Invert pan on waxed paper, leaving pan over rolls for a minute. Makes 12 rolls.

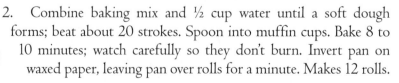

Quick & Easy Blueberry Muffins Oven 425°F

2   cups baking mix
¼   cups sugar
1   cup sour cream
2   large eggs, lightly beaten
½   cup chopped walnuts or pecans
1   cup blueberries

1. In medium bowl, combine baking mix and sugar. Combine sour cream and eggs and add to flour mixture, stirring just enough to moisten. Gently fold in nuts and blueberries. Spoon into sprayed muffin cups filling ¾ full. Bake 20 to 25 minutes or until tester inserted in center comes out clean. Remove from pan and place on rack to cool. Makes 12 muffins.

A baking mix comes in handy for these quick easy muffins. Serve with Roasted Chicken, Garlic Mashed Potatoes adn fresh broccoli or asparagus.

Jiffy Cornbread Muffins   Oven 350°F

1   box (8½-ounces) corn muffin mix
1   box (8½-ounces) yellow cake mix
2   large eggs, lightly beaten
2   tablespoons vegetable oil
⅓   cup milk

1. Place both mixes in a medium mixing bowl. Stir to combine and to break up any lumps. Add eggs, oil and milk along with ½-cup water. Stir just until moistened. Spoon into sprayed muffin cups. Bake 18 to 20 minutes or until tester inserted in center comes out clean. Makes 12 muffins.

If you like cornbread, you'll like this lighter, rather sweet version of one of our favorite recipes. If desired, you can add ½ cup fresh or frozen corn.

41

Sour Cream Muffins

Oven 400°F

This simple muffin recipe is easy to make and is great anytime. Serve for breakfast along with sausages and fresh fruit. Or serve with a nice spinach salad or a hot bowl of soup.

½ cups sugar
3 teaspoons baking powder
2 cups flour
½ cup chilled butter, sliced
2 large eggs, lightly beaten
½ cup sour cream

1. In medium mixing bowl, combine sugar, baking powder and flour. Cut butter into flour mixture, using a pastry blender or two knives, until mixture resembles small peas.

2. Add eggs and sour cream; stir until all the flour is moistened (batter will be quite stiff). Spoon into a sprayed muffin tin, filling about ⅔ full. Bake 18 to 20 minutes or until golden and tester inserted in center comes out clean. Makes 12 muffins.

Bacon & Corn Muffins

Oven 400°F

These cornbread muffins have a flavorful hint of onion, bacon and cheese. I find it really hard to eat just one.

Note: *If using the older smaller muffin tins, this recipe will make 12 muffins. If using the larger size most commonly used today, it will make 9 muffins.*

1 box (8½-ounces) corn muffin mix
⅓ cup milk
1 large egg
6 slices bacon, cooked and crumbled
⅓ cup finely chopped onion
¼ cup (1-ounces) Cheddar cheese, shredded

1. Place corn muffin mix in small mixing bowl. Add milk and egg; stir mixture just enough to moisten. Gently fold in the bacon, onion and cheese. Spoon into a sprayed muffin tin. Bake 10 to 15 minutes or until golden and cooked through. Makes 9 to 12 muffins.

Jalapeño Corn Muffins

Oven 375°F

1 box (8½-ounces) corn muffin mix
1 large egg, lightly beaten
⅓ cup milk
¾ cup (3-ounces) Monterey Jack cheese with peppers

1. Combine corn muffin mix, egg and milk in a medium bowl, mixing just until moistened. Spoon into a sprayed muffin tin.

2. Cut cheese into 6 cubes. Place one in each muffin cup pressing down with a spoon and making sure each is covered with batter. Bake 10 to 12 minutes or until golden and firm to the touch. Remove and serve hot. Makes 6 muffins.

Baking Powder Biscuits

Oven 450°F

2 cups flour
3 teaspoons baking powder
1 teaspoon salt
¼ cup shortening
¾ cup milk

1. Combine flour, baking powder and salt in a mixing bowl. Cut in shortening with two knives or a pastry blender. Add milk and stir until flour is moistened.

2. Turn out on lightly floured board and knead about 20 times. Roll out or pat to ½-inch thickness. Cut with biscuit cutter and place on ungreased baking sheet. Bake 8 to 10 minutes or until lightly browned. Makes 12 biscuits.

Biscuit Dough

❖❖❖

Biscuit Dough should be rolled or patted out evenly. If using a biscuit or cookie cutter, always press straight down. This makes for a better looking biscuit, scone or cookie.

You don't have a cookie cutter? Pat the dough into a square and cut into small squares with a knife.

Dough placed with edges touching will have a softer crust. Those placed slightly apart will be more brown and have more crust.

Easy, quick and amazingly, very good.

Note: *If not using a food processor, cut butter into flour until mixture is crumbly or butter pieces are smaller than a pea. Add sour cream and mix until all the flour is stirred into the dough. You may need to mix with your hands.*

You really can't beat a basic hot scone filled with butter and your favorite jam, but if you want, you can add any of the following ingredients for a different tasty treat: fresh lemon or orange peel, chopped nuts, chocolate or white chocolate chips, dried apricots, raisins, dried or fresh blueberries or dried cranberries.

Sour Cream Drop Biscuits
Oven 450°F

    1   cup self-rising flour
    ¼   cup butter, cut into small pieces
    ½   cup sour cream

1. Place flour and butter in a food processor. Using multipurpose blade, process quickly 3 to 4 times until mixture is crumbly. Add sour cream and process just until mixture is moistened. Dough will be thick.

2. Gently form into 8 balls and place on a baking sheet. Bake 12 to 15 minutes or until lightly browned and cooked through. Makes 8 biscuits.

Scones
Oven 400°F

    2   cups flour
    ¼   cup sugar
    1   tablespoon baking powder
    ½   teaspoon salt
    ½   cup chilled butter, cut up
    ¾   cup milk

1. In a medium mixing bowl, combine flour, sugar, baking powder and salt. Add butter and cut in with two knives or a pastry blender, until mixture resembles small crumbs. (This could also be done in a food proessor.)

2. Add milk and mix just until combined; mixture will be sticky. Place on a sprayed baking sheet. Flatten the dough into about a ¾-inch thick round. Cut into 8 wedges, but do not separate. If desired, sprinkle lightly with sugar. Bake 15 to 18 minutes or until lightly browned and cooked through. Makes 8 scones.

Cinnamon Rolls

Oven 350°F

1   package dry yeast
2   tablespoons sugar
2½   to 2¾ cups baking mix
⅓   cup cinnamon sugar
2   tablespoons butter, melted
2   cups powdered sugar

1. Dissolve yeast in ¾ cup warm water (110-115°F); pour into mixing bowl. Add sugar and baking mix; stir until well mixed, but slightly sticky.

2. Turn out onto a lightly floured surface and knead 4 to 5 minutes or until smooth. Roll into a 14x12-inch rectangle. Brush with melted butter. Sprinkle with cinnamon sugar. Roll up, starting with the long side; pinch dough to seal. Cut roll into 12 equal sections. Place in a sprayed muffin tin or on baking sheet and flatten to about a 3-inch circle. Bake 12 to 15 minutes or until lightly browned. Remove and place on cooling rack.

3. Combine powdered sugar with just enough water to make a thick glaze. Drizzle over warm rolls. Makes 12 rolls.

I love these cinnamon rolls with a cup of steaming hot coffee. They are a little different in that they aren't overly sweet or gooey. And, that's right, no "rising" necessary.

Cinnamon Sugar

½ cup sugar
2 teaspoons cinnamon

Combine and store in a tightly covered bottle or jar. Convenient to have on hand for breads, toast, coffee cakes and cookies.

Blueberry Drop Biscuits

Oven 375°F

1   cup flour
½   teaspoon salt
1½   teaspoons baking powder
2   tablespoons butter, chilled
½   cup milk
½   cup fresh blueberries

1. Combine flour, salt and baking powder in a mixing bowl. Cut in butter with two knives or a pastry blender. Add milk, stirring just enough to moisten. Carefully fold in blueberries. Drop by tablespoon onto a sprayed baking sheet. Bake 12 to 14 minutes or until lightly browned. Makes 12 biscuits.

Serve these easy to make biscuits anytime. If desired, substitute dried cranberries for the blueberries.

Variation: Omit tomatoes and top with assorted cheese such as Swiss, Mozzarella, Cheddar and Gorgonzola. Add a little chopped onion, oregano and freshly ground black pepper.

Tomato-Garlic Pizza Bread   Oven 425°F

   1   package (10-ounces) refrigerated pizza dough
   2   small garlic cloves, minced
  ¼   teaspoon dried oregano
   1   cup (4-ounces) Mozzarella cheese
   2   plum tomatoes, chopped

1. On a sprayed baking sheet, pat dough into about a 12x8-inch rectangle. Sprinkle with garlic, oregano, and then the cheese. Top with chopped tomato. Bake 10 to 12 minutes or until crust is golden and cheese has melted. Makes 6 to 8 servings.

Garlic Bread   Oven 350°F

   1   loaf French bread
  ½   cup butter, softened
   1   to 2 small garlic cloves, minced

1. Cut bread in slices or cut in half lengthwise. Place on baking sheet.

2. Combine butter and garlic, mixing well. Spread evenly on bread. Bake 8 to 10 minutes or until lightly toasted.

Tip: If a softer bread is desired, wrap in foil and bake.

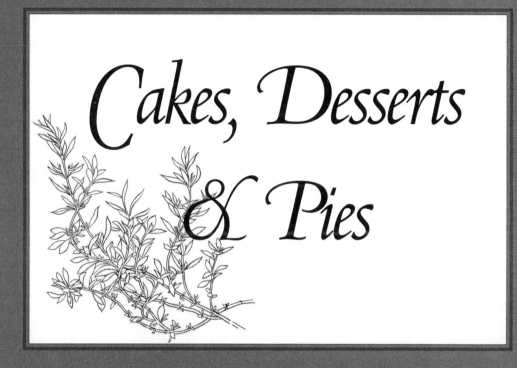

Cakes, Desserts & Pies

Date Nut Cake

Oven 375°F

8	ounces dates, finely chopped, about one cup
½	cup butter
1	cup firmly packed light brown sugar
1	teaspoon baking soda
1½	cups flour
1	cup chopped walnuts

1. Combine dates and butter with ¾ cup hot water. Let stand 10 minutes.

2. Meanwhile, combine sugar, baking soda and flour in a mixing bowl. Add to date mixture. Stir in walnuts. Pour into sprayed 8-inch baking pan. Bake 30 to 40 minutes or until tester inserted in center comes out clean. Let cool on rack. Makes 9 servings.

A wonderfully moist date cake. Serve plain, with ice cream or frosted with a buttercream or cream cheese frosting.

Sour Cream Chocolate Cake

Oven 325°F

3	squares (1-ounce each) semi-sweet chocolate
2	tablespoons butter
3	large eggs, separated
1½	cups sugar, divided
1	cup sour cream
1	cup flour

1. Melt chocolate in top of double boiler (or in microwave). Add butter and blend. Set aside.

2. Beat egg whites until soft peaks form. While continuing to beat egg whites, slowly add 1 cup of the sugar and beat until stiff, but not dry. Set aside.

3. In mixer bowl, beat egg yolks and the remaining ½ cup sugar until thoroughly mixed. Add chocolate mixture and sour cream. Alternately fold in flour and egg whites, about a third at a time, mixing only until smooth. Pour into a sprayed 13x9-inch baking pan. Bake 30 to 35 minutes. Cake should start to shrink from edge of pan. Cool. Frost with a thin layer of your favorite chocolate frosting. Or serve with vanilla ice cream. Makes 12 servings.

I think you will like this recipe. It makes a dense moist cake and slices beautifully.

Cooking Tip

A cake is done when the center springs back when lightly touched. The sides will also start to shrink from edge of pan.

49

Cherry Cake Squares

Oven 350°F

1	cup butter, softened
1½	cups sugar
4	large eggs
1	teaspoon lemon extract
2	cups flour
1	can (21-ounces) cherry or blueberry pie filling

1. Cream butter and sugar in large mixer bowl until light and fluffy. Add eggs, one at a time, beating after each addition. Add lemon extract. Stir in flour. Pour batter into a sprayed 15x10x1-inch jelly roll pan.

2. Mark off 20 squares. Put 1 tablespoon pie filling in center of each square. Bake 45 minutes or until tester inserted in center comes out clean. Cool and cut into squares. Makes 20 servings.

    Tip: If desired, sprinkle with powdered sugar before serving.

Variation: For a quick and easy coffee cake, prepare the cake batter and pour half of the batter into a greased Bundt cake pan. Sprinkle with ¼ cup cinnamon sugar. Pour remaining batter over top. You may have to increase baking time.

Or, place paper liners in muffin cups and fill a little over half full. Make a slight indentation in center and fill with cherry pie filling. Bake 30 to 35 minutes. Cool and drizzle with powdered sugar glaze.

Special Lunch Box Cake

Oven 300°F

2	cups sugar, divided
2	teaspoons baking soda
2	cups flour
2	large eggs, lightly beaten
1	can (17-ounces) fruit cocktail, undrained
¾	cup coarsely chopped walnuts

1. In mixing bowl, combine 1½ cups of the sugar, baking soda and flour. Add eggs and fruit cocktail. Mix well and pour into a sprayed 13x9-inch baking pan. Sprinkle remaining ½ cup sugar evenly over top. Sprinkle with nuts. Bake 60 minutes or until a tester inserted in center comes out clean. Makes 12 servings.

Gooey Butter Cake

Oven 325°F

2 cups flour, divided
3 tablespoons plus 1¼ cups sugar
⅓ cup, plus ¾ cup butter
1 large egg, lightly beaten
¼ cup light corn syrup
⅔ cup canned evaporated milk

1. In a mixing bowl, combine 1 cup of the flour and the 3 tablespoons sugar. Cut the ⅓ cup butter into the flour-sugar mixture until it resembles fine crumbs. Pat into the bottom of an ungreased 8x8-inch baking dish.

2. For filling, beat remaining ¾ cup butter until soft. Add remaining 1¼ cups sugar and beat until well mixed.

3. Combine egg and corn syrup; add to mixture and beat until just combined. Add the remaining 1 cup flour and milk alternately to the filling, mixing until just combined. Pour over crust and bake 30 to 35 minutes or until cake is firm. Place on rack to cool. Makes 9 servings.

I lived in St. Louis for a number of years and this was a favorite bakery creation. It is more like a dessert recipe than a traditional cake. If desired, sprinkle with powdered sugar and garnish with fresh sliced strawberries or assorted fresh fruit.

Cranberry-Nut Cake

Oven 350°F

1 cup, plus 1 tablespoon sugar
1 cup flour
⅔ cup coarsely chopped pecans
2 cups cranberries
2 large eggs, lightly beaten
½ cup butter, melted

1. In a mixing bowl, combine the 1 cup sugar and flour. Add pecans and cranberries, tossing to coat. Add eggs and butter and stir until thoroughly mixed.

2. Pour into a sprayed 8x8-inch baking dish. Sprinkle the 1 tablespoon sugar evenly over the top. Bake 30 to 35 minutes or until tester inserted in center comes out clean. Serve warm or room temperature. Makes 6 to 8 servings.

A quick cake that can be prepared in less than 10 minutes.

Variation: *Substitute blueberries for the cranberries.*

51

Mom's Fruit Cake   Oven 350°F

This is the fruit cake my brothers and I grew up on, then I went on to make the fancier kinds. I hadn't made this one for years, not until I started working on this book and now I am enjoying it all over again. It's very easy to make, you don't even have to get out your mixer and frosting isn't necessary.

1   cup mixed candied fruit
2   teaspoons baking soda
1   cup sugar
1   cup mayonnaise
1   cup chopped pecans
2   cups flour

1. Place the candied fruit in a 2 cup measuring cup. Sprinkle baking soda over top. Add just enough warm water to cover the fruit. Set aside.

2. In medium bowl, combine sugar, mayonnaise and nuts. Add candied fruit mixture. Stir in the flour. Pour into a lightly sprayed 13x9-inch baking pan. Bake 30 to 35 minutes or until tester inserted in center comes out clean. Makes 12 servings.

   Note: It's no wonder that a lot of people don't care for candied fruit or citron. Too often, the brands that are carried in the supermarket are inferior and dry. Good candied fruit should be fresh and moist. Often you can find this at your nicer Delicatessens, especially Italian ones. The last time I made this cake for my family I couldn't find candied mixed fruit, so I used glazed red and green cherries that I happened to have in the freezer. It was very good, the cake was moist, and even my grandchildren ate Great Grandma Warren's "fruitcake."

Dutch Cake   Oven 325°F

Each serving can be garnished with sliced almonds, or my favorite, assorted fresh fruit.

½   cup butter, softened
1   cup sugar
1   large egg
½   cup almond paste
1   cup flour

1. In mixer bowl, cream the butter and sugar until light and fluffy. Add egg and mix until blended. Add almond paste until blended. Slowly beat in flour. Spread in sprayed 9-inch pie dish. Bake 40 to 50 minutes or until golden. Serve warm or at room temperature. Makes 8 to 10 servings.

Pound Cake

Oven 350°F

1   pound butter, softened
1   box (16-ounces) powdered sugar, sifted
6   large eggs
1½ teaspoons vanilla extract
3   cups sifted cake flour

1. Cream butter and powdered sugar in large mixer bowl. Add eggs, one at a time, and beat well. Stir in vanilla extract and flour. Pour into a sprayed angel food cake pan. Bake about 1¼ hours or until tester inserted in center comes out clean. Cool. (While still slightly warm, sift additional powdered sugar over top.) Makes 10 to 12 servings.

Of all the pound cake recipes I have tried, this one seems to be a favorite.

Brownie Cupcakes

Oven 350°F

1   cup butter, softened
⅔   cup semi-sweet chocolate chips
1¾ cups sugar
4   large eggs
1   teaspoon vanilla extract
1   cup flour

1. Melt butter and chocolate chips in a large saucepan over low heat. Stir in sugar; mix well. Add eggs, vanilla and flour. Stir until blended and smooth. Pour into cupcake liners, filling three-fourths full. Bake 25 to 30 minutes or until tester inserted in center is just slightly moist. Makes 16 cupcakes.

Brownie fans will enjoy these. For variety, add 1¼ cups coarsely chopped walnuts to batter or sprinkle top of each cupcake with walnuts before baking.

Tip: If desired, when cool, drizzle with a small amount of glaze: Add a little water to powdered sugar until you get the desired consistency.

Cherry Cupcakes

Oven 350°F

1	cup butter
1½	cups sugar
4	large eggs
1	teaspoon vanilla extract
2	cups flour
1	can (21-ounces) cherry pie filling (or blueberry, apple)

1. In large mixer bowl, cream butter and sugar until light and fluffy. Add eggs, one at a time, beating well after each addition. Add vanilla. Add flour and mix until blended and smooth. Place paper liners in muffin tins and fill a little over half full. Make a slight indentation in center, fill with pie filling using about 3 cherries per cupcake. Bake 30 to 35 minutes or until light golden. Makes 22 cupcakes.

Tip: The amount of vanilla extract is correct, but if using a good brand of pure vanilla you may wish to decrease this amount.

Cream Cheese Cupcakes

Oven 300°F

3	packages (8-ounces each) cream cheese, softened
1¼	cups sugar, divided
5	large eggs
3	tablespoons vanilla extract, divided
1	can (21-ounces) cherry or blueberry pie filling
1	cup sour cream

1. In mixer bowl, combine cream cheese and 1 cup of the sugar. Add eggs and 2 tablespoons of the vanilla extract. Beat until thoroughly mixed, 3 to 4 minutes. Line muffin tins with paper cupcake liners. Fill ¾ full and bake for 30 to 40 minutes. Remove from oven and let cool 5 minutes (centers will drop while cooling).

2. Combine sour cream, the remaining ¼ cup sugar and remaining 1 tablespoon vanilla extract. Fill center of cupcakes with 1 tablespoon sour cream mixture. Spoon a dollop of pie filling on top. Return to oven and bake 5 minutes. Let cool in refrigerator.

Plum Cake

Oven 350°F

½ cup butter, softened
⅓ cup sugar
1 can (8-ounces) almond paste
2 large eggs, lightly beaten
1 cup flour
3 medium-firm red or black plums

1. In a mixer bowl, combine butter, sugar and almond paste. Beat until mixture is thoroughly blended and smooth. Add eggs and beat until well mixed and has a fluffy consistency. Add flour and beat on medium until blended.

2. Pour into a sprayed 10-inch spring-form pan. Cut plums in half, then each half into four wedges. Arrange in an attractive pattern over cake batter. Bake 40 to 45 minutes or until lightly browned. Let cool 10 to 15 minutes before removing rim. Serve warm or room temperature. Makes 8 servings.

You'll enjoy this beautiful cake when fresh plums are in season. This not-too-sweet dessert is wonderful with a steaming cup of coffee. Best eaten the same day made.

Strawberry Refrigerator Cake

1 package (18.25-ounces) white cake mix
1⅓ cups water
2 large egg whites
1 package (3-ounces) strawberry gelatin
1 cup boiling water
1 container (8-ounces) frozen whipped topping, thawed

1. Mix cake according to package directions, using the 1⅓ cups water and egg whites. Pour into a sprayed 13x9-inch baking pan. Bake 30 to 35 minutes or until cake tests done. Remove cake from oven; pierce all over with long tined fork.

2. Dissolve gelatin in boiling water and pour over cake. Cover and chill. Spread whipped topping over top of cake. If desired, garnish with fresh strawberries.

55

Little Molten Cakes

Oven 450°F

½ cup butter
1 bar (4-ounces) bittersweet chocolate
3 large eggs
½ cup sugar
⅓ cup flour
Vanilla, coffee or chocolate chip ice cream

Molten or sunken chocolate cakes are quite the rage right now. They remind me of a not quite cooked brownie. They have soft centers, and if not cooked too long, should be runny when you cut into them.

1. Melt butter and chocolate in a small saucepan or in the microwave oven. Stir to blend. Set aside.

2. In mixer bowl, beat eggs and sugar at medium speed, until thickened and light in color. Add flour and beat to blend. Stir in chocolate mixture. Pour into six lightly buttered 6-ounce ramekins, dividing batter evenly. Place in a shallow baking pan and bake 12 minutes, or until tops are somewhat dry and start to crack in the middle.

3. At this point, you can unmold cakes or serve in ramekins. To unmold, let stand 2 to 3 minutes, run a knife around edge and remove. Serve topped with ice cream. Makes 6 servings.

Cake Tips

❋❋❋

To make a good cake, you must follow a few simple rules. Unless you have made the cake before, you should follow the recipe exactly. Ingredients should be at room temperature. Use large size eggs and butter that contains at least 8 grams of saturated fat per tablespoon. Fill the cake pan with batter, then hold pan a few inches above the counter and drop a few times to prevent large air bubbles. Cool cakes on a rack for 10 minutes, then remove the pan and allow to cool.

Cake Mix Cakes

Cake mixes have come a long way since their introduction to the home cook in the 1940's. Today there are almost too many choices, but at least it gives us a wide variety of flavors and brands with which we can experiment and pick our favorites.

My only complaint is that in recent years, some of the cake mixes have developed this strong and unpleasant flavor which they say is caused by the use of artificial flavorings, mainly vanillin. This is detected mostly in white and yellow cake mixes and can sometimes be covered up by adding additional extracts, chocolate or coffee and liquids such as fruit juices, wine, Sherry or rum.

Many families today consider boxed cakes as made from scratch cakes, (as opposed to store bought cakes). So, enjoy the following recipes and try creating some of your very own family favorites.

Christmas Eggnog Cake

Oven 350°F

1	box	(18.5-ounces) yellow cake mix
¼	teaspoon	nutmeg
¼	cup	butter, melted
1½	cups	purchased eggnog
2	large	eggs
½	teaspoon	rum extract

1. Brush a 10-inch tube cake pan or Bundt pan with shortening. Sprinkle with flour; shake off excess.

2. Combine all the ingredients in a mixer bowl and beat until blended. Then beat on medium speed until batter is smooth, about 2 minutes.

3. Pour batter into prepared pan and bake 45 to 55 minutes or until tester inserted in center comes out clean. Cool in pan 10 minutes. Remove from pan and cool on rack. Makes 10 to 12 servings.

A very good light-textured cake made even better with a scoop of vanilla ice cream. Purchase cake mix without the pudding added. If cake is for company, lightly dust the top with powdered sugar or garnish with fresh fruit.

When you want to impress someone, but you don't have a lot of time to cook, make this quick and easy dessert using an angel food cake mix. You'll be impressed with this beautiful cake and so will they. It also has an added bonus of being low in fat. Serve with ice cream or fresh sweetened strawberries.

So moist you don't need frosting or ice cream. Perfect with a cup of coffee.

Almond Angel Food Cake   Oven 350°F

1	box (16-ounces) angel food cake mix
1½	teaspoons almond extract, divided
1½	to 2 cups sifted powdered sugar
⅓	cup sliced almonds

1. Prepare cake according to directions on package, adding 1 teaspoon almond extract along with the water. Pour into an ungreased 10-inch angel food cake pan with removable bottom. Bake 38 to 45 minutes or until golden and tester inserted in center comes out clean. Invert pan and cool.

2. Combine 1½ cups powdered sugar with 2 tablespoons water and the remaining ½ teaspoon almond extract. You want to be able to drizzle the frosting, so if too wet, add more powdered sugar. If too dry, add just a tiny bit more water. Drizzle over cake, allowing some of the frosting to drip over sides. Sprinkle top with almonds. Makes 12 servings.

Blueberry Orange Cake   Oven 350°F

2	oranges
1	box (18.25-ounces) lemon cake mix
⅓	cup vegetable oil
3	large eggs
1½	cups fresh or frozen blueberries

1. Wash oranges and grate 1 tablespoon peel. Squeeze oranges to make ½ cup juice. Place orange peel and juice in a large mixer bowl.

2. Add cake mix, oil, eggs and ½ cup water. Beat on low about 1 minute to combine ingredients. Beat on medium speed for 2 minutes. By hand, carefully fold in blueberries. Pour into a sprayed 13x9-inch baking dish. Bake 30 to 40 minutes or until tester inserted in center comes out clean. Place on rack to cool. Makes 12 servings.

Chocolate Cake with Peaches

Oven 350°F

1 box (18.25-ounces) Devil's food cake mix
⅔ cups sour cream
2 large eggs
1 teaspoon almond extract
   Sliced peaches with syrup

1. In large mixer bowl, combine first four ingredients with ½ cup water. Beat at low speed until combined. Continue to beat 2 minutes at medium speed.

2. Pour into a sprayed 10-inch springform pan and bake 40 to 45 minutes or until tester inserted in center comes out clean. Cool in pan 10 minutes. Remove ring and let cool on rack. Serve with peaches. Makes 12 servings.

You can fool anyone with this made from scratch taste - from a box.

Dome Cake

Oven 350°F

1 box (18.25-ounces) German chocolate cake mix
3 large eggs
1 cup sour cream
¼ cup oil
1 bottle (1-ounce) red food coloring
   Frosting of choice

1. In large mixer bowl, combine all ingredients along with ½ cup water. Beat at low speed until moistened. Then beat at medium speed for 2 minutes. Pour into a sprayed round 10-cup ovenproof glass or metal bowl and bake 55 to 65 minutes or until a tester inserted in center comes out clean. Place on rack and cool 15 minutes. Remove and cool on rack.

2. Frost with one of your favorite frostings or my favorite; Whipped Butter Frosting on page 62. (This frosting is delicious, but must be kept refrigerated.) Remove about 20 minutes before serving.

Forget layer cakes. This cake is easy to frost and pretty when sliced and served.

Variation: *Frost cake, then sprinkle entire surface with flaked coconut. I call this my Snowball cake and the grandchildren love it.*

59

Chocolate Chocolate Cake

Oven 350°F

An intensely dark chocolate cake with a dark chocolate frosting. It is a restaurant favorite changed somewhat to make it easier for the home cook.

2 boxes (18.25-ounces each) Dark Chocolate Fudge cake mix
3 large eggs
¾ cup mayonnaise
¾ cup brewed coffee
1½ cups Coca Cola®
Chocolate frosting on page 61 or purchased chocolate frosting

1. In mixer bowl, add 1 box cake mix and only 1½ cups of the second box of cake mix.

2. Combine eggs, mayonnaise, coffee and Coca Cola® beating until well-mixed. Add to cake mix and beat on low about 1 minute to combine ingredients. Beat on medium speed about 2 minutes until smooth. Pour into a sprayed 13x9-inch baking pan and bake 35 to 45 minutes or until a tester inserted in center comes out clean. Allow to cool before frosting. Makes 12 servings.

Triple Fudge Cake

Oven 350°F

This is a heavy spongy type cake, and is great for eating out of hand and for sack lunches.

1 package (3-ounces) regular chocolate pudding mix
2 cups milk
1 package (18.25-ounces) Devils food cake mix
½ cup semi-sweet chocolate chips
½ cup chopped walnuts

1. Prepare pudding mix with milk as directed on package. Remove from heat; blend dry cake mix into hot pudding. Mixture will be quite thick and spongy.

2. Pour into a sprayed 13x9-inch pan. Sprinkle with chocolate chips and nuts and bake 30 to 35 minutes.

Family Favorite Chocolate Frosting

¼ cup milk
¼ cup butter
1 cup semi-sweet chocolate chips
1 teaspoon vanilla extract
2½ cups sifted powdered sugar

1. Combine milk and butter in a small saucepan. Bring to a boil; remove from heat. Add chocolate chips and stir until smooth.

2. Place chocolate mixture, vanilla extract and powdered sugar in a mixer bowl. Beat until of spreading consistency. If necessary, thin with a few drops of milk.

My absolute favorite chocolate frosting. Don't add too much powdered sugar, because the frosting will thicken as it cools. Makes enough frosting for a 13x9-inch cake or 2 layer cake.

Cream Cheese Frosting

1 package (8-ounces) cream cheese, softened
½ cup butter, softened
1 teaspoon vanilla extract
1 box (16-ounces) powdered sugar, sifted

1. In mixer bowl, beat cream cheese until smooth. Add butter and vanilla and beat until mixed. Add powdered sugar, beating until smooth.

This a delicious frosting for Carrot Cake or cupcakes. Because of the cream cheese, it must be kept refrigerated.

Buttercream Frosting

¼ cup butter, softened
3 cups sifted powdered sugar
1 teaspoon vanilla extract
3 to 4 tablespoons milk

1. In small mixer bowl, cream the butter until smooth. Add sugar, vanilla and 3 tablespoons milk. Beat until creamy and thick enough to spread. It may be necessary to add more milk or more powdered sugar to get consistency desired. Makes enough frosting for a 13x9-inch cake.

Frosting can be changed by substituting different liquids for the milk such as lemon or orange juice, coffee, chocolate, etc.

61

This is one of my favorite frostings. The flavor is unique and delicious. It is the traditional frosting for Red Velvet Cake (more than six ingredients) but is equally as good on chocolate cake. It must be kept refrigerated.

If you have problems and the mixture looks curdled no matter what you do, switch your brand of butter. That is usually the culprit. Look for butter that has 8 grams of saturated fat per tablespoon.

Whipped Butter Frosting

    5   tablespoons flour
    1   cup milk
    1   cup sugar
    1   cup butter, softened
    1   teaspoon vanilla extract

1. Combine flour and milk in small saucepan (do not use aluminum). Cook over low heat until quite thick, stirring constantly. Remove from heat; cool completely.

2. Cream together sugar, butter and vanilla. Add cooled mixture and beat, beat, beat. When finished, frosting looks like thick whipped cream.

Penuche Frosting

    ⅓   cup butter
    ½   cup firmly packed light brown sugar
    3   tablespoons milk
    ¼   teaspoon vanilla extract
    2   cups sifted powdered sugar

1. Melt butter in small saucepan. Add brown sugar. Cook over medium heat, stirring constantly, until sugar melts. Add milk and bring to a boil. Remove from heat; let cool 10 minutes. Stir in vanilla and powdered sugar. Beat until blended and smooth. Add additional sugar if necessary. Makes about 1 cup.

Confectioner's Glaze

    1   cup sifted powdered sugar
    1   tablespoon hot water
    1½   teaspoons light corn syrup
    ¼   teaspoon vanilla extract

1. Combine ingredients in small mixing bowl; stir until blended and smooth. Consistency should be thin, but not run off cake. Add more powdered sugar or water, if necessary. Makes about ½ cup.

Rice Chex® Dessert

2½   cups crushed Rice Chex® cereal
1   cup firmly packed light brown sugar
1   cup cashews, split
½   cup butter, melted
1   cup Angel Flake coconut
½   gallon vanilla ice cream, softened

1. Combine first 5 ingredients; mix thoroughly. Spread half of mixture evenly in buttered 13x9-inch baking dish; pat down. Spread ice cream evenly over top. Sprinkle remaining cereal mixture over ice cream; pat lightly.

2. Cover and freeze. When ready to serve, remove from freezer and cut into squares. Makes 12 to 15 servings.

This recipe is worth the price of the cookbook. If strawberries are in season, it looks pretty to top each serving with a strawberry and a mint leaf.

Ice Cream Cake

1½   packages soft-type Ladyfingers, split
1   to 1½ quarts chocolate ice cream, softened
1   to 1½ quarts vanilla ice cream, softened
10   Heath® candy bars, coarsely crushed

1. Line sides and bottom of angel food cake pan (with removeable bottom) with Ladyfingers, rounded side out. Half fill pan with chocolate ice cream. Sprinkle half of the crushed candy over top. Add vanilla ice cream; sprinkle with remaining candy.

2. Cover with foil and freeze. Makes 12 to 14 servings.

When in their teens, this is the dessert my children wanted for their birthday cake. In fact they still do. Just add candles.

If you wish to make a smaller dessert, use half the ingredients and a 9x5-inch loaf pan lined with foil (for easy removal).

My favorite dessert? If I has to choose one dessert, this would be the one.

63

Quick Ice Cream Desserts

Grilled fresh pineapple slices with vanilla ice cream

Lemon sherbet or sorbet with sweetened raspberries

Vanilla ice cream and orange sherbet with a tablespoon of amaretto and a crisp butter cookie

Vanilla or chocolate swirl ice cream with sweetened sliced peaches

Layer vanilla ice cream and crushed Oreos®

Layer crushed vanilla wafers, vanilla ice cream and crushed Heath® bars

Brownies topped with ice cream and chocolate sauce

Angel Food Cake with ice cream and sliced mixed fruit

Layer ice cream with Caramel Sauce then top with crushed Heath® bars, nuts or toasted coconut

Quick Cheesecake Toppings

A purchased cheesecake served with your choice of
toppings is a lifesaver for the busy host or hostess.

Whole berry cooked blueberry sauce

Whole or chopped assorted fresh fruit

Chocolate sauce sprinkled with sliced almonds

Orange marmalade with Grand Marnier to taste

Melted seedless raspberry or blackberry jam

Caramel sauce

Shaved white chocolate

Fantastic Cheesecake

Oven 350°F

- ⅓ cup graham cracker crumbs
- 3 packages (8-ounces each) cream cheese, softened
- 4 large eggs
- 1¾ cups sour cream, divided
- 1¼ cups sugar, divided
- 4 tablespoons fresh lemon juice, divided

1. Butter a 9-inch spring form pan. Add graham cracker crumbs to pan and rotate to cover bottom and sides. Discard loose crumbs.

2. In mixer bowl, beat the cream cheese until smooth. Add eggs, one at a time, and mix well. Add ¾ cup of the sour cream, 1 cup of sugar and 2 tablespoons of the lemon juice. Mix until blended and smooth. Pour into spring form pan. Bake 35 to 40 minutes or until just firm (do not overbake, the center should still jiggle just a little).

3. Meanwhile, combine the 1 cup sour cream, ¼ cup sugar, and 2 tablespoons lemon juice. When done, remove cheesecake from oven and carefully spoon sour cream mixture over top. Return to oven and bake 5 minutes. Let cool on rack. Chill. Makes 12 servings.

Pistachio Dessert

Oven 350°F

- 50 Ritz® crackers, crushed
- ½ cup butter, melted
- 1 quart vanilla ice cream, softened
- 1 cup milk
- 1 package (3.4-ounces) instant pistachio pudding mix
- 1 container (8-ounces) frozen whipped topping, thawed

1. Combine cracker crumbs and butter. Pat evenly into a sprayed 13x9-inch baking dish. Bake 10 to 15 minutes. Remove from oven and let cool.

2. In mixer bowl, blend ice cream, milk and pudding mix. Pour over crust. Spread Cool Whip over top. Chill several hours or overnight. Makes 10 to 12 servings.

Try a delicious topping of Cherries Jubilee, sweetened strawberries, or a blueberry sauce with almond extract.

At first I wasn't going to put this recipe in the cookbook, mainly because of the problems I have been having with several brands of cream cheese. If you have problems with cheesecakes, especially if it is a recipe that has worked in the past, try using a different brand of cream cheese.

65

The first recipe I used to make Baklava was two pages long. This one is easier and just as moist and delicious. As you can see, it makes a lot, but it can be frozen.

Note: *It's important to measure the walnuts first, then grind them.*

Baklava   Oven 300°F

4½	cups walnuts, finely ground
3	cups sugar, divided
½	teaspoon cinnamon
1	box (16-ounces) Phyllo, thawed, at room temperature
1	pound butter, melted
1	tablespoon lemon juice

1. Combine walnuts, 1½ cups of the sugar and cinnamon. Set aside.

2. Butter a 15x10-inch jellyroll pan. Unroll Phyllo and place on flat surface. Cover with waxed paper or plastic wrap. Then cover with a slightly damp towel. (Phyllo must be kept covered at all times as it dries out quickly.) Lay 1 sheet of Phyllo in pan. You may have to fold one end over to fit pan. Brush with melted butter. Repeat layering until half of the Phyllo has been used.

3. Spread nut mixture evenly over top. Repeat layering with remaining Phyllo continuing to butter each layer.

4. With a sharp knife, cut through layers of Phyllo, cutting in a diamond shaped pattern, making cuts about 1½ inches apart. Bake 70 to 80 minutes or until golden brown.

5. Meanwhile, in medium saucepan, combine 1½ cups water with the remaining 1½ cups sugar and the lemon juice. Bring to a boil, stirring frequently to dissolve sugar. Lower heat and simmer 20 minutes. Let cool slightly. Spoon syrup over Baklava. Let stand 3 to 4 hours to absorb syrup. *Enjoy*

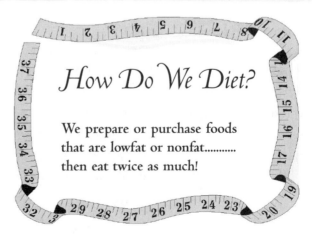

How Do We Diet?

We prepare or purchase foods that are lowfat or nonfat...........
then eat twice as much!

Cherries Jubilee

1	tablespoon sugar
1	tablespoon cornstarch
1	can (16-ounces) Bing cherries, pitted, save juice
4	strips orange peel
½	teaspoon lemon juice
¼	cup warm brandy

1. Combine sugar and cornstarch in chafing dish or saucepan. Slowly add liquid from canned cherries and blend. Cook over low heat until thickened, stirring constantly. Add cherries, orange peel and lemon juice; heat through.

2. Pour brandy over top and ignite. Serve over ice cream. Makes 4 servings.

This is an old recipe, but still a popular one. When you want to serve something spectacular, flame the cherries at the table and impress your guests. I usually double the recipe if serving 4 to 6 people.

Croissant Bread Pudding   Oven 350°F

2½	cups half and half
6	large eggs, lightly beaten
¾	cup sugar, divided
½	teaspoon cinnamon
8	croissants (day old works best)
¾	cup raisins

1. Combine half and half with the eggs. Combine ½ cup of the sugar with cinnamon; add to egg mixture. Pour into sprayed 11x7-inch baking dish.

2. Tear croissants into bite-size pieces. You should have about 7 cups. Add to custard, pressing down to cover. Sprinkle raisins over top. Sprinkle remaining ¼ cup sugar over raisins. Bake 40 to 45 minutes or until set. Serve warm with a little additional cream. Makes 6 servings.

Cherry Parfaits

1 cup heavy whipping cream
3 tablespoons sugar
1 teaspoon vanilla extract
1 cup sour cream
1 can (21-ounces) cherry pie filling

Whip cream in mixer bowl, adding sugar and vanilla. Fold in sour cream. In parfait glasses, spoon a small amount of pie filling, then the whipped cream, repeat. Chill.

Ice Cream Balls

❧

Form vanilla ice cream into balls and freeze. Roll in choice of: Angel Flake coconut, sliced almonds, chopped pecans, chocolate sprinkles.
Serve with: sliced strawberries, raspberries or peaches.

Strawberries Grand Marnier

❧

Combine 4 cups sliced strawberries, with ⅓ cup sugar (or to taste), 2-4 tablespoons Grand Marnier and 2 teaspoons freshly grated orange peel. Cover and chill before serving.

Easy Party Cake

1	Angel Food cake
2	cups whipping cream
¼	cup sugar
3	cups sliced strawberries, add sugar to taste

1. Whip cream, adding ¼ cup sugar or more to taste. Frost cake with whipped cream.

2. To serve, slice cake and spoon strawberries over each serving. Makes 10 servings.

Devonshire Cream and Berries

1	package (8-ounces) cream cheese, softened
½	cup sifted powdered sugar
⅓	cup whipping cream
1	teaspoon vanilla extract
1½	teaspoons Grand Marnier liqueur
	Fresh strawberries

1. In mixer bowl, whip cream cheese and powdered sugar until thoroughly blended and smooth. Add whipping cream, vanilla, and Grand Marnier; whip until light. Serve with berries. If not using right away, cover and chill. Makes 1½ cups.

Amaretto Strawberry Dessert

2 cups sliced fresh strawberries
4 tablespoons Amaretto liqueur
1 pint vanilla ice cream or nonfat frozen yogurt

1. In a mixing bowl, combine the strawberries and Amaretto and marinate at least two hours. When ready to serve, place a scoop of ice cream in each of 4 wine glasses or dessert bowls. Spoon strawberries over top. Makes 4 servings.

Taste strawberries and if not quite sweet enough you may want to add a little sugar. If desired, garnish with toasted coconut, toasted sliced almonds or shaved white chocolate.

Brownie Delight

1 package (20-ounces) fudge brownie mix
1 quart vanilla ice cream, softened
½ cup chopped pecans, or Heath® Bar Bits
2 to 3 cups sliced strawberries
¼ cup sugar or to taste

1. Prepare brownie mix as directed on package using a sprayed 13x9-inch baking dish. Cool completely.

2. Spread ice cream over brownies. Sprinkle with nuts or candy. Cover and freeze.

3. Meanwhile, combine strawberries and sugar. Cover and chill 1 to 2 hours. When ready to serve, cut into squares and top with strawberries and some of the juice. Makes 12 servings.

This combination of every-one's favorite ingredients, brownies and strawberries, is a "delight." You can use any brownie mix you have on hand, but in keeping with Six Ingredients or Less®, use a mix that requires water only. Omit strawberries if not in season and you still have a wonderful dessert.

Apple Raspberry Crisp — Oven 350°F

The raspberries add a nice touch of color and taste. If you want a really scrumptious dessert, top with a scoop of vanilla ice cream or frozen yogurt.

Variation: Use blueberries, pears, or dried cranberries in place of the raspberries.

8   cups peeled sliced apples (4 to 5)
1   cup fresh or frozen raspberries
½   teaspoon cinnamon
¾   cup flour
1   cup sugar
⅓   cup cold butter

1. Place apple slices in a sprayed 11x7-inch baking dish. Distribute raspberries over top. Sprinkle 3 tablespoons water over fruit.

2. In a small mixing bowl, combine the cinnamon, flour and sugar. Cut in butter with a pastry blender or two knives. Sprinkle over fruit. Bake 50 to 55 minutes or until light golden and apples are cooked through. Makes 8 servings.

Peach Cobbler — Oven 350°F

Nothing speaks "home cooking" like fruit cobbler. Delicious served with or without ice cream.

Variation: Add ¾ cup fresh blueberries or ½ cup dried cranberries.

½   cup butter, melted
2   cans (29-ounces each) sliced peaches, drained
¾   cup sugar
1   cup flour
2   teaspoons baking powder
1   cup milk

1. Pour melted butter into a 13x9-inch baking dish or 11x7-inch deep baking dish. Add peach slices.

2. In mixing bowl, combine sugar, flour and baking powder. Add milk and stir until blended. Pour over peaches, but do not stir. Bake 30 to 35 minutes or until golden. Makes 8 servings.

Deep Dish Fruit Cobbler

Oven 375°F

½   cup butter, melted
1   cup baking mix
1   cup sugar
1   cup milk
1   quart fruit, drained (peaches, blackberries, etc.)

1. Pour butter into an 11x7-inch baking dish. Stir in baking mix, sugar and milk. Pour fruit over top. Bake 35 to 40 minutes or until golden brown. Makes 6 servings.

This recipe has been in our family for more years than I remember, but at least two generations. It is still one of our favorite desserts. Serve it warm with vanilla ice cream.

Cherry-Pecan Ice Cream Dessert

2   quarts vanilla ice cream, softened
1   cup maraschino cherries, drained, save syrup
¼   cup of the cherry syrup
½   cup chopped pecans

1. Place ice cream in a large mixing bowl. Purée cherries (but leave tiny bits) and the ¼ cup syrup in a food processor or blender. Add to ice cream along with the pecans.

2. Pour into a 9x5-inch loaf pan lined with foil that extends over both ends of pan (makes removing easier). Cover and freeze overnight. Slice to make individual servings. Makes 8 to 10 servings.

For an impressive dessert, place each slice on an attractive dessert plate that has been drizzled with puréed fruit such as strawberries or raspberries. It's fun to be fancy once in awhile.

71

Ice Cream & Amaretto Dessert

FOR EACH SERVING:

    1   scoop vanilla ice cream
    1   tablespoon Amaretto liqueur
    2   tablespoons frozen whipped topping, thawed
    1   tablespoon toasted Angel Flake coconut

A great company dessert. There won't be a drop left. If desired, substitute sweetened whipped cream for the whipped topping.

1. Place scoop of ice cream in a small wine glass or dessert dish. Spoon Amaretto over top. Top with whipped topping. Sprinkle with coconut. Makes 1 serving.

Strawberry Shortcake   Oven 375°F

    1   can (10.8-ounces) Grands® biscuits
    ¼   cup butter, melted
    ¼   cup sugar
    1   tablespoon sliced almonds
        Fresh strawberries, sliced, sweetened

This is a wonderfully delicious way to use up those biscuits before the expiration date.

1. Dip each biscuit in melted butter and then into sugar to coat. Place on ungreased baking sheet. Sprinkle a few almonds over each biscuit. Bake 15 to 18 minutes or until cooked through and golden. Serve warm topped with strawberries. Makes 5 servings.

Steve's Perfect Pie Crust

4	cups flour
1	tablespoon sugar
2	teaspoons salt
1¾	cups shortening (do not substitute)
1	tablespoon cider or white vinegar
1	large egg

1. Combine flour, sugar and salt in a mixing bowl. Cut in shortening with two knives or a pastry blender. Combine vinegar and egg with ½ cup cold water; add to flour mixture. Stir until moistened and a dough is formed. Divide dough into 5 equal parts; shape each into a round flat patty ready for rolling. Wrap in waxed paper; chill at least 30 minutes.

2. When ready to use, place on lightly floured board; roll ⅛-inch thick and 2 inches larger than inverted pie pan. Makes 5 single crusts.

Pie Crust

2½	cups flour
½	teaspoon salt
¾	cup shortening
6	to 7 tablespoons ice water

1. Combine flour and salt in mixing bowl. With two knives or a pastry blender, cut in shortening until uniform, about the size of peas. Sprinkle with water, a tablespoon at a time, and toss with fork. Stir gently, just until dough forms a ball. Divide into 2 equal parts; place on lightly floured surface and roll to ⅛-inch thickness. Gently ease into pan to avoid stretching. Makes 2 single crusts.

This really is a reliable recipe. The dough can be refrigerated up to 3 days or can be frozen. Steve was a lifesaver one Thanksgiving when he made the pumpkin pies for me. The crust turned out flaky and the filling was delicious. You may not always need this large a recipe, but any left over could be formed into balls and frozen or even better yet, roll out to desired size, place on a baking sheet and freeze. Then wrap and freeze until ready to use. If freezing more than one, they can be layered with parchment paper between each layer.

A wonderfully versatile pie crust that is compatible with a variety of fillings.

Variation*: If desired, substitute chocolate wafer crumbs for the graham cracker crumbs.*

Baked Pie Shells

Aluminum pans work great for baking pies. Glass pans are also good, but remember to decrease the baking temperature by 25 degrees.

Fit dough loosely into pie pan and avoid stretching the dough. Prick all over bottom and sides with a fork. Bake at 425° for 5 minutes. Check crust to see if any areas have begun to swell, if so, gently press down. If necessary, repeat again. Total baking time should take 15 to 20 minutes for a golden crust, but watch carefully since every oven bakes differently.

Graham Cracker Crust   Oven 350°F

1¼ cups graham cracker crumbs
¼ cup sugar
⅓ cup butter, melted

1. Combine ingredients and press into bottom and sides of 9-inch pie pan. Bake 10 minutes. Cool.

Pretzel Pie Crust   Oven 350°F

¾ cup butter, melted
2⅔ cups crushed pretzels
3 tablespoons sugar

1. Combine ingredients and pat into two 9-inch pie pans or one 13x9-inch pan. Bake 10 minutes. Cool.

Meringue Shell   Oven 300°F

3 large egg whites, room temperature
⅛ teaspoon salt
½ teaspoon cream of tartar
1 cup sugar
½ teaspoon vanilla extract

1. In large mixer bowl, add egg whites, salt and cream of tartar; beat until soft peaks form. At low speed, gradually add sugar and beat until sugar is dissolved. Add vanilla and beat until very stiff and glossy. Spread on bottom and sides of sprayed 9-inch pie pan. Bake 40 minutes or until shell feels dry to the touch. Cool thoroughly on wire rack. Use as a base for ice cream topped with fruit, a cream or lemon pie filling or chocolate mousse.

An Apple a Day

You may have additional varieties in your area, but this is a good starting point.

Braeburn	Excellent all purpose apple. Good for eating out of hand or for cooking and baking. Also keeps well.
Cortland	A slightly tart versatile apple. Good for baking.
Elstar	A Sweet-tart flavor; versatile. Good for snacks, salad and baking.
Empire	Best for snacks and salads than for cooking.
Fuji	Good eating apple; sweet, crunchy and flavorful. A good choice for pies.
Gala	Good eating and baking apple.
Golden Delicious	Good eating apple. Perfect for sautéing and baking in casseroles. Great for applesauce and pies.
Granny Smith	Tart and firm apple. A favorite for pies.
Jonagold	Good all around eating, cooking and baking apple.
Jonathon	All-purpose. Good for cooking and baking. Really a good versatile apple.
McIntosh	Sweet-tart flavor. A favorite for snacking. Good for sauces, but not for pies because it loses its shape once cooked.
Red Delicious	A good eating apple, nice for salads.
Rome	Not a favorite for eating. Good for pies, breads, sauce, bread pudding and baking whole.

Tip: *Very good served with vanilla ice cream or whipped cream.*

Pecan Crunch Pie
Oven 350°F

3	large egg whites
1	cup sugar
1	teaspoon baking powder
1	teaspoon vanilla extract
1	cup crushed graham cracker crumbs
1	cup chopped pecans

1. Beat egg whites until stiff. Combine sugar and baking powder; beat into egg whites. Add vanilla. Fold in graham cracker crumbs, then pecans. Pour into buttered 9-inch pie plate. Bake 30 minutes or until cooked through. Cool.

Apple pie is always a favorite and this one is just a little bit different.

Sour Cream Apple Pie
Oven 400°F

¾	cup sugar, plus 2 tablespoons
3	tablespoons flour
1	cup sour cream
3	cups coarsely chopped apples (3 medium)
1	(9-inch) unbaked pie shell
1	teaspoon cinnamon

1. Combine the ¾ cup sugar, flour and sour cream; mix well. Add chopped apples. Pour into pie crust. Mix the remaining 2 tablespoons sugar with the cinnamon. Sprinkle evenly over apple mixture. Bake 15 minutes. Reduce heat to 350° and bake 25 to 30 minutes or until apples are tender. Cool. Makes 6 servings.

Apple Crumb Pie

Oven 400°F

1   (9-inch) unbaked pie crust
6   to 7 tart apples, peeled and sliced
1   cup sugar, divided
1   teaspoon cinnamon
¾   cup flour
⅓   cup butter

1. Arrange apple slices in pie shell. Combine ½ cup sugar and cinnamon; sprinkle over apples.

2. Combine remaining sugar and flour in a small bowl. With two knives or a pastry blender, cut in butter until crumbly. Sprinkle over apples. Bake 40 minutes or until apples are tender. Cover crust with foil if getting too brown toward end of cooking time. Makes 6 servings.

Although not a tart apple, the Golden Delicious makes a very good pie. Romes are probably my favorite. For another great apple filling, try a mixture of Golden Delicious, Granny Smith and Fuji apples.

Peanut Butter Pie

1   package (8-ounces) cream cheese, softened
1   cup creamy peanut butter
1   cup sugar
2   tablespoons butter, melted
1   cup whipping cream
1   (9-inch) baked pie crust

1. In mixer bowl, beat the cream cheese until smooth. Add peanut butter, sugar and butter; beat until smooth. Whip the cream and add to peanut butter mixture; mix well. Pour into pie crust. Chill until firm. Makes 6 to 8 servings.

A graham cracker crust can be substituted in place of the traditional pie crust. If desired, drizzle each serving with melted chocolate. "Very rich."

Linda's Cherry Pie

Oven 425°F

Pastry for 2-crust pie (9-inch)
1¼ cups sugar, divided
5 tablespoons cornstarch
¼ teaspoon cinnamon
2 cans (16-ounces each) tart cherries, pitted, save juice
1 tablespoon butter

1. In small saucepan, combine ¾ cup of the sugar, cornstarch and cinnamon until blended. Drain cherries, reserving one cup juice. Stir the juice into the sugar mixture. Cook over low heat, stirring frequently, until thickened.

2. Add remaining ½ cup sugar. Stir in cherries. Line a 9-inch pie pan with pastry; add pie filling. Dot with butter. Add top crust; cut slits in top. Bake 45 to 55 minutes or until golden. Makes 6 servings.

For a deeper red, add a few drops red food coloring.
Variation: *add ½ teaspoon almond extract with remaining ½ cup sugar.*

Fresh Strawberry Pie

1 (9-inch) baked pie shell
1 cup sugar
1 cup water, divided
3 tablespoons cornstarch
3 tablespoons strawberry gelatin
3 to 4 cups fresh whole small strawberries

1. Put the sugar in a small saucepan. In a small bowl, combine ¼ cup of the water with the cornstarch, stirring until smooth. Add to saucepan along with the remaining ¾ cup water; mix well. Cook over medium low heat until thickened, stirring frequently. Stir in gelatin.

2. Line pie shell with strawberries, pointed end up. Fill in where necessary with smaller berries. Pour sauce over top. Chill until set. Makes 6 servings.

One of the best strawberry pies and always a favorite among guests. Just pass around the whipped cream.

Make pie when the local berries are available. They are more uniform in size and much more flavorful.

78

Busy Day Pumpkin Pie

Oven 375°F

1   can (16-ounces) pumpkin
1   can (14-ounces) sweetened condensed milk
1   large egg
1   teaspoon pumpkin pie spice
1   teaspoon cinnamon
1   (9-inch) unbaked pie crust

1.   Combine first 5 ingredients and blend well. Pour into pie crust. Bake 50 to 55 minutes or until knife inserted just off center comes out clean. Let cool, then place in refrigerator until ready to serve.

This is one of those recipes that is even better the second day.

Amazing Coconut Pie

Oven 350°F

3   large eggs
¼   cup butter
1½   teaspoons vanilla extract
1   can (14-ounces) sweetened condensed milk
½   cup baking mix
1   cup Angel Flake coconut

1.   In blender or mixer, combine first 5 ingredients along with 1½ cups water; mix well. Pour into a sprayed deep-dish 10-inch pie plate. Sprinkle coconut over top. Bake 40 to 45 minutes or until mixture is set and knife inserted just off center comes out clean. Chill. Makes 6 servings.

Key Lime Pie

Oven 350°F

Key Lime pie is quite rich with a citrus tart flavor that is just perfect after a special meal. You can use a pastry or graham cracker crust, or try the Pretzel Crust on page 74. Serve with whipped cream and/or assorted fresh fruit.

1	9-inch baked pie crust of choice
½	cup lime juice (4 to 5 limes)
2	teaspoons grated lime peel
4	large egg yolks
1	can (14-ounces) sweetened condensed milk

1. Combine the last 4 ingredients until blended and smooth. Pour into pie crust. Bake 15 minutes or until center is just set. Let cool on rack, then chill until ready to serve. Makes 6 servings.

Daiquiri Pies

My daughter made these for Mother's Day one year. They make a delicious, not too heavy dessert. If you don't want to fool with a pie crust, just pour the filling into dessert dishes and top with whipped cream and toasted coconut.

2	baked (9-inch) pretzel pie crusts, see page 74
1	package (8-ounces) cream cheese, softened
1	can (14-ounces) sweetened condensed milk
1	can (6-ounces) limeade concentrate, thawed
⅓	cup light rum
1	container (4-ounces) frozen whipped topping, thawed

1. In mixer bowl, beat cream cheese until light and fluffy. Add condensed milk and limeade, mix well. Add rum. Fold in whipped topping. Pour into pie crusts. Chill at least 4 hours. Makes 2 pies.

Dreamsicle Pie

This yummy recipe reminds me of my childhood, when a Dreamsicle ice cream bar was so good on a hot summer day.

1	package (8½-ounces) plain chocolate wafers
¼	cup butter, melted
1	quart vanilla ice cream, softened
1	quart orange sherbet, softened

1. Crush wafers in blender or food processor. Reserve 1 teaspoon for top. Add melted butter; mix to blend. Press into bottom and sides of a deep 9-inch pie pan. Spread half of vanilla ice cream over crust. Spread sherbet over ice cream. Spread remaining ice cream over sherbet. Sprinkle reserved crumbs over top. Cover and freeze. Makes 6 servings.

Strawberry Margarita Pie

2⅔   cups Angel flake coconut, toasted
½   cup butter, melted
1   package (10-ounces) frozen strawberries in syrup, thawed
1   can (14-ounces) sweetened condensed milk
½   cup frozen margarita concentrate mix, thawed
2   cups (8-ounce container) frozen whipped topping, thawed

1. In a medium mixing bowl, combine toasted coconut and butter until thoroughly mixed. Press on bottom and sides of a 9-inch pie dish (do not cover the rim of the dish).

2. Combine strawberries (and juice), condensed milk and margarita mix in a medium bowl; stir until well mixed. Fold in the whipped topping. Pour into pie crust. Freeze pie. If not using right away, cover with plastic wrap to seal. Makes 6 servings.

A quick, yummy dessert that's quite addictive.

To Toast Coconut: *Spread coconut in a single layer on a 15x10-inch jelly roll pan. Bake at 325° for 10 to 15 minutes, stirring frequently, when it starts to brown around the edges. Bake until light golden in color.*

Almond Cream Cheese Pie   Oven 350°F

2   packages (8-ounces each) cream cheese, softened
⅔   cup plus 2 tablespoons sugar
3   large eggs
1½   teaspoons almond extract, divided
1   cup sour cream
1   can (20-ounces) blueberry or cherry pie filling, chilled

1. Beat cream cheese in large mixer bowl until light and smooth. Add ⅔ cup of the sugar and beat until well mixed. Add eggs, one at a time, beating well after each addition. Add 1 teaspoon almond extract and continue beating a couple of minutes to make sure there aren't any lumps. Pour mixture into a sprayed 10-inch deep pie dish. Bake 25 minutes. Remove from oven and let cool 10 minutes.

2. Meanwhile, combine sour cream, the remaining 2 tablespoons sugar and ½ teaspoon almond extract. Carefully pour over cheesecake, spreading to ¼ inch from edge. Bake 10 minutes. Let cool; cover with plastic wrap and chill. Serve with a dollop of pie filling. Makes 8 servings.

No crust — just light and delicious!

Chocolate Mint Pie

Oven 250°F

1   cup semi-sweet chocolate chips
2   tablespoons butter, softened
2   tablespoons powdered sugar
2   quarts chocolate chip mint ice cream, softened

1.   Line a 9-inch pie pan by pressing a 12-inch square of heavy-duty foil on bottom, sides and rim of pan. Sprinkle chocolate chips evenly over foil. Put in oven for about 5 minutes or until chocolate is soft. Remove from oven. Add butter and stir until melted. Add powdered sugar. Spread mixture over bottom and sides of pan. Chill until firm, about 30 minutes. Carefully remove foil and return shell to pan. Fill with softened ice cream. Freeze. Makes 6 to 8 servings.

Tip: Chocolate shell can be filled with your choice of ice cream and fillings. One of my favorites is a layer of chocolate and vanilla ice cream with a layer of crushed Heath® Candy bars in the middle and sprinkled on top. Another is a chilled lemon or chocolate filling. Garnish as desired.

Banana Split Pie

1   (9-inch) baked pie crust
3   bananas, sliced
1   tablespoon lemon juice
1   pint strawberry ice cream, softened
1½   cups frozen whipped topping, thawed
     Chocolate sauce

1.   Sprinkle bananas with lemon juice, stirring to coat. Arrange on bottom of pie crust. Spoon ice cream over bananas. Spread whipped topping over top. Freeze. Cover with plastic wrap if making several hours or days ahead. Remove from freezer 20 minutes before serving. Serve with chocolate sauce. Makes 6 servings.

Cookies & Candies

Cookies

Bar cookies, drop cookies, cut-out cookies, we love them all. Home baked cookies warm the heart and even though we are rushed for time, it's worth the effort to occasionally make our family favorites. As my grandson Ben said one day when I asked him if he wanted a cookie, "Grandma, are they homemade or the other kind?".

Finnish Jelly Fingers

Oven 375°F

1	cup butter, softened
¾	cup sugar
1	large egg
2½	cups flour
1	teaspoon baking powder
	Jam

1. In mixer bowl, cream butter and sugar. Add egg; beat thoroughly. Combine flour and baking powder. Add to butter mixture, stirring by hand. Cover and chill several hours or overnight.

2. Divide dough into 5 or 6 parts. Knead dough slightly to make it more workable. Roll into long ½-inch thick rolls. Carefully place on cookie sheet, allowing about 4 inches between rolls. With the side of your finger, make a well lengthwise down the roll, pressing almost to the bottom. Fill well with jam. Bake 10 to 12 minutes or until done but not brown around the edges.

3. Carefully place each roll on a breadboard. With a sharp knife, cut diagonally into 1¼-inch strips. Cool on rack. Makes 7 to 8 dozen.

How to store cookies?

Soft and crisp cookies should be stored separately. Use tightly covered containers to prevent the drying out of soft cookies and the softening of crisp cookies. Cookies and cookie dough can also be frozen.

I made hundreds of these for my daughter's wedding. They make a colorful addition to a cookie tray.

*T*he color of jam can be your choice; red, green, yellow, etc. If desired, drizzle the cookies with a powdered sugar glaze. Frozen cookies should not be frosted until ready to serve.

Cut out Cookies

⊞ ⊞ ⊞

Cut-out cookies (sugar cookies) are always fun to make. Young or old, it doesn't matter, we enjoy using the wonderful variety of cookie cutters available to us today.

The dough for cut-out cookies should be chilled before rolling out. Roll out only a small portion at a time and keep the rest chilled.

Roll dough on a lightly floured surface, rolling ⅛-inch thick or as specified in recipe. Cookie cutters should be dipped in flour or powdered sugar before cutting. Cookies can be served plain or decorated.

Best Sugar Cookies

Oven 375°F

2	cups butter, softened (do not substitute)
2	cups sugar
4	large eggs
2	teaspoons vanilla extract
1	teaspoon salt
6	cups flour

1. In mixer bowl, cream butter until smooth. Gradually add sugar, mixing well after each addition. Beat until light and fluffy. Add eggs and vanilla and mix well. Combine salt and flour. Add to creamed mixture, a little at a time and mix well. Cover and chill at least 6 hours.

2. On lightly floured surface, using a small amount of dough at a time, roll out to ⅛-inch thickness. Cut desired shapes with cookie cutters. Place on ungreased cookie sheets and bake 8 to 10 minutes or until just beginning to brown around edges. Makes about 6 dozen cookies depending on size of cookie cutters.

Easy Sugar Cookies

Oven 350°F

½	cup butter, softened
½	cup sugar, plus some to sprinkle on top
1	teaspoon vanilla extract
1	large egg yolk (reserve white)
1	cup flour

1. Combine ingredients in mixer bowl until blended.

2. Shape into small balls and place on ungreased cookie sheet.

3. Beat egg white slightly with fork. Dip fork in egg white and lightly press cookie. Sprinkle with additional sugar. Bake 8 to 10 minutes. They should not brown but should be light in color. Makes 2½ dozen.

Pecan Shortbread Cookies

Oven 350°F

1¼ cups butter, softened
1¾ cups powdered sugar, divided
3 cups flour
1 cup chopped pecans, divided
1 lemon (2 tablespoons juice, 1 teaspoon peel)

1. In a large mixer bowl, combine butter and ¾ cup of the powdered sugar and beat until light and fluffy. Add flour and beat just until blended. Stir in ½ cup of the pecans. Press dough into an ungreased 15x10-inch baking pan. Sprinkle with remaining ½ cup pecans and bake 20 to 25 minutes or until light golden – watch carefully. Place pan on wire rack and while hot, cut into squares and then cut each square diagonally in half. Let cool in pan.

2. Combine remaining 1 cup powdered sugar with lemon peel and just enough lemon juice to make a glaze. Drizzle cookies with the glaze; let set slightly, then remove from pan. Makes 48 cookies.

Everyone loves these little cookies. Put on the coffee pot and have friends over for coffee, cookies and great conversation.

Note: *Cut cookies evenly by making 3 lengthwise cuts and five crosswise cuts. You should then have 24 squares. Then cut diagonally, cutting each square in half, to yield 48 cookies.*

Chinese Cookies

1 cup butterscotch chips
1 cup semi-sweet chocolate chips
1 cup chopped walnuts
1 can (5-ounces) Chow Mein Noodles

1. Melt chips in top of double boiler; stir until blended and smooth. Remove from heat. Add walnuts and Chow Mein Noodles; gently stir until evenly coated. Drop by teaspoon onto waxed paper lined cookie sheet. Chill until firm. Store in refrigerator. Makes about 5 dozen.

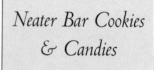

Neater Bar Cookies & Candies

Bar cookies are sometimes hard to remove from the pan and still maintain nice smooth edges. It helps if you line the pan with foil, extending the foil over the ends of the pan. Spray with cooking spray, then fill with cookie or candy mixture. When ready to cut, remove from pan and peel off the foil.

Coconut Macaroons

Oven 300°F

½ cup egg whites (about 4 large eggs)
¼ teaspoon salt
¾ cup sugar
1 teaspoon vanilla extract
4 cups shredded coconut

1. In medium saucepan, over low heat, combine egg whites, salt and sugar. Heat until warm, but not hot— you don't want to cook the egg whites. Remove from heat and stir in vanilla and coconut.

2 Drop into mounds, about the size of a walnut, onto greased baking sheet. Bake 20 to 25 minutes or until macaroons start to lightly brown on the bottom and around the edges. Cool on rack. Makes 36.

Variation: Add ¾ cup finely chopped dates and/or ½ cup chopped walnuts.

Raspberry Meringue Bars

Oven 350°F

¾ cup shortening
⅓ cup sugar, plus ½ cup sugar
2 large eggs, separated
1½ cups flour
1 cup raspberry preserves
⅓ cup finely chopped walnuts

1. In mixer bowl, cream shortening and ⅓ cup sugar . Add egg yolks and mix thoroughly. Stir in flour.

2. Pat mixture evenly into bottom of a 13x9-inch pan. Bake 15 minutes or until golden. Cool. Spread preserves evenly over crust. Beat egg whites until soft peaks form; gradually add the ½ cup sugar and beat until stiff but not dry; spread over preserves. Sprinkle with nuts. Bake 30 minutes. Makes 3 to 4 dozen.

Jan Hagel Cookies

Oven 350°F

1   cup butter, softened
1   cup sugar
1   large egg, separated
2   cups flour
½   teaspoon cinnamon
½   cup finely chopped walnuts or pecans

1. Cream butter, sugar and egg yolk in mixer bowl. Combine flour and cinnamon; stir into creamed mixture. Pat evenly into sprayed 15x10-inch jellyroll pan.

2. With fork, beat egg white with 1 tablespoon water; brush over dough. Sprinkle with nuts. Bake 20 to 25 minutes or until golden brown. Cut into bars while hot. Makes about 5 dozen.

Another method is to make drop cookies. Flatten slightly; brush with egg white glaze and sprinkle with nuts.

French Madeleines

Oven 425°F

4   large eggs
2   cups sugar
2   cups flour
1½   cups butter, melted
1   tablespoon vanilla extract
     Sifted powdered sugar

1. Combine eggs and sugar in top of double boiler. Heat until lukewarm. Remove from heat and place mixture in mixer bowl. Beat until cooled.

2. Add flour gradually, mixing well after each addition. Add melted butter and vanilla, mixing until smooth.

3. Use special shell shaped Madeleine molds which have been sprayed, or small 1½-inch sprayed muffin tins. Fill molds two-thirds full. Bake 8 to 10 minutes until just lightly browned around the edges. Remove from oven; let stand about a minute. Tap pan to release cakes; cool on rack. Makes 6 dozen.

These are absolutely delicious. They taste like crisp little butter cakes. Just before serving, sift powdered sugar lightly over top. The amount of vanilla extract called for is correct. Can freeze.

Mike's Babe Ruth Bars

When Mike had friends stay over, they always made these cookies and devoured every one of them.

1	cup sugar
1	cup light corn syrup
1	cup chunky peanut butter
6	cups Special K® cereal
1	cup semi-sweet chocolate chips
1	cup butterscotch chips

1. Combine sugar and corn syrup in a 2-quart saucepan. Place over medium heat and bring to a boil, stirring occasionally. Remove from heat. Add peanut butter. Stir in cereal until evenly coated. Press mixture into a sprayed 13x9-inch pan. Cool.

2. Melt chips in top of double boiler. Spread over cookie mixture. Cool; then cut into bars. Makes about 4 dozen.

Peanut Butter Drop Cookies   Oven 350°F

The basic cookie is very simple and delicious on its own. But, if the mood strikes you, you can always add a few extra ingredients.
Note: *This recipe does not contain flour!*

1	cup peanut butter
1	cup sugar
1	large egg
1	teaspoon baking soda

1. In mixing bowl, combine all ingredients and mix until well blended. Form into walnut size balls and place on ungreased cookie sheet. Bake 12 to 15 minutes or until golden. They should be slightly soft in the center. Makes about 18 cookies.

Variation: Add chocolate chips and/or chopped nuts. Or, after removing from oven, top centers with chocolate chips, an M&M® candy or a chocolate kiss. YUM!

Coconut Nut Bars

Oven 350°F

¼   cup butter, melted
1½   cups quick-cooking oats
1½   cups Angel Flake coconut
1   can (14-ounces) sweetened condensed milk
1   cup semi-sweet chocolate chips
½   cup chopped pecans or walnuts

1. Pour butter into a 13x9-inch baking dish. Sprinkle oats evenly over butter (most of the oats will not be coated). Sprinkle coconut over the top. Pour condensed milk over coconut. Sprinkle with chocolate chips and pecans. Press down slightly.

2. Bake 20 to 25 minutes or until just lightly browned. Cool before cutting into bars. Makes 30 bars.

You can play around with this recipe by using a variety of chips and nuts.

Quick Chocolate Bars

Oven 350°F

1   box (18.25-ounces) white cake mix
⅓   cup vegetable oil
2   large eggs
¼   cup butter
1   can (14-ounces) sweetened condensed milk
1   cup (6-ounces) semi-sweet chocolate chips

1. In a medium bowl, combine first three ingredients. Mix thoroughly with a stiff spatula or wooden spoon. Press two-thirds of the mixture into a sprayed 13x9-inch baking pan.

2. In small saucepan, melt butter over low heat. Add condensed milk and chocolate chips. Cook until mixture is melted, stirring until smooth. Pour evenly over crust. By hand, drop small pieces of dough over top. Bake 25 to 30 minutes or until lightly browned and chocolate filling feels somewhat firm. Cool and cut into bars. Makes 40 bars.

Remember the Chocolate Revel Bars that are so popular and get gobbled up almost as soon as they come out of the oven? Well, these are just about as good and a whole lot easier to make.

A delightful chocolate surprise in the center of each snowball.

Gifts

Cookies make great and much appreciated gifts. Package in attractive holiday tins, cookie jars, serving plates or baskets. Decorate with ribbon, tissue, colorful plastic wrap, or flowers, and perhaps include a cookie cutter, whisk or wooden spoon. If you are feeling really generous, including the recipe is a must.

Chocolate-Pecan Snowballs

Oven 400°F

1	cup milk chocolate chips
¾	cup powdered sugar, divided
⅓	cup chopped pecans
1¼	cups butter, softened
1	teaspoon vanilla extract
3	cups flour

1. In a small heavy saucepan, melt chocolate chips over very low heat. Stir in ¼ cup of the powdered sugar and then the nuts. Chill just until firm enough to roll into balls. Using about a level teaspoonful, roll mixture into 48 small balls. Chill until ready to use.

2. Meanwhile, in a large mixer bowl, beat butter until smooth. Add vanilla and flour and beat until smooth. If mixture is too soft, chill a few minutes. Otherwise, divide into 48 balls.

3. Flatten each ball and wrap it around a chocolate ball, enclosing completely. Place about 1 inch apart on an ungreased baking sheet. Bake 10 to 12 minutes or until lightly browned.

4. Remove from baking sheet and cool about 5 minutes on rack. Roll in remaining powdered sugar and place on rack. Let cool completely, then roll again in the powdered sugar. Makes 48 cookies.

Butterscotch Drop Cookies

2	cups butterscotch chips
½	cup creamy or chunky peanut butter
2	cups corn flakes

1. Melt butterscotch chips and peanut butter in top of double boiler. Remove from heat and gently stir in corn flakes to coat. Drop by teaspoon on waxed paper-lined cookie sheet. Chill until set. Makes 3½ dozen.

    Variation: Add raisins and/or peanuts.

Shortbread

Oven 350°F

1 cup butter, softened
½ cup sifted powdered sugar
¼ teaspoon salt
¼ teaspoon baking powder
2 cups flour

1. In mixer bowl, cream butter and powdered sugar. Beat until light. Combine remaining ingredients; add to butter mixture. Beat until thoroughly blended.

2. Divide mixture and pat evenly into two 9-inch pie pans. Prick all over with a fork. Bake 15 to 20 minutes or until a very light golden color. Cut into pie shaped wedges. Serve warm or cold. Makes 24 cookies.

Chocolate Walnut Brownies

Oven 350°F

1 cup butter
1⅔ cups semi-sweet chocolate chips, divided
2 cups sugar
3 large eggs
1 cup flour
1 cup coarsely chopped walnuts

1. Melt butter and ⅔ cup of the chocolate chips over very low heat. Remove from heat. Stir in sugar. Add eggs; stir until well mixed. Add flour and nuts.

2. Pour into sprayed 13x9-inch baking pan. Sprinkle with remaining 1 cup chocolate chips. Bake 30 to 35 minutes or until tester inserted in center comes out almost clean (do not over bake). Cool.

Mailing Cookies

Not all cookies travel well. Soft cookies, drop cookies and brownies are best. Also, miniature "fruitcakes". Thin, crisp cookies tend to crumble and break unless packaged with extra care.

Have available plenty of filler material such as bubble wrap, styrofoam popcorn or paper towels. Wrapping cookies back to back in plastic wrap and packing securely will minimize breakage. Be sure to mark the package Fragile.

Mom's Peanut Butter Cookies   Oven 350°F

1   cup peanut butter, smooth or crunchy
1   cup sugar
1   large egg
1   teaspoon vanilla extract
¼   cup semi-sweet chocolate chips
¼   cup chopped walnuts

1. Combine ingredients and mix well. Drop by teaspoon onto ungreased baking sheet. Bake 6 to 8 minutes or until the cookies are slightly soft in the center and lightly browned. Makes about 2½ dozen.

This is an unusual cookie because it doesn't have any flour in the recipe.

Raisin Crunchies

2   cups semi-sweet chocolate chips
½   teaspoon vanilla extract
1½   cups raisins
½   cup peanuts
1   cup corn flakes

1. Melt chocolate chips in top of double boiler, stirring until smooth. Remove from heat; stir in vanilla, raisins, peanuts and cereal. Drop by teaspoon onto waxed paper lined cookie sheet. Chill until firm. Makes about 3½ dozen.

Tip*: If desired, spread mixture into a lightly buttered 8x8-inch dish. Chill before cutting into squares.*

Peanut Butter & Oatmeal Bars   Oven 350°F

⅔   cup butter, melted
¼   cup plus ⅓ cup creamy peanut butter
¼   cup light corn syrup
1   cup firmly packed light brown sugar
4   cups quick-cooking oatmeal
1½   cups semi-sweet chocolate chips

1. In mixing bowl, combine butter, ¼ cup peanut butter, corn syrup, brown sugar and oatmeal. Press evenly into a sprayed 13x9-inch baking pan. Bake 10 to 12 minutes or until just starting to brown around the edges. Don't over bake or you won't be able to cut into nice neat bars. Place on rack and let cool while preparing frosting.

2. In a small saucepan, melt chocolate chips and the ⅓ cup peanut butter; stir to blend. Spread over cookie mixture and let cool. Cover and store in refrigerator until frosting is set. Makes about 30 bars.

It's a good thing this makes a large pan of cookies. You'll love the combination of chocolate and peanut butter.

Spritz   Oven 350°F

1¼   cups butter, softened
1   cup sugar
2   large eggs
2   teaspoons vanilla extract
½   teaspoon salt
3   cups flour

1. In mixer bowl, cream butter and sugar until light and fluffy. Add eggs, one at a time, beating after each addition. Add vanilla extract. Combine salt and flour and stir into mixture. Chill if necessary.

2. Press through cookie press onto an ungreased cookie sheet. Bake 8 to 10 minutes or until cooked through but not brown. Makes about 4½ dozen.

Spritz cookies are crisp buttery little gems that have adorned many a cookie tray. For color, try sprinkling with colored sugars or topping with a bit of maraschino cherry. For variety, dip half the cookie in melted chocolate.

When my children were small we did a lot of camping and, of course, a lot of eating. We often joined other friends who also had four children. When you have a large family, I think you sometimes tend to gravitate toward others with large families. Anyway, needless to say, we went through a lot of healthy, good for you food, but also a lot of desserts and cookies. We sometimes went through two batches of brownies a day - we just couldn't keep the adults away from them.

Patrick's Favorite Brownies   Oven 350°F

1   cup butter, softened
2   cups sugar
3   squares (1-ounce each) unsweetened chocolate, melted
4   large eggs
1½   cups flour

1. In mixer bowl, cream butter and sugar thoroughly. Add melted chocolate, then eggs. Stir in flour.

2. Pour into a sprayed 13x9-inch pan and bake 25 minutes or until tester inserted in center comes out clean. Do not over bake. Cool and cut into squares. Makes about 30 brownies.

Almond Butter Cookies   Oven 350°F

1   box (18.25-ounces) yellow cake mix
½   cup butter, melted
½   cup chopped almonds
3   large eggs, divided
1   box (16-ounces) powdered sugar, sifted
1   package (8-ounces) cream cheese, softened

1. In mixer bowl, blend cake mix, melted butter, almonds, and one egg. Pat mixture into a sprayed 13x9-inch baking dish.

2. Beat powdered sugar, cream cheese and remaining 2 eggs until well mixed; about 1 minute. Pour into baking dish, spreading evenly. Bake 40 to 45 minutes or until lightly browned. Cool. Cut into squares. Store in refrigerator. Makes 30 bars.

Chocolate Nut Bars

Oven 350°F

1 package (18.25-ounces) Devil's Food Cake mix
2 large eggs
½ cup butter, melted
1 cup semi-sweet chocolate chips
1 cup chopped walnuts or pecans, divided

1. Combine first 3 ingredients in mixing bowl, stirring until all dry ingredients are moistened. Add chocolate chips and ¾ cup of the nuts. Press into a sprayed 13x9-inch baking pan. Sprinkle with remaining ¼ cup nuts.

2. Bake 20 to 25 minutes or until tester inserted in center comes out clean. Cool and cut into bars. Makes 30 bars.

Lemon Nut Cookies

Oven 350°F

1 package (18.25-ounces) lemon cake mix
2 large eggs
½ cup vegetable oil
1½ teaspoons fresh lemon peel
⅓ cup finely chopped walnuts

1. In large mixer bowl, combine first four ingredients. Beat on low until thoroughly mixed. Drop rounded teaspoons about 2 inches apart onto ungreased cookie sheets. They should be slightly smaller than an unshelled walnut.

2. With finger, make an indentation in middle of each cookie, pressing almost to the bottom. Fill with chopped nuts. Bake 9 to 12 minutes. Cookies should not brown, but will flatten slightly just before done. Makes 48 cookies.

Cookie Tips

- Have eggs and butter at room temperature.
- Measure accurately using glass measuring cups for liquid and dry measuring cups for dry ingredients.
- Avoid using dark cookie sheets. They will absorb more heat and can cause over browning.
- Grease cookie sheets and baking dishes only if instructed to do so.
- Bake cookies on meduim rack.
- Cool cookies on a rack.
- Always cool baking sheet before cooking a new batch.

I had to hide these in the freezer or my children would eat them all in one sitting.

Mosaic Cookies

2   cups semi-sweet chocolate chips
½   cup butter
1   package (10½-ounces) colored miniature marshmallows
1   cup chopped walnuts
3½   cups Angel Flake coconut

1. In top of double boiler, melt the chocolate chips and butter. Place marshmallows and nuts in large mixing bowl. Pour melted chocolate over top; stir carefully to coat. Chill about 15 minutes for easier handling.

2. Sprinkle coconut on bread board. Spoon one third of chocolate mixture in a long row (about 10 to 12 inches) on top of coconut. Roll in coconut, shaping to make about a 12-inch roll. Place on waxed paper or foil; wrap and twist ends. Repeat with remaining mixture. Chill until firm. Slice to serve. Makes about 7 dozen.

These make a colorful addition to a tray of assorted holiday cookies.

Christmas Holly Cookies

35   large marshmallows
½   cup butter
1   teaspoon vanilla extract
1½   teaspoons green food coloring (approx.)
4   cups corn flakes
Red hot candies (for decoration)

1. Melt marshmallows and butter in top of double boiler; stir to blend. Stir in vanilla extract and enough food coloring to make a dark green. Remove from heat and gently stir in cereal.

2. Working quickly, drop by teaspoon onto waxed paper-lined cookie sheet. Decorate each cookie with 3 red hots for holly berries. Chill. Makes 3 dozen.

Chocolate Bon Bons

¼ cup butter, softened
1 cup peanut butter
2 cups sifted powdered sugar
1 cup finely chopped peanuts
2 cups semi-sweet chocolate chips
1 tablespoon melted paraffin

1. In mixer bowl, cream butter, peanut butter and powdered sugar. Stir in peanuts. If mixture is too soft, add a little more powdered sugar.

2. Roll into small balls and place on cookie sheet. Stick a wooden toothpick in center of each ball and freeze for at least one hour. (This will make the dipping process much easier.)

3. In top of double boiler, melt chocolate chips and paraffin and blend thoroughly. Remove 5 to 6 Bon Bons at a time from freezer. Dip one at a time in hot chocolate; remove excess by tapping edge of pan with side of toothpick. Place on waxed paper. Remove toothpick and fill in hole with additional chocolate, swirling to make a design. Place in refrigerator to set. Store in covered container in refrigerator or freeze. Makes about 7 dozen.

This is an easy recipe but time consuming. You can make the Bon Bons ahead and freeze. Then at your convenience, you can dip them in the chocolate.

Holiday Baking

*H*oliday baking can be an enormous task and it's the last thing you want to think about when you have a million other things to do.

Being organized is the best ingredient for stress-free cooking. Decide on the recipes you want to make that can be frozen. Depending on how much you want to do, starting in September and after the kids are in school, make a recipe or two a week and freeze. This will make for less stress in your life and your family will enjoy the goodies.

Chocolate Coconut Bars

Oven 350°F

1½	cups graham cracker crumbs
½	cup butter, melted
2⅓	cups Angel Flake coconut
1	can (14-ounces) sweetened condensed milk
2	cups semi-sweet chocolate chips
½	cup creamy peanut butter

1. Combine graham cracker crumbs and melted butter. Press into ungreased 13x9-inch baking dish. Sprinkle coconut over top. Pour condensed milk over coconut. Bake 25 to 30 minutes or until lightly browned.

2. Meanwhile, over low heat, melt chocolate chips with peanut butter. Pour over hot coconut layer. Cut into bars. Makes about 30 cookies.

Chocolate Peanut Squares

½	cup butter, melted
5½	double graham crackers, crushed fine
2	cups sifted powdered sugar
½	cup chunky peanut butter
1	cup semi-sweet chocolate chips

1. Pour melted butter over graham cracker crumbs, stirring to blend. Add powdered sugar and peanut butter; mix well. Pat into sprayed 8x8-inch pan, spreading evenly.

2. Melt chocolate chips in top of double boiler. Spread over top of mixture. Chill until firm, but not hard, about 30 minutes. Cut into squares. Cover and chill until ready to serve. Makes 25 squares.

Bar cookies can save a lot of time in the kitchen. These attractive bars are not only good to eat but make a nice addition to any cookie tray.

Delicious! Reese's Peanut Butter Cups® has competition. These can also be made ahead and frozen.

Cream Cheese Mints

1   package (8-ounces) cream cheese, softened
½   to 1 teaspoon desired flavoring
Food coloring
2   boxes (1 pound each) powdered sugar, sifted
Granulated sugar

1. In mixing bowl, beat cream cheese until soft. Add desired flavoring and coloring. Gradually add powdered sugar, mixing until dough is very thick and heavy, but not dry.

2. Roll in small balls; dip in granulated sugar. Press into small rubber molds; unmold.

Experiment to get the size ball needed to fill mold. If mixture tends to stick, add more powdered sugar. Mints should unmold easily without sticking. Place mints on plate and allow to dry somewhat before storing in covered container in refrigerator or freezer. Makes about 130 mints.

Use yellow coloring with lemon flavoring, pink with peppermint, and green with mint. Molds can be found in specialty kitchen shops and baker's supply houses or catalogs. These are wonderful mints for weddings, showers, luncheons, hostess gifts, etc.

Candied Walnuts

½   cup sugar
1   cup firmly packed light brown sugar
½   cup sour cream
1   teaspoon vanilla extract
3½ cups walnut halves

1. Combine sugar, brown sugar and sour cream in a heavy medium saucepan; stir to blend. Cook over medium heat, stirring constantly, until sugar is dissolved. Continue cooking, without stirring, to 238°F on candy thermometer.

2. Remove from heat; quickly stir in vanilla. Add walnuts and stir to coat. Turn out on waxed paper-lined baking sheet. Working with 2 forks, quickly separate walnuts. Let stand until coating is dry. Makes about 3½ cups.

Do try these, they are delicious. Bet you can't eat just one! For best results, don't try making these on a rainy day. If walnut halves are large, break in half. In fact, I usually break most of them in half.

Snowballs

1	cup semi-sweet chocolate chips
⅓	cup canned evaporated milk
1	cup sifted powdered sugar
½	cup finely chopped walnuts
1¼	cups Angel Flake coconut

1. Combine chocolate chips and milk in top of double boiler. Heat until melted, stirring to blend. Remove from heat. Stir in powdered sugar and walnuts. Chill slightly (until mixture just begins to hold its shape).

2. Drop by teaspoon onto mound of coconut. Roll in coconut; form into balls. Chill until set. Makes 2½ to 3 dozen.

Easy Toffee

2	cups finely chopped walnuts, divided
1	cup firmly packed light brown sugar
¾	cup butter
1¼	cups semi-sweet or milk chocolate chips

1. Sprinkle 1 cup of the walnuts evenly in well-buttered 8x8-inch dish.

2. Combine brown sugar and butter in small heavy saucepan. Bring to a boil over medium heat. Cook, stirring occasionally, to hard-ball stage, about 266° on a candy thermometer. Pour hot mixture evenly over walnuts.

3. Sprinkle chocolate chips over top. Sprinkle remaining 1 cup walnuts over the chocolate chips. Press mixture down firmly using a knife or metal spatula. Let stand until firm (or chill). Break into small pieces.

White Chocolate Clusters

12   ounces white chocolate
 3   cups coarsely chopped pecans or walnuts
⅓   cup semi-sweet chocolate chips

1. Melt white chocolate in top of double boiler or in a heavy saucepan over very low heat. Remove from heat and add pecans. Gently stir in the chocolate chips.

2. Drop by tablespoon onto waxed paper; cool. Makes about 48 candies.

   Variation: Omit chocolate chips and add dried cranberries, blueberries or other dried fruit.

Real white chocolate (as opposed to almond bark) has a very low melting point. If allowed to get too hot, it will be grainy and sometimes almost crunchy. If this happens, don't try to revive it, you'll have no choice but to throw it away. This is an expensive step to take, so remember...Low Heat.

Brian's Peanut Butter Candy

1   cup peanut butter, smooth or crunchy
1   cup light corn syrup
1   cup powdered milk
1   cup (or more) sifted powdered sugar

1. Combine all ingredients and mix until thoroughly blended. Shape into balls and roll in additional powdered sugar. Place on baking sheet and chill until set. Makes 3 dozen.

This or similar recipes have been printed over the years as See's® Fudge. I don't know how true that is, but I do know this has become one of my favorite fudge recipes. I had to experiment a bit to find the right temperature setting on my stove, which I found to be number five. This could vary from stove to stove. I also found that using a reliable cooking thermometer and cooking the sugar mixture to 234°F would ensure a perfect creamy fudge.

Ben's Favorite Fudge

¼	cup butter, sliced
1	cup semi-sweet chocolate chips
1¼	cups coarsely chopped pecans or walnuts
2	cups sugar
1	can (5¾-ounces) evaporated milk
10	large marshmallows

1. Place butter, chocolate chips and nuts in a large mixing bowl and set aside.

2. Place the sugar, milk and marshmallows in a heavy 3-quart saucepan. Bring to a boil over medium heat, stirring frequently. Cook about 6 minutes or until the temperature reaches 234°F, stirring constantly. Pour over ingredients in bowl and beat with a heavy wooden spoon or spatula until thoroughly mixed and butter and chocolate chips have melted. Pour into a buttered 8x8-inch baking dish. Chill until firm. Cut into about 36 squares.

Hint: It is much easier to remove the fudge and cut into neat squares if you first line the bottom and sides of the dish with foil; lightly butter foil. Then, when firm, turn the dish upside down to remove.

Variation: Use cashews or dry roasted peanuts. Mixed nuts are also very good. Cooking time may vary according to wattage of individual microwave ovens.

Microwave Peanut Brittle

1	cup sugar
½	cup light corn syrup
1¾	cups Spanish peanuts
1	teaspoon butter
1	teaspoon vanilla extract
1	teaspoon baking soda

1. In a 4 cup glass measuring cup (or microwave safe bowl), combine sugar and corn syrup. Cook on high 4 minutes. Add peanuts and cook 4 minutes. Add butter and vanilla; cook 1 minute. Quickly fold in baking soda. Quickly spread on greased cookie sheet to cool. Break into pieces.

Brunch & Lunch

Basic Omelet

3   large eggs
½   teaspoon salt
⅛   teaspoon pepper
1   teaspoon water
1   tablespoon butter

1. Slowly heat a 8 or 9-inch curved-sided nonstick skillet over medium heat. The pan must be hot enough for the butter to sizzle but not brown.

2. Combine first 4 ingredients in small bowl, mixing with fork until whites and yolks are just blended. Add butter to skillet; increase heat slightly. When melted, add eggs all at once. As eggs begin to set, pull edges slightly up and toward the center, letting uncooked egg flow underneath. When eggs are lightly set, fold in half and serve. Makes 1 omelet.

Any filling such as cheese, ham, onion, green pepper, mushrooms, etc. can be added to top of omelet just before the eggs start to set.

Ham & Cheese Omelet with Apple

FOR EACH OMELET:

1   tablespoon butter
½   Golden Delicious apple, peeled and diced
2   large eggs
⅓   cup diced ham
⅓   cup Swiss cheese, shredded

1. Melt butter in a 10-inch nonstick skillet. Add apple and cook until just tender. Remove from pan and set aside.

2. Combine eggs with 1 tablespoon water. Pour into skillet and cook until eggs begin to set. Then gently lift edges to allow egg to flow underneath. Continue until omelet is almost cooked through. Spoon apple, ham and cheese over one half the omelet. Let cook about 1 minute. Fold in half and gently slide onto plate. Makes 1 serving.

Keep cooked apple in the refrigerator for those days when you are really rushed.

Baked Ham Omelet   Oven 425°F

1	cup milk
6	large eggs, lightly beaten
½	cup flour
¼	teaspoon pepper
¾	cup chopped ham
¾	cup (3-ounces) Swiss cheese, shredded

1. Blend milk, eggs, flour and pepper in a food processor or blender until smooth. Pour mixture into a sprayed 13x9-inch baking dish. Bake 15 minutes. Sprinkle ham over top and bake 5 minutes more or until cooked through.

2. Sprinkle with cheese and bake about 1 to 2 minutes or until cheese has melted. Cut into 6 squares for light appetites or 4 squares for heartier appetites.

Preparing omelets for more than one or two can be quite a pain. This recipe is easier, and firmer than a regular omelet and very good.

Variation: *Use sausage and Pepper Jack cheese or bacon and Cheddar cheese.*

Frittata   Oven 400°F

6	large eggs
1	cup milk
1	tablespoon butter, melted
¼	teaspoon salt
⅛	teaspoon pepper
1	cup (4-ounces) Cheddar cheese, shredded

1. With wire whisk, beat first 5 ingredients until blended. Pour into a sprayed deep-dish 10-inch pie dish. Sprinkle cheese over top. Bake 20 minutes or until lightly browned and cooked through. Makes 4 servings.

Tip: *For variety, sprinkle top with parsley, ham, bacon, or sausage and cheese. Sliced vegetables and mushrooms can also be added.*

Ham & Cheese Bake

Oven 400°F

3 cups frozen hash browns, thawed
1 cup (4-ounces) Swiss cheese, shredded
1 cup finely diced ham
1 cup (4-ounces) Monterey Jack cheese with peppers, shredded
4 large eggs, lightly beaten
1 cup half and half

1. Place hash browns in a sprayed 1½-quart deep casserole. Bake 20 minutes. Remove from oven and reduce temperature to 350°. Sprinkle Swiss cheese over potatoes, then the ham and then the Monterey Jack cheese.

2. In a small mixing bowl combine the eggs and half and half. Pour over the cheese. Bake, uncovered, about 45 minutes or until center is set. Makes 4 servings.

   Note: It is sometimes hard to tell exactly when the center is set in this recipe. A knife inserted in the center should look fairly dry. The casserole will continue to cook somewhat in the center if allowed to stand about 10 minutes. Also good reheated.

Tired of the same old thing for breakfast? This recipe never fails to please. Serve as a breakfast, brunch or light dinner dish. Add fresh fruit or a fruit salad. A nice crisp roll or biscuit would also make a nice addition.

Heat and Hold Scrambled Eggs

¼ cup butter (do not substitute)
12 large eggs
1⅓ cups milk
1 teaspoon salt
⅛ teaspoon pepper
2 tablespoons flour

1. Melt butter in large skillet over low heat. Combine remaining ingredients in mixing bowl; mix until smooth. Pour mixture into skillet. As eggs cook, lift outside edges to allow uncooked eggs to flow underneath. Continue stirring until eggs are cooked, but still has a creamy texture. Serve, or cover and keep warm until serving time. Makes 6 servings.

Scrambled eggs, if allowed to stand any time at all, will become watery. This recipe allows you more time, thus avoiding any last minute calamities.

It doesn't take long to have this dish prepared and baking in the oven. Add sweet rolls or a coffee cake, sausage links and sliced strawberries or melon. What a treat. Surprise your family and make this a special meal for them.

Being able to prepare a dish the night before and bake the next day is right up there with slow-cooking for me. It makes a company breakfast or brunch so much easier. Just add fresh fruit, coffee and juice.

Hint: *If you are unable to find an 8-ounce loaf of bread, purchase a 16-ounce loaf and use the other half for dinner or French toast.*

Company Swiss Eggs

Oven 325°F

2	cups (8-ounces) Gruyere or Swiss cheese, shredded
¼	cup butter
1	cup whipping cream
½	teaspoon salt
⅛	teaspoon pepper
12	large eggs, lightly beaten

1. Sprinkle cheese in a sprayed 13x9-inch baking dish. Dot with butter.

2. Combine cream, salt and pepper. Pour half of cream over cheese. Pour eggs over top; add remaining cream. Bake 30 to 35 minutes or until eggs are set. Makes 8 to 10 servings.

Swiss Strata

Oven 350°F

1	loaf (8-ounces) French bread
1	cup ham, cubed or cut into slices
1	cup (4-ounces) Swiss cheese, shredded
6	large eggs, lightly beaten
1	cup whipping cream or half and half
1	cup milk

1. Tear bread into chunks and place in a sprayed 13x9-inch baking dish. Sprinkle with ham and cheese.

2. In medium mixing bowl, combine the eggs, whipping cream and milk. Pour over bread mixture. Cover and refrigerate overnight.

3. Bake, uncovered, 40 to 45 minutes, or until golden. Makes 8 servings.

Egg Surprise Muffins

Oven 375°F

1   can (16.3-ounces) Grands® buttermilk biscuits
7   large eggs
Salt and pepper
¾   cup (3-ounces) Monterey Jack cheese with pepper, shredded
Fresh or dried parsley for garnish

1. Press each biscuit into a 5-inch circle. Place in a sprayed muffin cup pressing on bottom and sides of each cup. Biscuits should extend slightly above the top of the cups.

2. Add ⅓ cup water to the eggs and lightly beat. Pour into a sprayed medium nonstick skillet. Sprinkle with salt and pepper. Cook, over medium low heat, stirring frequently, until cooked through. Remove from burner while eggs are still moist – they will continue to cook. Spoon into biscuit cups. Sprinkle with cheese, keeping the cheese inside the cups. Sprinkle with parsley and bake 11 to 13 minutes or until golden. Remove from cups and serve. Makes 8 muffins.

This recipe is surprisingly delicious as a family or a company dish. For brunch, serve with sausage links and fresh fruit. You can reheat in microwave (crust will be soft) or in the oven (crust will be crisper). Can be served with salsa. These muffins are wonderful hearty snacks for children. They can be cut in half and served warm and can be eaten out of hand.

Breakfast Bacon Pizza

Oven 450°F

1   can (8-ounces) refrigerated pizza dough
6   large eggs, scrambled, but still moist
2   tablespoons finely chopped onion
3   tablespoons finely chopped green pepper
8   slices bacon, cooked and crumbled
1   cup (4-ounces) Cheddar cheese, shredded

1. Unroll pizza dough and pat evenly onto a sprayed 12-inch pizza pan, forming a rim around the edges. Spoon the scrambled eggs over the crust. Sprinkle with onion, green pepper and then the bacon. Sprinkle cheese evenly over top. Bake 8 to 10 minutes or until crust is lightly browned. Makes 4 to 6 servings.

A deliciously quick and easy pizza for breakfast, lunch or dinner.
Hint: *This doesn't reheat well, so enjoy the first time around.*

Super Sunday Brunch

☙

Juice

Assorted Quiche

Fresh Fruit Bowl

Relish Tray

Bacon Quiche Pizza

Oven 425°F

 1 (9-inch) pie crust
 2 cups (8-ounces) Mozzarella cheese, shredded
 8 slices bacon, cooked and crumbled
1½ cups sour cream
 4 large eggs
 2 teaspoons dried parsley or 2 tablespoons fresh

1. Roll out or press pie crust to fit a 12-inch pizza pan, forming a ridge around the edge. Prick with a fork and bake 4 to 5 minutes. Remove from oven and sprinkle crust with cheese, then the bacon.

2. Combine sour cream and eggs. Add the parsley and pour over cheese. Bake 18 to 20 minutes or until lightly browned and cooked through. Makes 6 servings.

No Crust Spinach Quiche

Oven 350°F

 2 cups whipping cream
 6 large eggs
 ½ cup fresh white bread crumbs
 ½ teaspoon salt
 2 tablespoon frozen orange juice concentrate
 1 cup finely torn fresh spinach leaves

1. In mixing bowl, beat cream and eggs. Add remaining ingredients and pour into a sprayed quiche dish or a 10-inch, deep pie dish. Bake 35 to 40 minutes or until custard is set and lightly browned. Makes 6 servings.

Sausage Mushroom Quiche

Oven 375°F

¾ pound Italian sausage
8 ounces fresh mushrooms
1 (10-inch) pie crust
3 large eggs
1½ cups half and half
½ cup grated Parmesan cheese

1. Remove casings from sausage and slice the mushrooms. Add to medium skillet and cook until meat is cooked through. Drain off liquid.

2. Meanwhile, press crust into a deep 9-inch pie pan or a Quiche dish. Add meat mixture and spread evenly.

3. Slightly beat eggs to blend. Add half and half and Parmesan, stirring to mix. Pour over meat mixture. Bake 35 to 40 minutes or until knife inserted in center comes out clean. Makes 6 servings.

Hot Pepper Quiche   Oven 350°F

1   (9-inch) pie crust
2½ cups (10-ounces) Monterey Jack cheese with peppers,
    shredded
3   large eggs, lightly beaten
1   cup half and half

1. Sprinkle cheese in pie crust. Combine eggs and half and half; mix thoroughly and pour over cheese. Bake 40 to 45 minutes or until golden and mixture is set. Remove and let stand 10 minutes before cutting. Makes 6 servings.

A nice Southwestern touch. Serve with sausage links and fresh fruit.

Variation: *Add 1 cup chopped broccoli or 8 ounces cooked sausage.*

Mexican Quiche   Oven 350°F

8   large eggs, lightly beaten
¼   cup flour
1   teaspoon baking powder
2   cups (8-ounces) Monterey Jack cheese, shredded
¼   cup butter, melted
¼   to ⅓ cup canned diced green chilies

1. Place eggs in a large mixing bowl, beat to mix. Stir in flour and baking powder. Fold in cheese. Add butter and green chilies. Pour into a sprayed 10-inch quiche pan. Bake 30 to 35 minutes or until custard is set. Let stand 5 minutes before cutting. Makes 6 servings.

Forms its own crust!

Variations:
- *Add finely chopped red and green pepper instead of green chilies.*
- *Omit green chilies and use Monterey Jack cheese with jalapeños.*
- *Serve quiche slices topped with salsa.*

Quiche Lorraine

Oven 325°F

1	deep dish 9-inch pie crust
1½	cups (6-ounces) Swiss cheese, shredded
12	slices bacon, cooked, crumbled
4	large eggs, lightly beaten
1¼	cups whipping cream
½	cup milk

1. Sprinkle cheese evenly over pie crust. Sprinkle bacon over top.

2. Combine eggs, cream and milk, stirring until well mixed. Pour over bacon. Bake 40 minutes or until filling appears almost firm in center when pan is gently shaken. Makes 6 servings.

My favorite Quiche. Serve with fresh fruit or a spinach salad and toasted French bread.

Hint: *To prevent a soggy crust, you may prefer to pre-bake the piecrust. Prick crust with fork and bake at 400° for 10 minutes. Cool before adding filling.*

Southwestern Quiche

Oven 350°F

8	large eggs
¼	cup flour
1	teaspoon baking powder
2	cups (8-ounces) Monterey Jack cheese with peppers, shredded
¼	cup butter, melted

1. In mixing bowl, lightly beat the eggs. Combine flour and baking powder and add to eggs. Fold in cheese and then the butter.

2. Pour into a sprayed 10-inch quiche baking dish or deep 9-inch pie dish. Bake 30 to 35 minutes or until custard is set. Let cool 5 minutes before cutting. Makes 6 servings.

Sausage Brunch Soufflé

Oven 350°F

1½ pounds seasoned bulk pork sausage
6 slices white bread with crust, cubed
6 large eggs
2 cups milk
1 tablespoon dry mustard
1 cup (4-ounces) Cheddar cheese, shredded

1. Brown sausage and drain off fat.

2. Place bread cubes in sprayed 11x7-inch baking dish.

3. In mixing bowl, combine eggs, milk and mustard. Add sausage and pour mixture over bread cubes. Cover and chill several hours or overnight.

4. When ready to serve, bake 40 to 45 minutes or until lightly browned and mixture is set. Makes 6 servings.

Company Maple Sausages

16 pork sausage links
½ cup brown sugar
1 cup maple syrup

1. In a large skillet, brown sausages; drain off fat.

2. Combine brown sugar and maple syrup; pour over sausages. Bring to a boil, reduce heat and simmer until sausages are glazed and mixture has thickened. Makes 4 to 5 servings.

Sausage Gravy

12 ounces sausage
2 cups milk
¼ cup flour
Hot Biscuits

Cook sausage and remove from pan. Drain off all but 4 tablespoons drippings. Add flour and keep stirring until mixture is smooth. Bring to a simmer and cook about 1 minute. Add milk, a little at a time, stirring quickly to make a smooth gravy. Return sausage to pan. Taste for seasoning. You may or may not need salt and pepper. Serve over biscuits. Makes 4 servings.

Cinnamon Sugar Oatmeal

    2   cups quick oats (1 minute type)
    2   tablespoons sugar
    ½   teaspoon cinnamon
    ⅔   cup half and half
    Butter
    Light brown sugar

1. In medium saucepan, bring 2½ cups water to a boil. Stirring constantly, gradually add the oatmeal. Add sugar and cinnamon; mix well. Cook 1 minute.

2. Add half and half and bring to a boil. Pour into individual serving dishes. Top each with a dab of butter and a sprinkle of brown sugar. Makes 6 servings unless you are really hungry, then it makes 4 servings.

French Toast

    2   large eggs
    ½   cup whipping cream, half and half or milk
    ⅛   teaspoon salt
    6   slices French bread, cut ¾ to 1-inch thick
    Butter

1. Combine first 3 ingredients. Dip bread in egg mixture, coating well on both sides. Cook in generous amount of butter, about ⅛-inch deep, until golden brown on each side. Makes 2 to 3 servings.

Brunch Menu

❧

Omelets

Sausage Links

Assorted Muffins

Sliced Melons &
Fruits

Coffee

White Grape Juice
Spritzer

117

Pineapple Oatmeal

1 can (8-ounces) pineapple tidbits with juice
1 cup old-fashioned oats
4 teaspoons firmly packed light brown sugar
¼ teaspoon cinnamon
⅓ cup raisins
¾ cup milk

1. In a medium saucepan, combine pineapple with juice and 1½ cups water. Bring to a boil and add oats, brown sugar, cinnamon, and raisins. Cook 5 minutes. Remove from heat, cover and let stand 5 minues.

2. Spoon into serving bowls and top each serving with about 3 tablespoons of the milk. Makes 4 servings.

Eggs and Fried Bananas

I know this sounds like an odd combination, but it is truly wonderful. Cook eggs however you like them, over-easy, basted, etc. Slice bananas in half lengthwise and crosswise. Allow about 1 banana per person. Cook in heated butter in medium skillet until golden, turning once. Serve with the eggs.

Note: Bananas should be a little on the firm side. Over-ripe bananas will fall apart when cooked.

Swedish Pancakes

2	cups flour
4	large eggs
¼	cup sugar
½	teaspoon salt
2	cups milk
¼	cup melted butter, plus additional butter for cooking

1. In large mixer bowl, combine flour, eggs, sugar, salt and 1½ cups of the milk. Mix at medium speed until blended. Add remaining ½ cup milk and the ¼ cup butter. Cover and chill several hours or overnight. Batter should be fairly thin.

2. When ready to serve, if necessary, add a little more milk to the batter. Preheat medium skillet; add small dab of butter and spread to cover bottom. Pour about ¼ cup batter into skillet; spread thin by tipping pan, working quickly. When pancake appears a little dry on top, turn and cook other side. Roll up and keep warm while preparing remaining pancakes. Serve with syrup and fresh fruit. Makes about 12 large pancakes.

Since I'm not a morning person, I like the convenience of making the batter the night before, but if you are rushed for time, go ahead and eliminate this step.

Oven Pancake   Oven 425°F

½	cup flour
½	cup milk
2	large eggs
3	tablespoons butter

1. Combine flour and milk in a small mixing bowl, mixing with fork just until blended (batter will still be lumpy). Stir in eggs.

2. Place butter in a 9-inch pie pan and place in oven to melt.

3. Remove from oven; pour in batter. Bake 15 minutes or until puffed and golden. Serve immediately. Pancake will puff up, but will fall shortly after removing from oven. Makes 1 to 2 servings.

If you haven't had these pancakes before, you are in for a treat. They make a great breakfast or light dinner. Serve with fruit and bacon or sausage links or fill with peach slices, drizzle with apple syrup and sprinkle with powdered sugar.

Pancake Mix

7½   cups all-purpose flour
¼   cup baking powder
1   tablespoon plus 1 teaspoon salt
⅔   cup sugar

1. Combine ingredients in a large bowl. Stir to mix thoroughly. Store in an airtight container at room temperature. Makes about 8½ cups mix.

Pancakes (from "Pancake Mix")

1   large egg, lightly beaten
1   cup milk
2   tablespoons butter, melted
1¼   cups Pancake Mix

1. In mixing bowl, combine egg, milk and butter. Add Pancake Mix and mix until dry ingredients are just moistened. Batter should be slightly lumpy. If batter seems a little thin, add more mix. For medium-large pancakes, use ¼ to ⅓ cup batter for each pancake and bake on lightly oiled griddle or skillet, turning once, until golden brown. Makes 6 to 7 pancakes.

Tip: Double or triple recipe as needed.

During the last few years, a lot of our customers have been asking for more soup recipes. I can understand why. Soups are both filling and nutritious and can usually be made in just a few minutes. I have added several new recipes here and also in the Slow Cooker section.

Chicken Velvet Soup

⅓   cup butter
¾   cup flour
6   cups chicken broth, divided
2   cups milk
2   cups diced cooked chicken
Salt and pepper

1. Melt butter in heavy Dutch Oven or large saucepan. Add flour; stir quickly to blend. Cook over low heat until smooth. Add 2 cups of the chicken stock; stir to keep mixture smooth. Add milk. Cook, stirring frequently, until thickened.

2. Add remaining 4 cups chicken stock and the cubed chicken. Continue cooking until heated through. Add salt and pepper to taste. Makes 8 servings.

Tip: For a richer soup, use half milk and half cream.

121

I tend to make this soup quite often, especially when I have leftover chicken or turkey. You can substitute Cheddar cheese, but remember to keep the heat low to prevent mixture from curdling.

Chicken with Wild Rice Soup

1	package (6-ounces) long-grain and wild rice mix
1	can (10¾-ounces) condensed cream of potato soup,
4	cups milk
8	ounces process cheese spread, cubed
1½	cups cubed cooked chicken

1. In a 3-quart saucepan or pot, prepare rice as directed on package.

2. Add soup and mix until blended. Add milk and cook until heated through. Gradually add cheese, stirring until melted. Add chicken and gently cook until heated through. Makes 9½ cups.

Keep these ingredients on hand for a thick and hearty meal. Serve with warm sourdough rolls and a fresh vegetable tray.

Variation: *Use ¾ pound ground beef or turkey and tomatoes with green chilies.*

Bean Soup & Sausage

1	package (12-ounces) lowfat sausage
¾	cup chopped onion
1	can (15-ounces) black beans, drained
1	can (15-ounces) Great Northern beans, drained
1	can (14.5-ounces) diced tomatoes with basil, drained
1	can (14.5-ounces) beef broth

1. In a large saucepan, brown sausage and onion; drain off fat. Rinse beans and add to pan along with tomatoes and broth. Bring to a boil, reduce heat and simmer 15 minutes to blend flavor. Makes 6 cups.

Chicken Tortellini Soup

1   cup chopped onion
1   cup diced celery
1   package (9-ounces) cheese tortellini
6   cups half and half
24   ounces process cheese spread, cubed
4   cups cubed cooked chicken

1. In a small sprayed nonstick skillet, cook onion and celery until soft. Place in a large stockpot and add 6 cups of water.

2. Bring water to a boil; add tortellini and cook according to package directions. When pasta is cooked through, add half and half, cheese and chicken. Cook, stirring frequently, until heated through and cheese has melted. Stir from the bottom when serving (everything seems to settle there). Makes about 15 cups.

This recipe can easily be halved; in which case, you may still want to use all of the tortellini.

Some brands of process cheese can be shredded, but others are too soft and must be cubed. The shredded cheese will melt quickly and save a bit of time, but is usually more expensive.

Chicken Noodle Soup

2   cups cubed cooked chicken
2   cups mixed vegetables
½   cup chopped onion
6   cups seasoned chicken broth
2   ounces small egg noodles, uncooked

1. Place first four ingredients in a large pot. Bring to a boil and add the pasta. Bring to a boil again and cook on medium heat 12 to 15 minutes or until pasta is tender. Makes 10 to 12 cups.

The first chicken noodle soup I served as a newlywed was to my mother and father-in-law - and it was Campbells®. Soup and a roll. Fortunately, they were very gracious and didn't say anything, but I'm sure they had questions about whether or not I would ever learn to cook, or if I would just open a can.

*W*ant more soup recipes? Check out the Slow Cooker section.

Chili Corn Soup

3   large potatoes, peeled and cubed (5 cups)
2½ cups frozen corn, thawed
2   cans (15-ounces each) chili with beans
4   cups beef broth

1. In large saucepan, cover potato cubes with water and boil until just tender, about 15 minutes; drain.

2. Meanwhile, place remaining ingredients in a large pot or Dutch oven Add cooked potatoes. Bring mixture to a boil; reduce heat and simmer about 10 minutes to blend flavors. Makes about 10 cups.

French Onion Soup

5   medium onions
3   tablespoons butter
4   cups beef broth
Salt and pepper
Toasted French bread slices or croutons
1   cup (4-ounces) Swiss or Mozzarella cheese, shredded

1. Thinly slice onions; separate into rings.

2. Heat butter in a 3-quart saucepan or pot and cook onions until tender and light golden. Add broth. Season with salt and pepper. Bring to a boil, reduce heat and simmer 10 minutes.

3. Top bread slices with cheese. Place under broiler and cook until cheese is melted and lightly browned. Pour soup into serving bowls and top with bread. Makes 4 servings.

Quick Soup Ideas

• Add ⅓ cup salsa to a can of cream of tomato soup.
• Add salsa to black bean soup and top with shredded Cheddar cheese.
• Cream soups- add 1 tablespoon dry white wine or sherry per serving.

Company Egg Drop Soup

    3   cups chicken broth
    2   large eggs, beaten
  ⅓   cup fresh snow peas cut on the diaganol into narrow strips
  ¾   cup sliced fresh mushrooms
  ⅓   cup chopped water chestnuts
    1   tablespoon light soy sauce

1. Place broth in a large deep saucepan (you need this to prevent splattering when stirring in the eggs). Bring to a boil. Gradually add the eggs, stirring briskly after each addition. Add remaining ingredients and cook until mushrooms are tender. Makes about 4 cups.

If desired, you can still make a delicious soup using just the first 3 ingredients.

Wild Rice & Cheese Soup

    1   package (6.2-ounces) long-grain and wild rice mix
  ½   cup chopped onion
1½   cups chicken broth
2½   cups half and half
    1   can (10¾-ounces) condensed cream of potato soup
    2   cups (8-ounces) Cheddar cheese, shredded

1. In saucepan, cook rice according to package directions; set aside.

2. Meanwhile, in a 3-quart saucepan, cook onion in a small amount of water until soft. Add chicken broth, half and half and soup. Heat, but do not boil (the cheese will curdle). Gradually add the cheese, stirring with each addition. Continue stirring until cheese is melted. Add the cooked rice. Makes 10 cups.

Nothing warms the body like a hot bowl of soup on a cold winter night. For a complete meal, add a sandwich or salad and toasted bread or hot rolls.

Note: *If you want to eliminate a good portion of the sodium, omit the seasoning packet that comes with the rice, you will still have plenty of flavor.*

To expand the recipe you can add thinly sliced celery and any leftover vegetables such as peas and corn. Serve with French bread.

A vegetable soup can become a heartier main dish by adding cooked ground beef, chicken or leftover pot roast. If you like even more flavor use seasoned canned tomatoes.

Note: Canned diced tomatoes are sometimes a larger dice than you may want for soup. They can be cut in the can, by using kitchen shears or lightly pulsed in a blender or food processor.

Ground Beef Soup

1½	pounds lean ground beef
1	medium onion, chopped
2	cups cubed potatoes
1½	cups sliced carrots
1	can (1 pound 12-ounces) tomatoes, cut up
	Salt and pepper

1. Brown ground beef and onion; drain off fat.

2. Put meat mixture, potatoes, carrots and tomatoes in a large stockpot. Add 2 to 3 cups of water. Cook 1 hour or until vegetables are tender. Add salt and pepper to taste. Makes 6 servings.

Vegetable Chowder

¾	cup chopped onion
2	cups peeled, cubed potatoes
1	can (28-ounces) diced tomatoes
2	cups mixed vegetables
	Salt and pepper to taste

1. In a sprayed 3-quart saucepan or stockpot, cook onion until soft, but not brown. Add potatoes, tomatoes, and 3 cups water. Bring to a boil, reduce heat and simmer 15 minutes.

2. Add vegetables and cook 10 to 15 minutes or until potatoes are tender. Add salt and pepper to taste. Makes about 8 cups.

Broccoli-Cheese Soup

1½	cups fresh broccoli, chopped
¼	cup finely chopped onion
5½	cups milk
2	tablespoons butter
1	tablespoon flour
2	cups (8-ounces) Swiss cheese, shredded

1. In a large saucepan, cook broccoli and onion in the milk until vegetables are tender.

2. Meanwhile, in a small saucepan, melt the butter. Stir in flour and heat until mixture is smooth, stirring frequently. Add to milk mixture. Bring mixture to a boil, reduce heat, and simmer 3 to 4 minutes, stirring frequently. Remove from heat and gradually add the cheese, stirring to melt. Makes 6 servings.

Soup should not be allowed to boil after adding cheese. Some cheese has a tendency to curdle if added too quickly and if exposed to too high heat.

Quick Broccoli Soup

¾	cup onion, finely chopped
2	cups fresh broccoli florettes
1	cup milk
1	can (10¾-ounces) condensed cream of chicken soup
1	cup (4-ounces) Cheddar cheese, shredded

1. Place onion and ½ cup water in a 1½-quart saucepan. Bring to a boil and cook until onion is tender. Add broccoli pieces; cover and simmer 2 to 3 minutes or until broccoli is just tender.

2. Combine milk and soup, mixing until smooth. Add to broccoli. When mixture is quite warm, but not boiling, add cheese a little at a time, stirring until melted. Cook gently, until heated through, but do not allow to boil. Makes 3½ cups.

Lunch or dinner can be ready in less than 30 minutes. Just add bread and raw vegetables for a very satisfying meal.

Variation: *Some brands of reduced fat sausage are spicier than the regular sausage. If substituting ground beef, you may want to add additional seasoning or perhaps a can of Mexi-corn with it's wonderful flavor of red and green peppers.*

Sausage-Corn Chowder

12	ounces reduced fat sausage
¾	cup chopped onion
1	can (10¾-ounces) condensed chicken soup with herbs
1¾	cup milk
1	can (15-ounces) cream corn

1. In a large saucepan, cook sausage and onion, breaking sausage up into small pieces; drain off fat.

2. Combine soup and milk until smooth. Add to sausage along with the corn. Cook until heated through. Makes 5½ cups.

Clam Chowder

1½	quarts chicken broth
2	cups finely chopped clams
2	cups small diced potatoes
½	cup small diced carrots
4	cups half and half
	Salt and pepper

1. Combine first 4 ingredients in large saucepan. Cook until vegetables are tender and mixture has thickened.

2. Stir in half and half. Add salt and pepper to taste. Makes 6 to 8 servings.

Tired of Washing Dishes?

❖ ❖ ❖

Almost any kind of soup is delicious served in bread bowls. Use 6 to 8 inch rounds of sourdough or French bread. Cut 1-1½ inches off the top, remove the soft bread and fill with soup. No dishes!

Baked Potato Soup

4   large baking potatoes, baked, then peeled and cubed
2   tablespoons butter
¾   cup finely chopped onion
2   tablespoons flour
2   cups half and half
Salt and pepper to taste

1. Melt butter in large saucepan and cook onion until tender.

2. Combine flour with ¼ cup of the half and half, mixing until smooth. Add to mixture in saucepan. Add ½ cup water, salt and pepper. Bring mixture to a simmer, not a boil, and cook until heated through. Add the potatoes and then stir in the remaining half and half. Continue cooking over low heat until hot, but do not boil.

Creamy Potato Soup

8   slices bacon
1   cup finely chopped onion
4   cups cubed potatoes
2   cans (10¾-ounces) condensed cream of chicken soup
2   soup cans milk
Salt and pepper

1. In 3-quart saucepan, cook bacon until crisp; remove bacon and set aside. Pour off all but 1 tablespoon fat; add onion and cook until tender.

2. Add potatoes and about 1½ cups water or enough to cover. Cook, covered, until potatoes are tender, 15 to 20 minutes.

3. Combine soup and milk; stir until smooth. Add to potato mixture. Heat through, but do not boil. Add salt and pepper to taste. Add bacon just before serving or sprinkle on top as a garnish. Makes 6 servings.

You may have had a similar soup served in a restaurant topped with (in order):

Dollop of sour cream
Shredded cheese
Chives
Bacon

Beef Roll-Ups

Spread 10-inch flour tortillas with herb-flavored cheese spread or mayonnaise. Top with sliced roast beef, Monterey Jack cheese, shredded lettuce and thinly sliced tomatoes. Roll up tightly and serve.

You will probably have some of the meat left over. It can be reheated and served over baked potatoes, or used as a filling for flour tortillas. Or, also buy a can of 5 biscuits and make additional turnovers.

Gourmet Chicken Sandwiches

16 thin slices cooked chicken or turkey
1 can (20-ounces) pineapple spears, reserve 1 tablespoon syrup
8 slices raisin bread, buttered
⅓ cup mayonnaise
2 tablespoons finely chopped pecans

1. Arrange chicken slices on each of 4 slices of bread. Top with well drained pineapple spears.

2. Combine mayonnaise, the 1 tablespoon pineapple syrup, and pecans. Spread mixture evenly over remaining 4 slices of bread. Cut sandwiches in half and serve. Makes 4 sandwiches.

Beef-Sauerkraut Turnovers   Oven 350°F

1 pound lean ground beef
1 cup chopped onion
1 can (8-ounces) sauerkraut, drained
1 teaspoon salt
1 teaspoon caraway seeds
1 can (16.3-ounces) buttermilk Grands® Biscuits

1. Brown ground beef and onion; drain. Add sauerkraut, salt and caraway seeds; mix well. Cool.

2. Roll or pat each biscuit into a 5-inch circle. Top each with ⅓ cup meat mixture. Fold over to form a turnover. Press edges firmly to seal. Prick top 3 or 4 times and place on baking sheet. Bake 12 to 15 minutes or until golden. Makes 8 servings.

Banana-Muffin Treat   Broil

    4   English muffins
    Butter
    2   bananas, sliced
    8   slices Swiss cheese
    8   slices bacon, cooked, cut in half

1. Toast, then lightly butter the muffins and place on a baking sheet. Arrange banana slices on muffins. Top with a slice of cheese. Criss-cross 2 slices bacon on top of cheese. Place under broiler just long enough to melt the cheese. Makes 2 to 4 servings.

Burger Towers

    2   pounds lean ground beef
    1   teaspoon seasoned salt
    2   large tomatoes
    4   ounces small mushrooms
    2   tablespoons butter
    3   hamburger buns, split and toasted

1. Lightly mix ground beef with salt. Shape into 6 patties about 1-inch thick. Pan-fry, grill or broil over medium heat, cooking to no less than 160°.

2. Meanwhile, cut each tomato into 3 thick slices. Sauté mushrooms in butter until tender. Place a meat patty on each bun half; top with tomato slice and garnish with mushroom caps. Makes 6 servings.

Bagels
⊞ ⊞ ⊞

Turkey Club Bagel
Arrange sliced turkey, bacon, cheese, sliced tomatoes and mayonnaise on a fresh bagel.

Gourmet Bagel
Arrange hot corned beef and pastrami, Swiss cheese and Thousand Island dressing on a bagel of your choice.

Egg Salad Bagel
Combine chopped hard-boiled eggs with salt, dill weed, chopped almonds and mayonnaise. Serve on bagels.

Bacon Cheeseburgers   Grill

1   pound lean ground beef
1   medium onion, cut into 4 ¼-inch slices
Salt
4   slices Cheddar cheese
4   hamburger buns
4   slices bacon, cooked, halved crosswise

1. Make 4 ground beef patties and place on medium-hot grill along with the onion slices. Cook over direct heat, turning meat patties and onion slices halfway through cooking time. Cook until meat is cooked to no less than 160° and onion is tender. Top meat with cheese slices last 2 minutes of cooking time.

2. Place meat on buns and top with onion and bacon. Serve with your choice of condiments. Makes 4 servings.

Swiss Burgers   Grill

1   pound lean ground beef
2   tablespoons sour cream
¼   teaspoon dried dill weed
4   slices Swiss cheese
4   hamburger buns, toasted

1. Combine first 3 ingredients just until mixed. Shape into 4 patties and place on medium-hot grill over direct heat. Cook, turning once, until cooked to no less than 160°. Top with cheese the last 2 minutes of cooking time. Serve on buns with your choice of condiments. Makes 4 servings.

What's in the Beef?

Hamburgers, because they are made with "ground" beef, must be cooked well-done. To ensure safety, cook to 160° and check temperature with an accurate meat thermometer with a sensor in the tip, thus reducing any margin for error. "No Pink" in the center doesn't always mean it has cooked long enough. Don't take chances. This applies to any recipe using ground beef: meatloaf, Salisbury steak, meatballs, etc.

Stuffed Burgers   Grill

> 1½ pounds lean ground beef
> 1   cup (4-ounces) Cheddar cheese, shredded
>   Barbecue sauce of your choice
> 4   large-size hamburger buns, toasted, if desired
>   Sliced pickles
>   Lettuce

1. Divide meat into 8 equal portions. Shape each portion into thin patties. Sprinkle cheese in center of half the patties. Press remaining patties over cheese and press edges to seal, enclosing all of the cheese.

2. Place on grill and cook until meat is cooked to no less than 160°, turning once or as needed to cook through, brushing with the Barbeque sauce toward end of cooking time. Serve on buns with sliced pickles and lettuce. Makes 4 servings.

CHOICE OF FILLINGS:

- Herb flavored cheese spread
- Crumbled Roquefort cheese or dressing
- Flavored butters
- Thinly sliced mushrooms sauteed in butter
- Thinly sliced onion or green pepper slices
- Pizza sauce and Mozzarella cheese
- Thinly sliced pepperoni and Mozzarella cheese
- Sliced or chopped ham and Swiss cheese
- Thinly sliced red peppers and Monterey Jack cheese
- Monterey Jack cheese with peppers

Beef and Cheese Roll-ups

1   container (5-ounces) soft spread Herb cheese
8   slices Deli roast beef
4   (10-inch) flour tortillas
¾   pound sliced Monterey Jack cheese
    Shredded lettuce

1. Spread cheese spread on tortillas. Top with meat slices, cheese and lettuce. Roll up tightly and serve, or wrap tightly with plastic wrap and chill until ready to serve. Makes 4 servings.

The nice thing about tortilla roll-ups is that you can use almost any combination of foods. Use your favorite ingredients and you just might come up with some fantastic sandwiches. Keep in mind that in order to roll the sandwich, you need to use thin slices of meat and cheese and it works best if the lettuce is shredded or you can use a flat lettuce and there shouldn't be a problem.

Ways to Reduce the Fat in Sandwiches

- Mustard instead of butter, mayonnaise or pesto
- Reduced fat or nonfat mayonnaise
- Nonfat cream cheese
- Reduced fat or nonfat sliced cheese
- Tuna packed in water
- Less meat and cheese and more lettuce, sprouts and tomato
- Nonfat or very low fat breads and rolls
- Thin sliced meats rolled or folded on bread to make layers of meat appear thicker
- Lower fat meats, such as chicken, turkey and ham

Open-Faced Smoked Salmon Sandwich

> 1 loaf French bread (long narrow loaf)
> ¼ cup butter, softened or olive oil
> 4 to 6 ounces thinly sliced smoked salmon
> 8 slices Mozzarella or Provolone cheese
> Chopped fresh parsley for garnish

1. Slice the bread, at an angle, into 6-inch long slices, making 8 slices. Spread one side of each slice with butter or oil. Place on baking sheet and broil until lightly toasted.

2. Remove from oven and top with salmon slices. Arrange cheese slices over salmon, cutting to fit. Return to broiler to melt the cheese. Sprinkle with parsley. Makes 8 servings.

Smoked Salmon

⊠ ⊠ ⊠

There are two methods for smoking salmon. There is hot smoking, which is probably the most popular method and cold smoking which is much more complicated. Hot smoked salmon is darker in color and difficult to slice. It also tends to be quite dry if not properly smoked. Cold smoked salmon actually looks uncooked, but it is much easier to slice.

Vegie Pita Sandwich

FOR EACH SANDWICH:

> 1 Pita bread
> Cream cheese, softened
> Thinly sliced cucumber
> Shredded lettuce
> Sliced Swiss cheese
> Thinly sliced tomatoes

1. Spread inside of each Pita with a thin layer of cream cheese. Add remaining ingredients and enjoy. Makes 1 sandwich.

Are you tired of doing the same old thing for picnics? Give this a try, it's a little different and great for those hungrey appetites.

Note: You can vary the type and size of the bread loaf as well as the filling.

Prepare these for picnics, kid's birthday parties, and after the game. Sandwiches can be made ahead and reheated.

Bread Bowl Sandwich

SANDWICH FOR TWO:

1   (5 to 6 inch) round loaf sour dough bread, unsliced
1   tablespoon mayonnaise
3   ounces Deli sliced turkey
1   small plum tomato, sliced
    Lettuce

1. Cut a 1 to 1½-inch slice from top of bread. Remove bread from center, leaving a ¼-inch shell. Spread inside of shell with mayonnaise. Arrange folded slices of turkey on bottom. Top with tomato slices, then lettuce. Replace top. Cut in half to serve. Makes 2 servings.

Sloppy Joes

2   pounds lean ground beef
1   cup finely chopped onion
¾   cup chili sauce
3   tablespoons prepared mustard
1   to 2 teaspoons chili powder, or to taste
    Hamburger buns

1. In a large skillet, cook ground beef and onion until browned; drain off fat. Add chili sauce, mustard and chili powder along with ½-cup water. Bring to a boil, reduce heat and simmer 15 to 20 minutes or until liquid is absorbed, stirring occasionally. Serve on buns. Makes 6 to 8 sandwiches.

Breakfast Ham Sandwich

Broil

2   English muffins, toasted
Dijon mustard
4   slices sliced Deli ham
4   eggs, poached
4   slices Cheddar cheese

1. Spread muffins with mustard. Top with ham, folded to fit. Top with egg, then cheese. Place under broiler to melt cheese. Makes 2 to 4 servings.

Serve with fresh fruit, coffee and orange juice.

Tortilla Turnovers

Oven 400°F

1   pound lean ground beef
1   cup thick and chunky salsa
6   flour tortillas
6   tablespoons chopped onion
2   cups (8-ounces) Cheddar cheese, shredded

1. In medium skillet, brown ground beef, mashing meat slightly so you have small pieces of meat rather than large. Drain off fat. Add salsa; bring to a simmer and cook 15 minutes or until liquid is absorbed.

2. Place tortillas on ungreased baking sheets. Just off center of each, place a portion of the meat mixture. Sprinkle with onion and cheese. Bake just until the cheese melts. This takes only a minute or so. Remove from oven and fold each tortilla in half like a turnover. Press edges to seal. Makes 6 servings.

Taco Burgers

Brown 1 pound ground beef with 1 package taco seasoning mix and cook as directed on package; drain. Serve on hamburger buns with shredded cheese, shredded lettuce and chopped tomatoes.

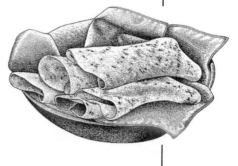

Sausage patties and maple syrup sounds a little weird, but that's how some kids like them.

Sausage Biscuits

1   can of 5 (10.8-ounces) buttermilk biscuits
5   sausage patties
5   slices Cheddar or American cheese
   Maple syrup (optional)

1. Bake biscuits according to package directions.

2. Meanwhile cook sausage; drain.

3. Cut biscuits in half horizontally. Place a sausage patty on each biscuit half; then a slice of cheese and top with the other biscuit half. Serve with Maple syrup, if desired.

English Muffin Treats   Broil

Tip: *When cutting sandwiches, use a sharp or serrated knife to avoid squashing the bread.*

2   English muffins, split and toasted
   Mayonnaise
4   (¼-inch) tomato slices
4   thin onion slices
4   slices of Cheddar cheese
4   slices of bacon, cooked and cut in half

1. Spread muffins with mayonnaise. Layer with slices of tomato, onion and cheese. Place under broiler to melt cheese. Top each with 2 strips of bacon and serve. Makes 4 sandwiches.

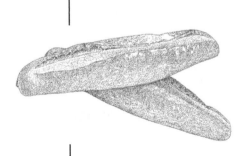

Favorite Barbecue Pork Sandwich

Kraft® Original barbecue sauce
Hot pepper sauce
Thinly sliced Grilled Pork Loin Roast, see page 178.
Shredded green cabbage
Hamburger buns

1. Several hours ahead or day ahead, combine barbeque sauce and several drops of hot sauce to taste. Cover and store in refrigerator.

2. When ready to serve the sandwiches, heat the sliced meat and warm the buns. Spread sauce on buns, top with sliced pork and then top meat with shredded cabbage. If at this point the sandwiches have cooled off, place briefly in the microwave to reheat.

I have tried other prepared and purchased barbecue sauces with this sandwich, but Kraft® seems to work the best. And for that little zing, you do need the hot sauce too.

Tuna Burgers   Oven 350°F

1	can (6-ounces) tuna, drained
¼	cup finely chopped celery
½	cup (2-ounces) Cheddar cheese, shredded
½	small onion, finely chopped
⅓	cup mayonnaise (or to moisten)
6	hamburger buns

1. Combine first 5 ingredients, tossing with just enough mayonnaise to moisten. Fill buns with mixture. Wrap each separately in foil or place in baking pan and cover with foil. Bake 20 minutes or until heated through. Makes 6 sandwiches.

Panini
❖ ❖ ❖

What is it? A panini is nothing more than a grilled sandwich, ususally made with foccacia bread. They are dressed up a bit with seasonings and sometimes cooked on a special grill which conpresses the sandwich and cooks from both sides, but a skillet will work fine. Try with assorted Deli meats, cheese, sliced vegetables, chicken or turkey breast and assorted breads.

Special Turkey Sandwich

FOR EACH SANDWICH:

2   slices sourdough bread
1   tablespoon cream cheese, softened
2   tablespoons cranberry sauce
2   ounces Deli sliced turkey
Lettuce leaves

1. Spread one side of each bread slice with cream cheese. Spread with cranberry sauce. Add turkey and lettuce. Makes 1 sandwich.

Turkey & Swiss Sandwich

2   tablespoons mayonnaise
8   slices pumpernickel or 7-grain bread
8   slices Deli sliced turkey
8   slices bacon, cooked
4   slices Swiss cheese
4   to 8 thin slices tomato

1. Spread mayonnaise on bread slices. Layer with turkey, bacon, cheese and tomato. Top with bread slice. Makes 4 sandwiches.

Easy Hot Chicken Sandwich

Prepare frozen breaded chicken breast patties as directed on package. (These are convenient to have on hand.) Spread hamburger buns or French rolls with Ranch dressing, Italian dressing or your choice of spread and layer sandwich with chicken, sliced tomatoes and lettuce.

French Toasted Sandwiches

4 thin slices ham (to fit bread)
4 thin slices cheese (to fit bread)
8 slices bread
2 large eggs, lightly beaten
½ cup milk or cream
Butter

1. Place a slice of ham and cheese between each 2 slices of bread, making 4 sandwiches.

2. Combine eggs and milk. Dip sandwiches in egg mixture. Brown on both sides in heavy skillet or on grill, using butter as needed. Makes 4 sandwiches.

Polish Sausage Sandwiches

1 tablespoon olive oil
¾ cup chopped onion
¼ cup chopped green pepper
⅓ cup drained sauerkraut
2 cooked Polish sausages, heated
2 hot dog buns or hard rolls

1. Heat oil in small skillet. Cook onion and green pepper until just tender. Add sauerkraut and heat through. Place sausages on buns and top with vegetable mixture. Makes 2 servings.

Focaccia Bread
❖ ❖ ❖

Focaccia bread makes great sandwiches. Make recipe on page 31 which is very easy if made in a bread machine. Slice bread in half horizontally and make individual sandwiches or make one large sandwich, then cut into wedges. Let your taste buds take over and use any ingredient that sounds good to you (within reason, of course). Sandwiches can be served hot or cold, depending on the type of ingredients used.

Chicken-Pineapple Sandwiches

Chicken can be served on lettuce leaves as a salad or in melon halves garnished with strawberries or raspberries.

2 cups finely diced cooked chicken
1 can (8-ounces) crushed pineapple, drained
¼ cup chopped slivered almonds
Mayonnaise
Lettuced leaves
Choice of bread

1. In a small bowl, combine first 3 ingredients . Add just enough mayonnaise to moisten. Spread on half the bread slices; top with lettuce. Place remaining bread slices on top. Cut sandwiches in half diagonally. Makes 4 to 6 sandwiches.

Deli Sub Sandwich

A meal in itself, but if you are really hungry, add a green salad or a cup of fresh fruit.

4 Hoagie rolls
½ pound Deli sliced roast beef
8 slices Jarlsberg cheese, halved diagonally
3 plum tomatoes, thinly sliced lengthwise
Italian dressing

1. Split rolls and top each bottom half with some of the sliced beef. Add cheese. Arrange tomato slices over top. Drizzle with dressing. Top with remaining bread. Makes 4 servings.

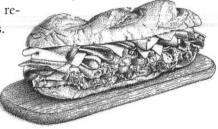

Reuben Burgers
Broil

1¼ pounds lean ground beef
French bread
Butter
1 cup sauerkraut, drained
4 slices Swiss cheese

1. Shape ground beef into 4 oblong patties and broil until meat reaches 160°, turning once.

2. Cut French bread into ¾-inch slices, to fit meat patties. Butter and toast bread. Place on a baking sheet. Top with beef patty and sauerkraut. Place cheese slices over top and place under broiler to melt cheese. Makes 4 servings.

Note: *If bread is a narrow loaf, cut slices on a diagonal to fit the size of the meat patties. Or, if you enjoy more crust with your sandwich, cut bread in half lengthwise, then in half cross-wise, making four pieces of bread.*

Cheeseburger Turnovers
Oven 375°F

½ pound lean ground beef
¼ cup chopped onion
½ teaspoon salt
⅛ teaspoon pepper
1 can (10.8-ounces) Grands® refrigerated biscuits
5 Cheddar cheese slices

1. In small skillet, brown ground beef and onion; drain. Season with salt and pepper.

2. Meanwhile, roll out biscuits on a floured surface, to a 5-inch circle. Place ground beef mixture on one side, top with cheese and fold biscuits over pressing firmly to seal. Prick top in 3 or 4 places and place on a baking sheet. Bake 10 to 12 minutes or until lightly browned. Makes 5 turnovers.

A half pound of ground beef will give you 5 sandwiches. Larger appetites will want two, but one should be enough for smaller appetites and children. These can also be reheated in the oven at 350°.

Sausage Turnovers   Oven 375°F

1   package (12-ounces) sausage
½   cup chopped onion
1   can (4-ounces) mushroom pieces, drained
1   cup (4-ounces) Monterey Jack or Cheddar cheese
1   can (16.3-ounces) refrigerated Grands® Biscuits

1. Brown sausage and onion in a large skillet; drain. Add mushrooms and heat through.

2. Roll each biscuit into a 5-inch circle. Place ⅛ of the meat mixture just off center on biscuit. Sprinkle with some of the cheese. Fold one side over filling, stretching to fit; press edges firmly to seal, pricking 3 or 4 times with a fork. Place on baking sheet and bake 10 to 15 minutes or until lightly browned. Makes 8 turnovers.

Grilled Roast Beef Sandwich

3   tablespoons mayonnaise
1   tablespoon Dijon mustard
8   slices sourdough bread
4   slices Monterey Jack or Swiss cheese
Deli roast beef, 10 to 12 slices
Butter, softened

1. Combine mayonnaise and mustard and spread on 4 of the bread slices. Top with cheese and roast beef. Cover with remaining bread. Butter both sides of sandwiches.

2. Cook sandwiches on a hot grill or in a large skillet until golden. Makes 4 sandwiches.

I don't know who likes these more, the kids or their parents. These are so convenient to have on hand in the freezer for lunch, dinner or a snack. For work or school, pack a few of these right from the freezer and microwave at lunch time.

Tip*: These are quite a treat for the busy mother who is tired of feeding her children the same things day after day. Use you imagination and fill with a variety of fillings. Make a cheeseburger or taco (no lettuce). Fill with scrambled eggs and ham, bacon or sausage. Add chicken or tuna salad. Use leftovers, etc.*

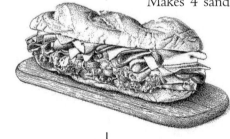

Picnic Turkey Sub

1   loaf French bread
1   container (8-ounces) herb or garlic cream cheese
½   to ¾ pound sliced turkey
¼   pound sliced cheese
Shredded lettuce
2   tomatoes

1. Cut bread in half lengthwise.

2. Stir cream cheese to soften. (If too thick, you can thin with a small amount of milk.) Spread on bread.

3. Layer turkey, cheese, lettuce and thinly sliced tomatoes on bottom half of bread. Top with second half of bread and slice into individual sandwiches. Makes 6 sandwiches

Flavored cream cheese gives these sandwiches just the zest they need to become a family favorite.

Open Face Bacon Cheese Sandwich   Broil

PER SANDWICH:

1 slice sourdough bread, toasted on one side
Sliced Cheddar cheese
Sliced Tomato
2 slices bacon, cooked
Parsley, for garnish (optional)

1. Cover bread with cheese; top with tomato slice. Place under broiler and boil just until cheese melts. Top with bacon and serve.

Tortilla Pizzas

Oven 400°F

Flour tortillas make a great crust for quick pizzas. You may be surprised at how good they are. Toppings are endless, just use your imagination and have fun.

Flour tortillas
Pizza sauce, purchased or page 306
Mozzarella cheese, shredded
Choice of meat
Choice of vegetable
Grated Parmesan cheese

1. Place tortillas on baking sheet and bake 5 to 6 minutes or until lightly toasted. Remove from oven and turn over. Spread with pizza sauce, sprinkle with cheese. Top with meat and/or vegetables. Sprinkle with Parmesan.

2. Increase heat to 450° and bake 10 to 12 minutes or until cheese is melted and pizza is lightly browned.

MEAT CHOICES:
Cooked ground beef, Cooked sausage, Canadian bacon, Pepperoni, Bacon, Ham, Chicken

VEGETABLE CHOICES:
Sliced tomatoes, Onions, Mushrooms, Red, yellow or green pepper, Ripe olives, Avocado, Artichokes

Artichoke & Cheese Pizza

Oven 425°F

- 2 teaspoons olive oil
- 1 large onion, thinly sliced, separated into rings
- 2 cups (8-ounces) Mozzarella cheese, shredded
- 1 10 to 12 inch pizza crust or bread shell
- 1 can (9-ounces) artichoke hearts, drained
- ⅓ cup freshly grated Parmesan cheese

1. Heat oil in medium skillet and cook onion until soft, stirring frequently. Drain off any liquid.

2. Sprinkle 1 cup of the Mozzarella cheese over pizza crust. Top with artichoke hearts, onion and the remaining Mozzarella. Sprinkle with Parmesan cheese.

3. Bake 10 to 12 minutes or until pizza is heated through and cheese is melted. Makes 4 to 6 servings.

Pizza Party

Pizza parties are a lot of fun as guests become involved with creating and baking their own pizza. As the host, you can provide a variety of pizza crusts, toppings and cheese, and let others bring the salad and dessert.

Hint: Make the pizza dough recipe on page 33. Press into 9-inch pie pans and have guests fill with desired toppings.

Chicken Pesto Pizza

Oven 425°F

- 1 refrigerated pizza crust (10-ounces) or bread shell
- ⅓ cup pesto
- 1½ cups (6-ounces) Mozzarella cheese, shredded
- 1½ cups cubed cooked chicken
- 1 jar (6-ounces) marinated artichokes, drained
- 3 plum tomatoes, chopped

1. Place pizza crust on baking sheet and spread with pest Sprinkle with remaining ingredients in order given an bake 10 to 15 minutes or until crust is golden brown an cheese is melted. Makes 4 to 6 servings.

Use your choice of meat, and sliced mushrooms, olives or green onion, if desired.

Deep Dish Pizza   Oven 425°F

3	cups baking mix
¾	cup cold water
1½	pounds lean ground beef
½	cup finely chopped onion
1	jar (14-ounces) pizza sauce or spaghetti sauce
1	package (12-ounces) Mozzarella cheese, shredded

1. Mix baking mix and water until soft dough forms; beat 20 strokes. Place on floured board and knead about 20 times. With floured hands, press dough evenly on bottom and up sides of a sprayed 15x11-inch jelly roll pan.

2. Lightly brown ground beef and onion; drain off fat. Spread pizza sauce over dough. Distribute meat over top. Sprinkle with cheese. Bake about 20 minutes or until lightly browned. Watch cheese carefully the last 5 minutes. Makes 6 to 8 servings.

Pizza Dough

Make your own pizza dough or use refrigerated canned pizza dough, large biscuits, English muffins, tortillas, frozen bread dough, or easiest of all, purchased baked pizza crusts. Pizza crusts can be prebaked or unbaked. If unbaked, the cooking time will be a few minutes longer. Check closely the last few minutes.

Pizza Toppings

• Barbecue sauce, cooked chicken, chopped red onion and Mozzarella cheese.

• Pesto sauce, cooked chicken, chopped tomatoes, and Mozzarella cheese.

• Pizza sauce, cooked chicken, Canadian bacon, pineapple tidbits and Mozzarella cheese.

• Pizza sauce, cooked sausage, onion, green pepper and Mozzarella cheese.

• Pizza sauce, chopped plum tomatoes, fresh basil, Parmesan or Mozzarella cheese.

• Pizza sauce, sausage, pepperoni, mushrooms and Mozzarella cheese.

• Pizza sauce or olive oil, artichoke hearts, coarsely chopped onion, green peppers and Mozzarella cheese.

• Lots of Mozzarella cheese topped with chopped red pepper and whole basil leaves.

• Mozzarella and Cheddar cheese, artichoke hearts, red pepper strips and sliced ripe olives.

Meats & Seafood

Company Beef Casserole

Oven 350°F

- 1½ pounds lean ground beef
- 1 jar (15½-ounces) spaghetti sauce
- 12 ounces small egg noodles
- 1 package (3-ounces) cream cheese, softened
- 1 cup sour cream
- 16 ounces Mozzarella cheese, shredded

1. Brown ground beef; drain. Add spaghetti sauce; simmer 20 minutes.

2. Meanwhile, cook noodles; drain.

3. Beat cream cheese until smooth. Add sour cream; mix well. Spread half the noodles in sprayed 13x9-inch baking dish. Cover with half the cream cheese mixture; top with half the cheese. Spread all the meat sauce over cheese. Layer remaining noodles, cream cheese mixture and cheese. Bake 30 minutes or until heated through. Makes 12 servings.

Popover Pizza Casserole

Oven 425°F

- 1 pound ground beef
- 2 cups pizza sauce
- 1 package (12-ounces) Mozzarella cheese, shredded
- 1 cup flour
- 1 cup milk
- 2 large eggs

1. In medium skillet, lightly brown ground beef; drain off fat. Add pizza sauce and bring to a boil. Lower heat; cook 2 to 3 minutes. Pour into sprayed 13x9-inch baking pan. Sprinkle cheese over top.

2. Combine flour, milk and eggs; mix well. Pour over cheese. Bake 25 to 30 minutes or until heated through. Makes 6 servings.

If desired, cook on outdoor grill and serve with a mushroom sauce. For mock Filet Mignon, wrap 1 slice of bacon around each patty before cooking. Serve with baked potatoes and tossed green salad.

Salisbury Steak   Broil

1½ pounds lean ground beef
¾ cup quick cooking oats
¼ cup finely chopped onions
1 large egg, beaten
½ cup tomato juice
  Salt and pepper to taste

1. Combine ingredients in large mixing bowl. Shape into 4 thick oval patties. Place on broiler rack and cook to 160°, turning once. Makes 4 servings.

Cornbread Salsa Bake   Oven 400°F

1 box (8½-ounces) corn muffin mix
1 large egg
⅓ cup milk
1 pound lean ground beef
1 cup thick and chunky salsa
1 cup (4-ounces) Cheddar cheese, shredded

1. In a bowl, combine muffin mix, egg and milk, stirring just until moistened. Spread in a sprayed 8x8-inch baking dish. Bake 10 to 12 minutes or until golden.

2. Meanwhile, lightly brown ground beef; drain off fat. Add salsa and simmer 7 to 8 minutes or until excess liquid has cooked off. Pour over baked cornbread. Sprinkle with cheese.

3. Return to oven just long enough to melt the cheese. Makes 6 servings.

   Note: If desired, serve additional salsa to spoon over the top.

Quick Meat Loaf

Oven 350°F

1½   pounds lean ground beef
1½   teaspoons salt
¼   teaspoon pepper
½   cup quick-cooking oats
¼   cup milk
1   large egg

1.   Combine ingredients and shape into loaf in a sprayed 13x9-inch baking dish. Bake 45 to 60 minutes or until meat reaches 160°. Makes 6 servings.

Serve with mashed potatoes, broccoli and a molded fruit salad.

Southwestern Meat Loaf

Oven 350°F

1½   pounds lean ground beef
¾   cup thick and chunky salsa
1   large egg, lightly beaten
10   saltine crackers, crushed
¾   cup (3-ounces) Cheddar cheese, shredded

1.   Combine ingredients in a large bowl and mix just until blended. Place in a sprayed 9x5-inch loaf pan. Bake 60 to 70 minutes or until meat reaches at least 160°. Carefully pour off fat; let stand about 5 minutes for easier slicing. Makes 6 servings.

Wondering what in the world to do with that bit of left over salsa. Try it in meatloaf for a southwestern touch. Makes a great sandwich too.

Note: *Recipe can be baked in the oven, if desired, at 350° for about the same amount of time.*

Hamburger Chili Dish

1	pound lean ground beef
2	cups coarsely chopped onion
1	can (14½-ounces) stewed tomatoes with liquid
2	teaspoons chili powder
1	teaspoon salt
½	cup uncooked rice

1. In large skillet, lightly brown ground beef and onion; drain. Add tomatoes (cut up, if too large) and remaining ingredients. Add 1 cup water. Bring to a boil; reduce heat and simmer, covered, for 30 minutes. Uncover; cook 10 minutes or until most of the liquid is absorbed. Makes 4 servings.

An excellent lasagna recipe that doesn't take all day to make. If desired, make 2 smaller dishes and serve one for dinner and freeze one for later. The lasagna can be prepared and then frozen or baked and frozen and reheated at another time.

Everyone's Favorite Lasagna

Oven 350°F

2	pounds lean ground beef
1	tablespoon light brown sugar
1	jar (32-ounces) chunky spaghetti sauce with mushrooms
10 to 12	lasagna noodles, cooked
2½	cups (10-ounces) Cheddar cheese, shredded
3	cups (12-ounces) Mozzarella cheese, shredded

1. Brown ground beef in large skillet; drain off fat. Stir in brown sugar and spaghetti sauce. Bring to a boil; reduce heat and simmer 20 minutes.

2. Meanwhile, cook noodles according to directions on package. Spread about ½ cup of the meat sauce in sprayed 13x9-inch baking dish. Layer starting with noodles, then sauce, Cheddar cheese and Mozzarella cheese, making 2 layers of everything. Bake 30 minutes or until hot. Makes 10 to 12 servings.

Beef Rice Casserole

Oven 350°F

1½ pounds lean ground beef
½ cup chopped onion
1½ cups uncooked long grain rice
1 can (10¾-ounces) condensed cream of mushroom soup
1 can (10¾-ounces) condensed cream of celery soup
2 soup cans water

1. Brown ground beef and onion; drain off fat. Spoon into a sprayed 2-quart casserole. Add the uncooked rice.

2. Combine soups in mixing bowl; gradually stir in water until blended and smooth. Pour over rice mixture. Bake 1 hour and 15 minutes or until liquid is absorbed and rice is tender. Makes 6 to 8 servings.

Your Own Seasoned Taco Meat

You won't have to purchase expensive seasoning mixes for this recipe (provided you have the other seasonings among your collection of spices).

Use for Tacos, Taco Burgers, Mexican Pizzas, Meat Turnovers and a topping for baked potatoes.

1¼	pounds lean ground beef
1½	cups chopped onion
1½	teaspoons garlic salt
2	teaspoons chili powder
¼	teaspoon cumin
¼	teaspoon crushed red pepper flakes, or to taste

1. In medium skillet, brown ground beef and onion; drain. Add 1 cup water along with remaining ingredients. Bring to a boil, reduce heat and simmer 18 to 20 minutes or until liquid is absorbed.

Tacos

1	pound lean ground beef
1	package (1¼-ounces) taco seasoning mix
6	to 8 taco shells or corn tortillas, cooked
	Shredded Cheddar cheese
	Shredded lettuce
	Salsa

1. Brown ground beef; drain. Add seasoning mix and ¾ cup water. Reduce heat; simmer about 15 minutes or until liquid is absorbed.

2. Spoon filling into taco shells, sprinkle with shredded cheese and lettuce. Top with salsa. Makes about 8 tacos.

Ground Beef Salsa Dinner

8	ounces rotini noodles
1½	pounds lean ground beef
1	cup chopped onion
2	cups salsa
1	can (11-ounces) Mexicorn, drained
1	cup (4-ounces) Cheddar cheese, shredded

1. Cook pasta according to package directions; drain.

2. Meanwhile, in a 12-inch deep skillet, brown ground beef and onion; drain. Add salsa and corn; heat through. Add pasta then sprinkle with cheese. Cover and cook 5 minutes or until cheese is melted. Makes 6 to 8 large servings.

This recipe will be a standby for many busy cooks. It makes a lot, which also makes for wonderful leftovers. To make ahead: Cook as directed and spoon into a sprayed 13x9-inch baking dish. When ready to serve, bake at 350° for 30 minutes. Add cheese and bake about 5 minutes.

Southwestern Chili

1	pound lean ground beef
1	can (15-ounces) dark kidney beans, drained
1	can (14.5-ounces) diced tomatoes, undrained
1	cup thick and chunky salsa
¾	teaspoon chili powder (or to taste)
	Salt and pepper

1. In a large skillet, brown ground beef; drain. Add kidney beans, tomatoes and salsa. Add chili powder and stir until well mixed. Bring to a boil; reduce heat, cover and simmer about 15 minutes. Taste for flavor, and if desired, season with salt and pepper. Makes 4 to 6 servings.

A delicious warming chili to be served on a cold blistery day.

Beefy Salsa Chili

Add a pound of ground beef to these pantry items and you have a family meal in less than 30 minutes.

1   pound lean ground beef
1   cup chopped onion
1   can (15-ounces) Chili Makins®
1   can (14½-ounces) ready-cut tomatoes, undrained
1   cup thick and chunky salsa
1   can (15-ounces) black beans, drained

1. In a large skillet, brown ground beef and onion; drain. Add remaining ingredients. Bring to a boil. Reduce heat, and simmer 10 to 15 minutes to blend flavors and heat through. Makes 4 large servings.

Hamburger Hash

Another dinner that can be ready in about 30 minutes. Add bread, fresh raw vegetables and fruit.

1   pound lean ground beef
1   can (11-ounces) Mexi-corn, undrained
4   cups frozen cubed potatoes, thawed
¾   cup beef broth
    Salt and pepper to taste

1. In a large skillet, brown ground beef; drain.

2. Add corn, potatoes and broth. Cover and cook over medium heat about 15 minutes or until potatoes are tender, but not too soft. Makes 4 to 6 servings.

Hamburger Hot Dish

Oven 350°F

1½ pounds lean ground beef
¾ cup finely chopped onion
1 cup sour cream
1 can (10¾-ounces) condensed cream of mushroom soup
1 can (10¾-ounes) condensed cream of chicken soup
4 cups noodles, cooked, drained

1. Brown ground beef and onion in large skillet; drain off fat. Stir in remaining ingredients.

2. Pour into sprayed 3-quart casserole or 13x9-inch baking dish. Bake 45 minutes or until heated through. Makes 6 to 8 servings.

Layered Hamburger Bake

Oven 350°F

2 pounds lean ground beef
Prepared mustard
Salt and pepper
Thin onion slices
Sliced tomatoes
Sliced green pepper rings

1. Pat half of the ground beef into a deep 8 or 9-inch round cake pan. Spread with a little mustard; sprinkle with salt and pepper. Cover with onion slices, then tomato slices and green pepper rings.

2. Pat remaining ground beef evenly over top. Arrange additional tomato slices over ground beef. Bake 30 minutes or until ground beef reaches 160°. Makes 6 servings.

You can do all kinds of things with this casserole. Add any combination of chopped green pepper, pimiento, olives, corn, etc. Use regular or spiral shaped noodles, top with buttered soft breadcrumbs or grated cheese. Or, just follow the recipe. If really in a hurry, heat ingredients in skillet and omit step two.

Note: If a smaller or larger recipe is desired, decrease or increase ingredients and size of pan accordingly.

Italian Meatballs

Oven 400°F

Meatballs are easy to cook when you bake them in the oven.

Note: If desired, make smaller meatballs, spear with a pick and serve as an appetizer.

1	pound lean ground beef
½	cup fine dry bread crumbs
1	teaspoon Italian seasonings
1	large egg, lightly beaten
2¼	cups purchased chunky spaghetti sauce, divided
2	ounces Mozzarella cheese, cut into 16 cubes

1. In large mixing bowl, combine ground beef, bead crumbs, Italian seasoning, egg and ¼ cup of the spaghetti sauce. Mix lightly.

2. Shape a small amount of mixture around each cheese cube, making 16 meatballs (the cheese should be completely enclosed). Place on a shallow baking pan and bake 18 to 20 minutes.

3. Meanwhile, heat remaining spaghetti sauce, add meatballs and serve over pasta. Makes 4 servings.

Basic Meatballs

Oven 425°F

Use for spaghetti, stroganoff, appetizers, etc. Meatballs may be frozen before or after baking. If more seasoning is desired, add parsley, basil, oregano or thyme.

3	pounds lean ground beef
3	large eggs, lightly beaten
½	cup milk
4	slices bread, processed to make soft crumbs
½	cup finely chopped onion
	Salt and pepper

1. Combine ingredients. Chill mixture if too soft to form into balls. Shape into desired size meatballs and place on a 15x10-inch pan. Bake 15 to 20 minutes or until temperature reaches at least 160°. Makes 6 dozen small meatballs.

Stuffed Green Peppers

Oven 325°F

1½ pounds lean ground beef
1 cup chopped onion
½ cup cooked rice
Salt and pepper to taste
4 large green peppers
2 cans (8-ounces each) tomato sauce

1. In a skillet, brown ground beef and onion; drain. Add cooked rice and season to taste.

2. Meanwhile, cut green peppers in half lengthwise. Remove seeds. Place cut side up, in sprayed 13x9-inch baking dish. Fill with meat mixture. Pour tomato sauce over top. Add ¼ cup water to baking dish. Bake 60 minutes or until peppers are tender. Makes 4 servings.

Note: Any leftover meat mixture can be spooned around the green peppers.

Skillet Lasagna

10 ounces mafalda pasta
1 pound lean ground beef
1 jar (15.5-ounces) chunky spaghetti sauce
1 tablespoon firmly packed light brown sugar
1 cup (4-ounces) Mozzarella cheese, shredded

1. Cook pasta according to package directions; drain.

2. Meanwhile, cook ground beef in a deep 10" or 12" skillet; drain off fat. Stir in spaghetti sauce and brown sugar. Bring to a boil, reduce heat and simmer 10 to 15 minutes. Drain pasta and add amount needed to sauce. You may or may not need all of the pasta. Stir to mix well and then heat through. Sprinkle with cheese. Cover and heat long enough to melt the cheese. Makes 6 to 8 servings.

A quick version of a family favorite. Serve with a salad and toasted French bread and you have a meal in minutes.

Note: Mafalda pasta looks like tiny lasagna noodles about 1-inch long.

A young mother, who doesn't think she can cook, told me she made these for a special friend. She was thrilled that it was so easy and so attractive that she told another friend that she absolutely had to buy this book. This encouraged her to venture out and try other recipes that she was reluctant to try before.

Chili Bowl   Oven 350°F

FOR EACH SERVING:

Small round loaf bread, unsliced
Melted butter
Prepared or canned chili, heated
Chopped onion
Shredded Cheddar cheese
Sour cream

1. Cut a 1 to 1½-inch slice off the top of the bread. Remove three-fourths of bread from center forming a bowl. Brush inside with melted butter. Bake 6 minutes, to lightly toast the bread. Remove from oven.

2. Fill with hot chili. Sprinkle with onion and cheese. Top with sour cream. Makes 1 serving.

Chili-Cornbread Casserole   Oven 400°F

2   cans (15-ounces each) chili with beans
1   can (11-ounces) Mexican corn
1   box (8½-ounces) corn muffin mix
1   large egg
⅓   cup milk

1. Heat chili and corn in medium saucepan. Pour into a sprayed 11x7-inch baking dish. Mix cornbread according to package directions and spread as evenly as possible over the chili. Bake 12 to 15 minutes or until golden. Makes 4 to 6 servings.

Chili Without the Beans

2 pounds lean ground beef
1 medium onion, finely chopped
4 teaspoons chili powder
1 garlic clove, minced
½ teaspoon oregano, crushed fine
2 cans (16-ounces each) tomatoes, with liquid, chopped

1. Brown ground beef and onions; drain. Stir in chili powder, garlic, oregano and tomatoes. Simmer 2 to 3 hours. Makes 4 to 6 servings.

Chili Bake
Oven 425°F

⅓ cup butter
5 large eggs, lightly beaten
½ cup yellow cornmeal
¾ cup flour
1¼ cups milk
2 cans (15-ounces each) chili with beans

1. Place butter in a 10-inch cast iron or ovenproof skillet. Place in oven to melt.

2. Meanwhile, combine eggs, cornmeal, flour and milk until smooth. Remove skillet from oven. Carefully pour batter into pan. Spoon chili into center leaving about a 1½-inch margin around the edge. Bake 18 to 20 minutes, or until puffed and lightly browned. Serve right away. Makes 6 servings.

Beef and Wild Rice

1 (6-ounces) pkg long grain and wild rice mix
1 pound ground beef
1 cup chopped onion

Prepare rice according to package directions, but omit the butter. Meanwhile, cook ground beef and onion in a large skillet; drain off fat. Add cooked rice, mix well, and heat through.

Ground Beef Deluxe

Broil

I like to serve these patties with scalloped potatoes, corn on the cob, toasted French bread and Raspberry-Apple Crisp.

1   pound lean ground beef
1   teaspoon salt
⅛   teaspoon pepper
4   tomato slices
4   strips of bacon, cooked and crumbled
4   slices cheese

1. Season ground beef with salt and pepper. Shape into 4 patties. Broil or grill on both sides until temperature reaches at least 160°. Top each with a tomato slice, sprinkle with bacon and top with a cheese slice. Continue cooking until cheese is melted. Makes 4 servings.

Southwestern Beef & Rice

Can be made in about 15 minutes and is a lot better than Hamburger Helper.

1   pound lean ground beef
1   cup cooked rice
1   can (15-ounces) kidney beans, drained
1   cup thick and chunky salsa
½   cup (2-ounces) Cheddar cheese, shredded

1. In a large skillet, brown ground beef; drain off fat. Add rice, kidney beans and salsa; heat through. Add cheese and stir just until melted. Makes 6 servings.

Spaghetti Cheese Casserole

Oven 350°F

1	package (12-ounces) thin spaghetti
1	pound lean ground beef
1	cup chopped onion
2½	cups spaghetti sauce with mushrooms
2	cups (8-ounces) Cheddar cheese, shredded
2	cups (8-ounces) Mozzarella cheese, shredded

1. Cook pasta according to package directions. Meanwhile, in a large skillet, cook ground beef and onion until browned; drain. Add spaghetti sauce, bring to a boil, reduce heat and simmer 10 to 15 minutes.

2. Drain pasta; add meat mixture and toss to mix. This doesn't mix very well so you will need to rearrange some of the meat in the casserole. Place half of the mixture in a sprayed 13x9-inch baking dish. Top with half of each cheese. Add remaining meat mixture. Sprinkle with remaining cheese. Dish will be quite full. Bake 20 to 30 minutes or until heated through. Makes 8 generous servings.

My grandchildren like this casserole because it has fewer tomato chunks (ugh!) and more cheese (yum!).

Ground Beef Stovetop Dinner

1	package (7.2-ounces) rice pilaf or beef-flavored rice mix
1	pound lean ground beef
½	cup chopped celery
¾	cup chopped onion
½	cup (2-ounces) Cheddar or Monterey Jack cheese, shredded

1. Cook rice according to directions on package. Meanwhile, brown ground beef, celery and onion in a deep 10-inch skillet; drain off fat. Add rice; if necessary, cook a little longer to heat through. Sprinkle cheese over top. Cover and let stand until cheese has melted. Makes 6 servings.

Nothing fancy here, but you'll enjoy this quick and easy recipe on those days when you have to eat and run.

Dinner Nachos

Oven 400°F

¾ pound lean ground beef
⅓ cup taco sauce
4 cups tortilla chips
1 small tomato, coarsely chopped
⅓ cup sliced ripe olives
2 cups (8-ounces) Cheddar cheese, shredded

1. Lightly brown ground beef; drain. Add taco sauce.

2.   Spread tortilla chips on a 12-inch pizza pan or large baking sheet. Spoon meat over top. Sprinkle with tomato, olives and then cheese. Bake 10 minutes or until cheese is melted. Serves 2 for dinner; 4 for snacks.

Ground Beef & Onion

1 pound lean ground beef
½ cup fresh bread crumbs
1 teaspoon salt
⅛ teaspoon pepper
2 tablespoons butter
2 large onions, thinly sliced

1. Combine ground beef, bread crumbs, salt and pepper. Shape into 4 oval patties.

2. Melt 2 tablespoons butter in a large skillet; add onion and cook until tender and lightly browned. If desired season with salt. Remove and keep warm. Add meat patties to skillet and cook to 160°. Arrange on serving dish and top with onions. Makes 4 servings.

Easy Goulash

❋ ❋ ❋

Easy, but good.

Great for boating and camping.

1 pound lean ground beef
1 can kidney beans, drained
1 can vegetable soup

Brown ground beef in skillet; drain off fat. Add kidney beans and soup. Simmer 15 to 20 minutes. Makes 6 servings.

Skillet Ground Beef & Potatoes

1	pound lean ground beef
½	cup chopped onion
3	cups frozen O'Brien potatoes, thawed
1¼	cups salsa

1. In a large skillet, brown ground beef and onion; drain. Add potatoes and cook 8 to 10 minutes or until tender. Add salsa and heat through. Makes 4 large servings.

This hearty dish of meat and potatoes can be prepared quickly and is sure to please hungry appetites.

Southwestern Muffin Cups

Oven 375°F

1	pound lean ground beef
¾	cup thick and chunky salsa
1	package (16.3-ounces) Grands® buttermilk biscuits
¾	cup (3-ounces) Cheddar cheese, shredded

1. Brown ground beef in medium skillet; drain. Add salsa and bring to a boil. Reduce heat and simmer while preparing biscuits.

2. On cutting board or other smooth surface, pat each biscuit into a 5-inch circle. Spray cooking spray in 8 of the muffin cups. Press a biscuit into each one, pressing well onto bottom and up sides of each cup, extending over the top a little.

3. Spoon equal amounts of ground beef mixture into muffin cups. Sprinkle with cheese making sure the cheese stays inside the biscuits. Bake 10 to 12 minutes or until biscuits are golden. Makes 8 servings.

Note: Can be reheated in microwave oven, but the crust will be soft.

Hamburger Salsa Dish

❀ ❀ ❀

A great family recipe when you have less than 30 minutes to cook dinner. Also good reheated.

- 1 pound lean ground beef
- 1 can (10¾ ounces) Southwest style Chicken Vegetable soup
- ¾ cup frozen corn
- ½ cup thick & chunky salsa

Brown ground beef in a large skillet; drain. Add remaining ingredients along with ½ cup water. Cook 10 to 12 minutes, over low heat. Makes 4 servings.

When cooking meats, I highly recommend you invest in an accurate thermometer. The one that I like best has an external display that you can place on your counter with a cord attached to a probe that you insert into the meat. You simply set the desired temperature and the thermometer will beep to alert you when it has reached that degree. Do not rely on thermometers that have preset temperatures for Rare, Medium Rare, etc., we usually find these settings to be too high. Probably the most important thing to remember when cooking roasts, turkey, or a whole chicken is to allow time for the meat to stand after roasting. Your meat will be juicier and easier to carve.

Beef Roasting Chart

Beef Cut	Oven Temp	Lbs	Approx. Total Cooking Hours	Remove when temperature reaches
Eye Round Roast	325° F	2-3	Med. Rare: 1½ to 1¾	135° F
Rib Eye Roast (small end)	350° F	4-6	Med. Rare: 1¾ to 2 / **Med: 2-2½**	135° F / **140° F**
		6-8	Med. Rare: 2¼ / **Med: 2½-2¾**	135° F / **140° F**
Rib Eye Roast (large end)	350° F	4-6	Med. Rare: 2-2½ / **Med: 2½-3**	135° F / **140° F**
		6-8	Med. Rare: 2¼-2½ / **Med: 2½-3**	135° F / **140° F**
Rib Roast (prime rib)	350° F	6-8	Med. Rare: 2¼-2½ / **Med: ¾-3**	135° F / **140° F**
		8-10	Med. Rare: 2½-3 / **Med: 3-3½**	135° F / **140° F**
Round Tip Roast	325° F	4-6	Med. Rare: 2-2½ / **Med: 2½-3**	140° F / **150° F**
		6-8	Med. Rare: 2½-3 / **Med: 3-3½**	140° F / **150° F**
Tenderloin Roast	425° F	2-3	Med. Rare: 35-40 min. / **Med. 45-50 min**	135° F / **140° F**
		4-5	Med. Rare: 50-60 min. / **Med. 60-70 min**	135° F / **140° F**
Tri-Tip Roast	425° F	1½-2	Med. Rare: 30-40 min. / **Med. 40-45 min**	135° F / **140° F**
Ground Beef				160°F

Basic Pot Roast

Oven 350°F

1   3 to 4 pound rump, chunk or round beef roast
Flour
¼   cup oil
1   large onion, cut into 8 wedges
Salt and pepper to taste
1½   teaspoons of thyme or an herb blend

1. Brown meat in oil in heavy pot or Dutch oven. Add remaining ingredients along with 1 cup water. Cover; bake 2 to 2½ hours or until meat is tender. Add more water if necessary. If desired, potatoes and carrots can be added last hour of cooking time. Makes 6 to 8 servings.

Rib-Eye Roast

Oven 350°F

1   (5-5 ½-lb) rib-eye roast, small end
½   teaspoon lemon pepper

1. Place roast, fat side up, on a rack in a shallow roasting pan. Sprinkle with lemon pepper.

2. Place roast in oven and bake to desired degree of doneness. See Meat Chart on page 168. Cover with foil and let stand 15 to 20 minutes before slicing.

Pepper Roast

Oven 350°F

2   pound sirloin tip roast
2½   teaspoons seasoned salt
3   teaspoons fresh coarsely ground black pepper

1. Rub surface of roast with salt and pepper mixture. Place on rack in roasting pan. Bake 30 minutes per pound or until meat thermometer registers 135° for medium rare or 140° for medium. Cover with foil and let stand 10 to 15 minutes for easier carving. Makes 4 servings.

A rib-eye roast is one of the most expensive roasts you can buy. The rib bones are removed as well as any other bones, and all the fat and all the cap meat is removed, leaving only the tender eye meat. Some argue that you don't get the flavor you normally would get from the attached bones, but I doubt if most of us would notice the difference. A rib-eye roast makes a wonderful entree for company and holiday entertaining. And slicing is a breeze.

169

Standing Rib Roast

Oven 350°F

1   standing rib roast (4 ribs)
Seasoning, if desired

1. Place roast, rib side down, on rack in a shallow roasting pan. Sprinkle with seasoning, if desired. Bake to desired degree of doneness. See Meat Chart, page 168.

2. Cover lightly with foil and let roast stand 15 to 20 minutes before carving. Allow ¾ to 1 pound per person.

Beef: **To determine degree of doneness, beef should have the following appearance:**

Rare-130°   Meat will be soft in center and still red. Very moist, but probably not much more than lukewarm in center.

Medium-Rare-135° Meat will be pink in center, but darker around the edges. Somewhat firmer than rare, but still very juicy. Also considered safer than meat cooked to rare stage.

Medium-150°   Meat may still be somewhat pink in center, but with more darker meat around the edge. The texture is more firm than medium-rare.

Medium-Well-165° Meat will be darker throughout with very little, if any pink in center. Depending on cut of meat, can be quite dry.

Well Done-170°   Don't! But if you insist, know that the meat will be overcooked and also very dry unless that particular cut of meat has a lot of fat.

What Size to Buy

2 Rib Roast
4 to 5 pounds and
should serve 4 to
6 people.

4 Rib Roast
7 to 9 pounds and
should serve 8 to
10 people.

Beef Tenderloin with Mustard Caper Sauce

Oven 425°F

- 1 beef tenderloin (3 pounds), purchase the butt section
- 2 tablespoons butter, divided
- 3 green onions, divided
- 2 cups heavy cream
- 3 tablespoons Dijon mustard
- 1½ tablespoons capers, drained

1. Remove tenderloin from refrigerator and trim, if necessary, and pat dry. Melt 1 tablespoon of the butter and brush over meat. Place on rack in a small roasting pan. Bake about 35 to 44 minutes or until meat thermometer registers 135° for medium rare (or 140° for medium.) Remove from oven and cover lightly with foil. Let stand 10 to 15 minutes before carving.

2. Meanwhile, melt the remaining 1 tablespoon butter in a medium saucepan and cook 1 tablespoon chopped white part of the onion, until soft. (Thinly slice some of the green part of the onion and set aside for garnish.) Add cream and bring to a boil. Reduce heat and simmer 10 to 15 minutes or until mixture thickens, stirring occasionally. Remove from heat and add Dijon mustard and capers.

3. Spoon some of the sauce on each dinner plate and top with a slice of beef tenderloin. Sprinkle with sliced green onion for garnish. Makes 6 servings.

Keeping it Warm

* * *

This wonderful sauce can be made 1 to 2 hours ahead and kept warm in a well-insulated thermos. Leftover sauce can be gently reheated. In addition to beef tenderloin, the sauce can be served with pork chops, pork tenderloin, beef and pork kabobs, beef fondue, and prime rib.

Note: *You must use pasteurized heavy cream or the sauce may not thicken.*

Menu

Beef Tenderloin with Mustard Caper Sauce

Scalloped Potatoes Deluxe

Lemon Broccoli

Caesar Salad

Hot Rolls

Ice Cream Amaretto Dessert

Beef Fajitas

This is a popular recipe in restaurants as well as home entertaining. Chicken breasts halves can be substituted for the beef. Favorite condiments served with Fajitas are: Guacamole, salsa, chopped onion and tomato or sour cream. Or try the Onions and Pepper Sauté on page 325.

> 1   pound skirt steak, flank steak, or sirloin steak
> ½   cup fresh lime juice
> ¾   teaspoon garlic salt
> ½   teaspoon freshly ground black pepper
>   Flour tortillas, warmed

1. Place beef in shallow dish. Combine next 3 ingredients and pour over meat. Cover and refrigerate several hours or overnight.

2. Remove meat from marinade; drain thoroughly. Cook to desired degree of doneness. Meat can be grilled, broiled or cooked in a skillet with a small amount of oil. Slice diagonally into strips. Serve with warm flour tortillas. Makes 4 servings.

Beef Stroganoff

> 1½   pounds beef tenderloin or sirloin
> 6   tablespoons butter, divided
> 1   cup chopped onion
> ¼   cup flour
> 1¾   cups beef broth
> 1   cup sour cream

1. Cut meat across the grain into ¼-inch strips about 1½-inches long.

2. Heat butter in large skillet. Add onion and cook until tender; remove and set aside. Add remaining butter to skillet. Add half the meat and lightly brown; remove and repeat with remaining meat. Return all the meat to skillet, but do not drain off fat.

3. Add onion and flour to skillet; stir to mix. Slowly add the broth, stirring until smooth. Cook until thickened, stirring occasionally. Reduce heat. Add sour cream and heat through, but do not boil or it may curdle. Serve over rice or noodles. Makes 4 servings.

Stuffed Flank Steak

Oven 350°F

1   to 1½ pound flank steak
¾   pound bulk Italian sausage

1. Place steak on waxed paper, rounded side down. Pound to flatten slightly.

2. Crumble sausage over steak to within 1 inch of edge. Starting with the short end, roll meat tightly. Tie with string (or dental floss) in 5 to 6 places, making sure ends are tied to enclose filling. String should be tight, making a compact loaf. Place seam side down on rack in roasting pan. Bake 75 to 85 minutes or until both meats are cooked through. Slice into ¼-inch slices to serve. Makes 6 servings.

For a two ingredient recipe, this one has a lot of flavor. Any left over steak makes delicious sandwiches.

Teriyaki Steak

1   1 to 1½ pound flank steak
1   cup firmly packed light brown sugar
1   cup soy sauce
5   slices fresh ginger
1   garlic clove, minced
½   cup pineapple juice

1. Combine ingredients in shallow dish. Marinate at least 2 hours or overnight in refrigerator.

2. Broil or grill to desired degree of doneness, basting frequently with marinade. Makes 4 servings.

Flank Steak

⚅ ⚅ ⚅

Flank steak is a tender & flavorful meat with virtually no waste. In most cases, it should be broiled or grilled over high heat and thinly sliced across the grain. Never cook beyond medium rare or it can become dry and tough.

Flank steak combines well with numerous marinades and seasonings ensuring added flavor at a savings of cost and time.

Broiled Sirloin Steak

Broil

1   sirloin steak, 1½ inches thick
1   tablespoon Worcestershire sauce
¼   cup butter, melted
1   teaspoon salt
⅛   teaspoon pepper
½   teaspoon garlic powder

1. Place steak on rack in a roasting pan.

2. Combine remaining ingredients. Brush steak generously with the sauce. Broil about 3½-inches from broiling unit 8 to 10 minutes. Turn steak, brush with sauce and broil 8 to 10 minutes, depending on desired degree of doneness. Transfer to a hot serving platter; pour remaining butter sauce over top. Makes 4 to 6 servings.

The steak can be grilled over direct heat, basting with the butter sauce. If desired, use individual sirloin steaks or steaks of choice.

Steak & Mushroom Sauce

2   New York steaks
¼   cup butter
½   cup chopped onion
8   mushrooms, sliced
2   teaspoons Worcestershire sauce
2   tablespoons brandy

1. Melt butter in a large skillet. Brown steak quickly on one side. Reduce heat; add onion and mushrooms. Cook 2 minutes. Turn steaks and cook about 6 minutes or to desired degree of doneness.

2. Add Worcestershire sauce and brandy. Cook about 2 minutes. Makes 2 servings.

If you want to impress your guest, you can flame the brandy after adding it to the skillet. But, watch carefully - I've heard of singed eyebrows and curtains burning!

Pepper Steak

2	New York cut steaks, about 1½ inches thick
2	tablespoons black peppercorns, coarsely ground
1	teaspoon salt
3	tablespoons butter
3	tablespoons oil
⅓	cup cognac

1. Sprinkle both sides of steak with peppercorns, pressing into the meat. Let stand 15 to 20 minutes.

2. Sprinkle one side of meat with salt. Heat butter and oil in skillet over medium-high heat. Place steaks, salted side down, in the hot oil and cook for 3 minutes. Salt steaks, turn, and cook 3 minutes. Reduce heat to medium; cook about 3 minutes on each side. Check for desired degree of doneness and cook longer, if necessary, bearing in mind, that they will continue to cook when removed from the skillet. Remove and keep warm. Remove pan from heat, add cognac and carefully ignite; pour over steaks.

Beef Jerky   Oven 150°F

1	flank steak
½	cup soy sauce
½	teaspoon garlic powder
1	teaspoon lemon pepper

1. Cut flank steak lengthwise (with the grain) in long thin strips no more than ¼-inch thick. Combine remaining ingredients in mixing bowl. Add meat; marinate 1 hour. Baste occasionally if meat is not completely covered with sauce.

2. Arrange meat strips on rack; place on cookie sheet. Bake 12 hours. The time can vary a little depending on how your oven bakes. Meat should be cooked through and dry, but not brittle. Cool and store in a covered container.

Menu

≈

Pepper Steak

Asparagus & Red Peppers

Garlic Mashed Potatoes

Pear-Gorgonzola Cheese Salad

Easy Dinner Rolls

Almond Angel Food Cake

Beef Kabobs

Grill

1¼ to 1½ pounds top sirloin
1 cup dry white wine
⅔ cup vegetable oil
⅓ cup soy sauce
2 large garlic cloves, crushed
2 medium onions, cut into 12 wedges

1. Cut meat into 1½-inch cubes. You will need 16 cubes (4 per kabob).

2. In medium bowl, combine wine, oil, soy sauce and garlic. Add meat and toss to coat. Cover and marinate in refrigerator at least 2 hours. Drain the marinade into a small saucepan; bring to a boil and cook 5 minutes.

3. Meanwhile, thread meat alternately with onion on skewers, starting and ending with meat. Place kabobs on grill and cook about 3 minutes per side or until desired degree of doneness, basting frequently with the marinade. Makes 4 servings.

Tip: Place a scoop of rice on center of plate. Top with a Beef Kabob, then spoon peas on both sides.

Wooden Skewers

Wooden skewers can be used for Kabobs, but they must first be soaked in water for at least 20 minutes.

Swiss Steak

Oven 350°F

2 pounds round steak, 1 inch thick
¼ cup flour
Salt and pepper
3 tablespoons oil
½ cup chopped onion
1 can (16-ounces) tomatoes, with juice, cut up

1. Combine flour, salt and pepper; pound into meat. Brown meat on both sides in hot oil in large Dutch oven or skillet. Top with onion and tomatoes. Bake, covered, for 1¾ hours or until tender. Add water if necessary. Makes 4 to 6 servings.

Tip: If desired, add ¼ cup chopped green peppers the last 15 minutes.

Leg of Lamb   Oven 350°F

5 to 7 pound leg of lamb, bone-in
Flour
Salt and pepper

1. Rub lamb with a little flour, salt and pepper. Place on rack and bake about 1½ hours or until meat thermometer registers 145° for medium-rare or 155° for medium. Remove from oven and cover with foil to keep hot. Let stand 10 minutes before carving. Makes 6 servings.

Company Lamb Chops   Broil

4 lamb chops, 1½ inches thick
1 teaspoon salt
¼ teaspoon pepper
3 tablespoons prepared mustard
3 tablespoons honey

1. Trim fat from lamb chops. Season with salt and pepper. Broil 7 minutes on one side; turn and broil 6 minutes or to desired degree of doneness. Do not overcook; it's okay if lamb is pink in the center.

2. Combine mustard and honey; spread over lamb chops. Broil 2 minutes longer. Makes 4 servings.

Lamb is delicious served with apple mint or jalepeno jelly.

177

Grilled Pork Loin Roast

Grill

Makes delicious barbecue sandwiches, see page 139.

Makes delicious barbecue sandwiches, see page 139.

1   3 pound boneless pork loin
Salt and pepper or Dry Rub

1. Sprinkle roast with salt and pepper. Place fat side up, on low-heat grill, over indirect heat. Cover and cook slowly, about 1½ to 2 hours or until meat thermometer reads 145°. Cover with foil and let stand 10 to 15 minutes. Makes 6 to 8 servings.

Dry Rub

A dry rub is a mixture of dry ingredients spread or sprinkled on meat before cooking. It adds a lot of flavor, especially on grilled meats. This one is my daughter's absolute favorites.

2 tablespoons salt
2 tablespoons sugar
2 teaspoons pepper
2 teaspoons paprika
2 teaspoons fresh lemon peel

Amounts can be increased, as needed. I use approximately 1 recipe per rack of ribs.

Note: *Best not to use dried lemon peel.*

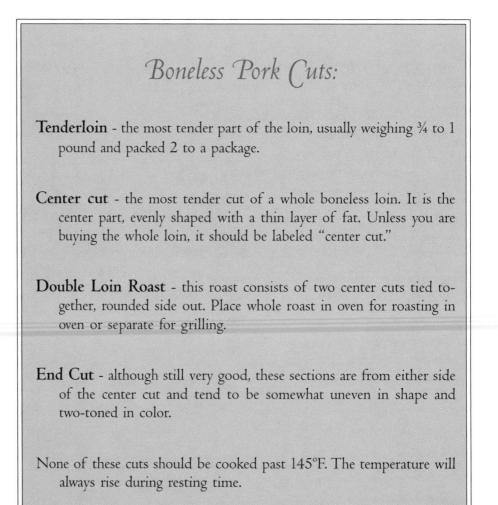

Boneless Pork Cuts:

Tenderloin - the most tender part of the loin, usually weighing ¾ to 1 pound and packed 2 to a package.

Center cut - the most tender cut of a whole boneless loin. It is the center part, evenly shaped with a thin layer of fat. Unless you are buying the whole loin, it should be labeled "center cut."

Double Loin Roast - this roast consists of two center cuts tied together, rounded side out. Place whole roast in oven for roasting in oven or separate for grilling.

End Cut - although still very good, these sections are from either side of the center cut and tend to be somewhat uneven in shape and two-toned in color.

None of these cuts should be cooked past 145°F. The temperature will always rise during resting time.

Pork Roasting Chart

Cut	Oven Temp	Lbs	Approximate Cooking Time Per Pound	Remove when temperature reaches
Crown Roast	350° F	6-10	20 minutes per pound	145° F
Center Loin Roast	350° F	3-5	20 minutes per pound	145° F
Boneless Top Loin Roast	350° F	2-4	20 minutes per pound	145° F
Whole leg (fresh ham)	350° F	12	20 minutes per pound	145° F
Boston Butt	350° F	3-6	45 minutes per pound	145° F
Tenderloin	425° F	½-1½	25-35 minutes total	145° F
Half Ham (precooked)	325° F	6-8	1 hour total	130° F -140° F
Ground Pork				160°

Lemon Pepper Pork Chops

❧

4   loin pork chops, ½ to ¾-inch thick (about 8 ounces each)
1½ tablespoons olive oil
Lemon pepper
1   cup chicken broth

Trim pork chops and pat dry. Brown quickly over medium high heat, about 2 minutes per side. Sprinkle with lemon pepper. Add broth and cook over low heat until temperature reaches 145°, about 5 to 6 minutes.

Boneless Pork Loin Roast   Oven 350°F

1   4-4½ lb boneless pork loin
Salt and pepper
1   teaspoon dried rosemary

1. Wash and trim meat, but do not dry. Place on rack in roasting pan and sprinkle with salt, pepper and rosemary.
2. Bake 1½ to 2 hours or until meat thermometer reaches 145°. Remove from oven and cover with foil. Let stand 10 to 15 minutes before slicing. Makes 6 to 8 servings..

Purchase a single roast (not two tied together); hopefully it will have a layer of fat on top. This is a very tender flavorful cut of meat as long as it isn't overcooked. It also has the added bonus of being low in fat.

179

Baked Herb Pork Chops   Oven 450°F

4   loin-cut pork chops, about ½-inch thick
Salt and pepper
1   tablespoon red wine or red wine garlic vinegar
1   tablespoon Dijon mustard
1   teaspoon Italian seasoning

1. Rinse pork chops and pat dry. Sprinkle both sides lightly with salt and pepper. Place in a sprayed 8x8-inch baking dish.

2. Combine remaining ingredients and brush over meat. Bake, covered, for 10 minutes. Remove from oven, turn pork chops, and continue baking, uncovered 5 to 8 minutes or until temperature reaches 145°. (Do not overcook or meat will be dry and tough.) Makes 2 to 4 servings.

Chicken Fried Pork

2   thick cut boneless pork chops
Salt and pepper
½   cup flour
Vegetable oil

1. Cut pork lengthwise into 2 thin chops. Place between plastic wrap and pound to ¼-inch thickness. Sprinkle both sides with salt and pepper. Dredge in flour, coating both sides and shaking off excess.

2. Heat ¼-inch oil in a heavy large skillet. Add pork and fry until nicely browned, about 3 to 4 minutes on each side. Makes 4 servings.

    Note: If gravy is desired, pour off all but 2 tablespoons of the fat. Add 1 cup milk. Heat until boiling, scraping up all the browned bits. Cook until thickened. (No need to add flour, as the flour from the cooked pork chops is usually enough to thicken.)

Quick Grill

Grill ½-inch thick pork chops over medium high heat, covered, about 6 to 7 minutes per side. Baste frequently, especially the last few minutes, with your favorite barbecue sauce.

This recipe is similar to Chicken Fried Steak (Beef), only here I have used pork. It can be made for any number of servings, using any size boneless pork, pounded to ¼-inch thickness.

Note: *For a traditional southern dinner, serve with mashed potatoes, green beans, biscuits and how about Peach Cobbler on page 70.*

180

Stuffing-Topped Pork Chops

Oven 350°F

 4 loin cut pork chops, 1-inch thick
 3 cups herb seasoned bread cubes
 ¼ cup chopped onion
 ¾ cup vegetable or chicken broth
 ¼ cup butter, melted
 1 can (10¾-ounces) condensed cream of mushroom soup

1. Trim pork chops of excess fat. Rinse and pat dry. Lightly brown on both sides in a large sprayed skillet. Place in a shallow roasting pan.

2. In mixing bowl, combine bread cubes with the onion, broth and butter. Let stand 3 or 4 minutes for the liquid to soften the bread somewhat. Divide into four equal amounts. Roll each into a rather compact, but not firm, ball. Place on pork chops and pat to cover most of the meat.

3. Combine soup with ½ can water, mixing until smooth. Spoon over and around pork chops. Cover tightly with foil and bake 25 minutes. Remove foil and bake, uncovered, 15 minutes or until tender. Watch carefully and do not overcook. The internal temperature when removing from oven should be no higher than 145°. The temperature will then continue to rise.

A lot of flavor with just a few ingredients.

Note*: The onion is somewhat crisp in this recipe. If desired, after browning the pork chops, add onion to skillet and cook until soft.*

Variation*: For special dinners, I sometimes add ⅓ cup chopped pecans to the stuffing mixture.*

Is it Safe?

❈ ❈ ❈

The fear of trichinosis, which can make you extremely sick, was at one time, associated with eating undercooked pork. Today, the safety of pork has greatly improved. The trichinosis organism is destroyed at an internal temperature of 137° which is well below the recommended temperature of 150° to 165°. Bear in mind that the meat will continue to cook after removing from the oven. For more moist meat, I have found that removing the pork from the source of heat when it reaches 145° works best. Roasts should be covered and allowed to stand 10 to 15 minutes. The temperature will rise as it stands.

The first time I had these ribs was in a local restaurant and they swore these were the only ingredients they used. They are very tender, moist and delicious. You must try them.

Note: *The ribs are just as delicious cooked on a grill as in the oven (maybe even better).*

Delicious Baby Back Ribs

Oven 400°F

Desired amount of baby back ribs
Salt
Freshly ground black pepper

1. Remove excess fat and trimmings from ribs. Rinse and pat dry. Sprinkle both sides rather generously, but not heavily with salt and pepper. Place in shallow baking pan, meaty side down, in a single layer. Bake 30 minutes. Turn ribs and bake 20 to 30 minutes or until cooked through and tender. The cooking time may vary according to the number of ribs and how hot your oven bakes.

Oven Spareribs

Oven 350°F

3 to 4 pounds pork spareribs
½ cup ketchup
½ cup firmly packed light brown sugar
2 tablespoons Worcestershire sauce
1 tablespoon white vinegar
Dash hot pepper sauce

1. Cut spareribs into 2-rib servings. Place ribs in a large roasting pan, meaty side down. Bake 45 minutes.

2. Turn ribs, meaty side up. Combine remaining ingredients and brush over ribs. Bake 20 to 30 minutes or until cooked through and tender. Makes 4 to 6 servings.

Stuffed Spareribs

Oven 400°F

2   racks baby back ribs
Salt and pepper
½   cup butter
1¼ cups chopped onion
¾   cup chopped celery
1   package (8-ounces) seasoned bread cubes

1. Trim ribs of excess fat, rinse and pat dry. Sprinkle lightly with salt and pepper and set aside.

2. Melt butter in a large 12-inch skillet. Add onion and celery and cook until just tender. Add bread cubes and 1 cup water, toss until bread cubes are moistened.

3. Place one rack of ribs, meaty side down, on a shallow roasting pan. Spoon stuffing evenly over ribs. Top with remaining rack of ribs, meaty side up. Press down slightly to cover and check to make sure the stuffing is inside the ribs and not spilling out the sides. Bake 50 to 60 minutes (no need to turn) until nicely browned and cooked through. Cut into 2 rib servings, cutting through the bottom ribs. Makes about 6 servings.

Mustard Glazed Ham

Oven 325°F

1   4 to 6 pound ham
½   cup firmly packed light brown sugar
¼   cup orange juice
½   teaspoon dry mustard

1. Place ham on rack, fat side up. Bake 20 minutes per pound or until heated through, temperature should reach 140°.

2. Meanwhile, combine remaining ingredients. Brush ham generously with glaze during last 30 minutes of baking time. Continue basting every 10 minutes. Let stand 20 minutes before slicing. Serve with Orange-Raisin Ham Sauce, page 310. Makes 8 to 12 servings.

Menu

❧

Stuffed Spareribs

Almond Rice Pilaf

Lemon Broccoli

Jiffy Cornbread Muffins

Dome Cake

Quick Glaze

❧

Pour 3 cups apple cider or Coca Cola® over ham; basting occasionally during the last hour to glaze.

Ham & Cheese Bake   Oven 400°F

3   cups frozen hash browns, thawed
1   cup (4-ounces) Swiss cheese, shredded
1   cup finely diced ham
1   cup (4-ounces) Monterey Jack cheese with peppers, shredded
4   large eggs, lightly beaten
1   cup half and half

1. Place hash browns in a sprayed 1½-quart casserole. Bake 20 minutes. Remove from oven and reduce temperature to 350°. Sprinkle Swiss cheese over potatoes, then the ham and then the Monterey Jack cheese.

2. In a small mixing bowl, combine the eggs and half and half. Pour over cheese. Bake, uncovered, about 45 minutes or until center is set. Makes 4 servings.

Tired of the same thing for breakfast. This recipe never fails to please. Serve as a breakfast, brunch or light dinner dish.

Note: It is sometimes hard to tell exactly when the center is set. A knife inserted in the center should look fairly dry. The casserole will continue to cook somewhat in the center if allowed to stand about 10 minutes. Also good reheated.

Cashew Ham Bake   Oven 300°F

1   large ham slice, 1-inch thick
½   cup orange marmalade
¼   cup coarsely chopped cashews

1. Place ham on rack in a roasting pan. Bake 30 minutes.

2. Spread marmalade over top and sprinkle with cashews. Bake 15 minutes. Makes 4 to 6 servings.

Note: Serve with buttered peas, Dinner Hash Browns, and a crisp green salad.

Ham Noodle Casserole

Oven 350°F

8 ounces ¼-inch wide egg noodles
1 cup finely chopped onion
2 large eggs
1 cup sour cream
¾ cup (3-ounces) Swiss or Monterey Jack cheese, shredded
1½ cups cubed cooked ham

1. Cook noodles according to directions on package; drain. Meanwhile, cook onion in a small nonstick skillet until tender.

2. In mixing bowl, combine eggs and sour cream. Add onion, cheese and ham. Add noodles and mix well. Pour into a sprayed 2-quart casserole. Cover and bake 35 minutes. Uncover and bake 10 minutes or until heated through and mixture is set. Makes 6 servings.

For a quick economical meal, this is an excellent way to use up any leftover ham.

Casserole Dish or Baking Dish... Do you know the difference?

A **Casserole Dish** is usually a round, square or oval deep dish and is referred to in quart sizes such as a 2-quart casserole dish.

A **Baking Dish** is usually rectangle, square or oval and is a shallow dish no more than 2 to 3 inches deep. They are usually refered to in measurements such as a 13x9-inch baking dish or pan.

185

Italian Sausage Dinner

4 to 6 Italian sausages
1 tablespoon oil
2 medium onions, sliced, separated into rings
1 green pepper, cut into strips
5 plum tomatoes, sliced
Salt and pepper

This hearty and flavorful dish can be prepared quickly and is great anytime. Serve with hot bread to sop up the juices.

1. Brown sausages in hot oil in medium skillet. Add onion and green pepper and continue cooking until vegetables are just tender. Add tomatoes and season with salt and pepper. Cook until heated through. Makes 4 servings.

Italian Sausage Spaghetti

1 pound Italian sausage
1 green pepper, cut into small squares
1½ cups coarsely chopped onion
2 to 2½ cups spaghetti sauce
10 ounces spaghetti (or desired amount)
Grated Parmesan cheese

1. In large skillet, lightly brown sausage; add green pepper and onion and cook until cooked through. Add spaghetti sauce. Bring to a boil, lower heat and simmer 10 to 15 minutes.

2. Meanwhile, cook spaghetti as directed on package. Serve sauce over spaghetti. Sprinkle with Parmesan cheese. Makes 4 servings.

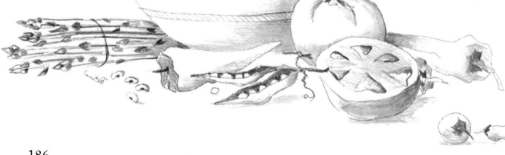

Baked Hot Dogs and Sauerkraut Oven 350°F

    1 jar (32-ounces) refrigerated sauerkraut, drained
    2 teaspoons caraway seeds
    8 hot dogs
    1½ cups (6-ounces) Swiss cheese, shredded

1. Place well-drained sauerkraut in sprayed 10x7-inch baking dish.
   Sprinkle with caraway seeds and toss with a fork to mix. Place hot dogs
   over sauerkraut and sprinkle with cheese. Bake 25 to 30 minutes or
   until heated through and cheese is melted. Makes 4 (or more) servings.

The caraway seeds and Swiss cheese soften the tartness of the sauerkraut.

Franks & Cornbread Oven 400°F

    1 large egg
    ⅓ cup milk
    1 package (8½-ounces) corn muffin mix
    4 hot dogs
    ½ cup (2-ounces) Cheddar cheese, shredded
    1 can (16-ounces) chili with beans (optional)

1. Combine first 3 ingredients, mixing just until moistened. Spoon into
   a sprayed 8x8-inch baking dish.

2. Cut hot dogs in half lengthwise, but do not cut all the way through.
   Open flat and place on top of batter, cutting, if necessary, to fit dish.
   Sprinkle with cheese. Bake 15 to 20 minutes or until golden.

3. Meanwhile, heat chili. Cut cornbread into squares. Top each serving
   with some of the chili. Makes 4 servings.

Convenience foods are here to stay. Enjoy them for what they have to offer us, especially on those busy days when nothing else will do.

Salmon Steaks   Broil

4   salmon steaks, about 6 ounces each
2   tablespoons oil
2   tablespoons fresh lemon juice
1   small garlic clove, minced
2   tablespoons minced fresh basil

1. Pat salmon steaks dry with a paper towel and place on a broiler pan, skin-side down.

2. Combine remaining ingredients and brush some of the mixture over the salmon. Broil, about 8 to 10 minutes, or until steaks test done, basting once or twice with the sauce. You do not have to turn the steaks. Makes 4 servings.

Tip: *I have found that a fish that has been stuffed may take somewhat longer than the 10 minutes per inch cooking time usually required.*

Cooking Time for Fish

Measure fish at its thickest point
Estimate 10 minutes total cooking time per inch

Total cooking time applies to whatever cooking method is being used—baking, broiling, frying, etc. If baking a salmon or other fish and the fish measures 3 inches at its thickest point, bake 30 minutes at 450°. If broiling a steak 1½-inches thick, divide the total time and broil 7½ minutes on each side. Test with a wooden toothpick; if it comes out clean and dry, fish is done. Cooking times may vary somewhat according to the thickness and size of the fish, the temperature of the fish at cooking time and how hot your oven bakes. Watch carefully though, and remember that the fish will continue to cook somewhat after removing from heat. The internal temperature of fish should be 137 degrees.

Baked Salmon with Sour Cream

Oven 450°F

2½ **pound salmon fillet**
Salt and pepper
2 **tablespoons fresh lemon juice**
1 **cup sour cream**
2 **teaspoons finely chopped onion**

1. Place fillet in shallow baking dish. Season with salt and pepper; sprinkle with lemon juice. Spread sour cream over top; sprinkle with chopped onion. Bake 10 minutes per inch measuring at its thickest point. Makes 6 servings.

Teriyaki Salmon Steaks

Broil

4 **salmon steaks, 1-inch thick**
¼ **cup oil**
2 **tablespoons lemon juice**
2 **tablespoons soy sauce**
½ **teaspoon dry mustard**
½ **teaspoon ground ginger**

1. Place salmon steaks in shallow dish. Combine remaining ingredients; pour over steaks. Let stand at room temperature 1 hour, turning occasionally. Drain, reserving marinade. Place steaks on rack in broiling pan; broil steaks 5 minutes; turn and brush with marinade. Broil steaks 5 minutes more, brushing occasionally with the sauce. Check for doneness. Makes 4 servings.

Poached Salmon

❊ ❊ ❊

Poached salmon is great for a low-fat diet as well as for adding to pastas, salads, soups and sandwiches.

Add desired number of salmon fillets to a pot of simmering water along with a little bit of salt, some herbs , if desired, and even a little bit of wine wouldn't hurt (optional). Cook only until salmon loses its color and is cooked through.

This is such an easy way to bake a whole salmon. If you want you can add lemon slices, garlic cloves, onion, dill weed, etc. to the inside of the salmon.

Company Baked Salmon

Oven 450°F

Whole salmon, rinsed and wiped dry
Salt and pepper
Bacon slices

1. Sprinkle inside of salmon with salt. Salt and pepper outside. Place on large sheet of heavy-duty foil in shallow baking pan.

2. Place bacon slices inside salmon and crosswise over top. Wrap foil to seal. Bake 10 minutes per inch measuring salmon at its thickest point. Test for doneness. If wooden toothpick is dry, salmon should be done.

Salmon Loaf

Oven 350°F

1	can (14-ounces) salmon
1	can (10¾-onces) condensed cream of mushroom soup
1½	cups soft breadcrumbs
¼	cup finely chopped celery
2	tablespoons finely chopped onion
2	large eggs

1. Combine ingredients and spoon into sprayed 7x5-inch loaf pan. Bake 45 to 50 minutes or until center is firm. Let stand 5 minutes. Turn out on serving plate. Makes 4 to 6 servings.

"Fresh" Canned Shrimp

Canned shrimp
1   teaspoon salt

1. Drain shrimp; rinse several times. Place in a quart jar; cover with ice water and the 1 teaspoon salt. Chill overnight. Drain shrimp and pat dry with paper towels.

   Shrimp will taste almost as good as fresh. Use in shrimp cocktail, salads, soups, main dishes, etc.

Bacon Prawns   Broil

Bacon - 1 slice per prawn
Raw Prawns - allow 3 to 4 per person
Melted butter with parsley or desired herbs

1. Partially cook bacon, until limp, but not crisp. Drain on paper towels.

2. Shell prawns, except for the tails and de-vein. Wrap a bacon strip around each prawn; secure with a wooden toothpick. Place on broiler rack, baste with butter mixture and cook, turning once, until prawns are opaque and turn pink. Brush occasionally with butter mixture.

Jumbo prawns are so large you need allow only 3 to 4 per person. Try cooking the prawns on a grill and serve with corn on the cob and rice pilaf.

Easy Baked Shrimp   Oven 450°F

2   pounds uncooked jumbo shrimp, peeled, deveined, butterflied
⅓   cup butter, melted
2   tablespoons olive oil
¼   cup fresh lemon juice
3   medium garlic cloves, minced

1. Place shrimp in a 13x9-inch baking dish. Combine remaining ingredients and pour over shrimp. Gently toss to coat. Spread evenly over pan and bake 6 to 10 minutes or until shrimp is pink and cooked through. Makes 4 servings.

This is a delicious recipe, but also quite expensive. For a more affordable dish, substitute medium-size shrimp for the jumbo. Sauté shrimp in a large skillet and you can call it Shrimp Scampi.

Serve with tartar sauce, coleslaw and Au Gratin Potatoes.

Breaded Butterflied Shrimp

1 pound shrimp
Salt an pepper
1 large egg, lightly beaten with 1 tablespoon water
½ cup fine dry breadcrumbs
Oil

1. Remove shells from shrimp, leaving tails intact; de-vein. Cut two-thirds of the way through the center of each shrimp and flatten. Season with salt and pepper. Dip in crumbs, egg and again in crumbs.

2. Deep fry in oil (350°) for about 3 minutes or until golden. Drain and serve. Makes 3 servings.

Definition of:

Shrimp-
Widely available and comes in a variety of sizes.

Prawns-
Because of their large size, prawns are often served stuffed. They are usually sold 6 to 8 per pound.

Scampi-
Usually refers to shrimp sautéed in garlic butter.

Shrimp Scampi

2 pounds shrimp, peeled and cleaned
⅓ cup oil
2 small garlic cloves, minced
1 teaspoon salt
½ teaspoon pepper
¼ cup fresh lemon juice

1. Heat oil in large skillet. Stir in garlic, salt, pepper and lemon juice. Add shrimp. Cook until shrimp turns pink. Reduce heat and cook until liquid is almost absorbed (do not overcook shrimp). Serve hot. Makes 4 to 6 servings.

Tip: For added color, sprinkle with chopped parsley or garnish dish with parsley sprigs.

Crab Divan

Oven 350°F

1 can (6½-ounces) crab, drained
2 cups broccoli florettes, cooked
½ cup mayonnaise
1 teaspoon prepared mustard
1 tablespoon finely chopped onion
½ cup (2-ounces) Cheddar cheese, shredded

1. Arrange broccoli in bottom of a sprayed 1-quart casserole. Distribute crab evenly over top.

2. Combine mayonnaise, mustard and onion; spread over crab. Sprinkle with cheese. Bake 20 to 30 minutes or until heated through. Makes 4 servings.

Quick Crab Cakes

2 cups flaked crab meat
1 tablespoon lemon juice
1 large egg, lightly beaten
Salt and pepper to taste
1 cup fine breadcrumbs, plus extra
Oil

1. Combine first 5 ingredients in mixing bowl; mix well. If mixture is too wet, add more breadcrumbs, if too dry, add a little water. Shape into 6 patties; dip in additional breadcrumbs. Brown lightly on both sides in hot oil. Makes 3 servings.

Halibut-Shrimp Bake

Oven 350°F
Broil

4	small halibut steaks or fillets
½	cup fresh lemon juice
½	cup butter, melted
½	cup sour cream
½	cup (2-ounces) Cheddar cheese, shredded
⅓	cup tiny shrimp, cooked

1. Place halibut in a shallow baking pan. Combine butter and lemon juice; pour over halibut. Bake 10 to 12 minutes or until fish tests done.

2. Top each steak or fillet with some of the sour cream. Sprinkle with cheese. Place under broiler and cook just until cheese melts. Garnish top with shrimp. Makes 4 servings.

Trout Amandine

Broil

4	trout (about 8-ounces each)
½	cup butter, melted
⅓	cup slivered almonds
1	tablespoon lemon juice

1. Wipe trout dry with paper towels. Brush both sides with melted butter. Place on sprayed broiler pan. Broil 4 inches from heat, about 8 to 10 minutes or until fish tests done, being careful not to overcook. (Do not try to turn fish.)

2. Meanwhile, brown almonds lightly in remaining butter; add lemon juice. Pour over fish. Makes 4 servings.

Mushroom Fillet Dish

Oven 400°F

2 pounds fillets (white fish)
1 medium onion, finely chopped
8 ounces fresh mushrooms, sliced
1 cup (4-ounces) Swiss cheese, shredded
Salt and pepper
1 cup whipping cream

1. Sprinkle onion evenly in a sprayed 11x7-inch baking dish. Arrange three-fourths of the mushrooms over onions. Sprinkle with half the cheese. Place fillets over the top; sprinkle with salt and pepper. Add remaining mushrooms and cheese. Pour cream over top. Bake 20 minutes or until cooked through. Makes 4 to 6 servings.

Baked Halibut

Oven 450°F

4 halibut steaks, 1-inch thick
3 tablespoons fresh lemon juice
1 teaspoon salt
½ teaspoon paprika
½ cup chopped onion
2 tablespoons butter

1. In shallow dish, combine lemon juice, salt and paprika. Add halibut, turning to coat. Marinate 1 hour, turning steaks after first half hour.

2. Meanwhile, sauté onion in butter until tender.

3. Place halibut in a sprayed 11x7-inch baking dish; top with onion. Bake 10 minutes or until fish flakes easily with a fork. Makes 4 servings.

Delicious served over hot buttered toast, rice or noodles.

Tuna Mornay

2   cans (6½-ounces each) tuna, drained
¼   cup butter
¼   cup flour
2   cups milk
¼   cup (1-ounce) Swiss cheese, shredded
   Salt and pepper

1. Melt butter in medium saucepan. Stir in flour and cook for 1 minute. Remove from heat; add milk, stirring to blend. Return to heat, continue cooking, stirring frequently, until thickened. Add cheese; stir until melted. Add salt and pepper to taste. Stir in tuna and heat through. Makes 4 servings.

Tuna Cashew Casserole   Oven 350°F

1   can (6½-ounces) tuna, drained
1   can (10¾-ounces) condensed cream of mushroom soup
1   cup thinly sliced celery
¼   cup finely chopped onion
1   can (3-ounces) Chow Mein Noodles
1   package (3-ounces) cashews, split

1. Combine soup with ¼ cup water. Add remaining ingredients, reserving ⅓ of the Chow Mein Noodles. Pour mixture into a sprayed 2 quart casserole. Sprinkle reserved noodles over top. Bake 30 minutes or until heated through. Makes 4 to 6 servings.

Tuna Rice Casserole

Oven 350°F

1   can (6½-ounces) tuna, drained
1   can (10¾-ounces) condensed cream of mushroom soup
1   cup cooked rice
1   small onion, chopped
1   cup crushed potato chips

1. Gently combine ingredients until mixed. Spoon into a sprayed 1-quart casserole. If desired, top with additional crushed potato chips. Bake 30 to 45 minutes or until heated through. Makes 4 servings.

Easy Bake Parmesan Sole

Oven 450°F

4   fillet of sole
2   tablespoons butter
⅓   cup dry breadcrumbs
2   tablespoons grated Parmesan cheese
1   teaspoon paprika

1. Wash fillets; brush both sides with melted butter.

2. Combine remaining ingredients in a pie dish. Dip fillets in crumbs and place in a sprayed shallow baking pan. Bake 10 minutes or until fish flakes easily with a fork. If coating is dry, brush with a little melted butter. Makes 4 servings.

Red Snapper with Mushrooms and Peppers

Broil

1 pound fillet of red snapper
1 tablespoon light soy sauce
¼ teaspoon ground ginger
2 medium pepper, 1 red and 1 green, julienned
6 ounces fresh mushrooms, sliced

1. Place fillet in shallow baking pan. Combine soy sauce and ginger; brush over fish. Place under broiler and cook 8 to 10 minutes, depending on thickness of fish, or until fish flakes easily with a fork.

2. Meanwhile, in large sprayed non-stick skillet, cook peppers and mushrooms until crisp tender. Serve vegetables over fish. Makes 4 servings.

Scallops & Ginger

1¼ pounds bay scallops
¼ cup butter
3 to 4 slices fresh ginger
Salt and pepper

1. Rinse scallops and pat dry.

2. Heat butter in medium skillet. Add ginger and sauté briefly. Add scallops and continue to cook until scallops are heated through. Add salt and pepper to taste. Makes 4 servings.

Poultry & Pasta

Turkey Roasting

*F*resh or frozen - it's up to you. Fresh turkey is a little bit higher priced, but will not take up days worth of refrigerator space to thaw. Frozen turkey will need to be defrosted. The safest recommended method is to thaw turkey in the refrigerator. Allow 24 hours for each 5 pounds. For example a 15-pound turkey will take 3 days to thaw. If you are running tight on space or time, an alternative method is to thaw the turkey in cold water. Allow approximately 30 minutes per pound, and change water every hour or two.

*W*hen your turkey is thawed, you may prepare it for roasting. First, be sure to remove the paper sack inside of the turkey containing the giblets. Remove any other pieces, such as the neck, that may be inside the turkey. Next, rinse the turkey both inside and out. Dry with paper towels. (Be sure to thoroughly clean all surfaces that have come into contact with the raw turkey.) If stuffing, do so now. Do not pack dressing in bird, but rather, put in loosely. Tie drumsticks together with string or tuck under the folds of the skin.

FOLLOW ONE OF THE TWO ROASTING METHODS:

Foil Wrapped Method

Using wide, heavy-duty foil, cut 2 long strips. Place one piece length-wise in large shallow roasting pan and one piece crosswise in pan. Place turkey, breast side up, on top of foil. Brush with oil or butter. Bring 2 opposite ends of foil up over turkey; fold ends together to seal. Bring remaining two ends of foil up and seal. Bake at 450°.

POUNDS	HOURS	REMOVE FROM OVEN
8-12	1¼-2	170°F (thigh)
12-16	2-2¼	170°F (thigh)
16-20	2¼-2½	170°F (thigh)
20-24	2½-2¾	170°F (thigh)

*F*or stuffed turkeys, you may find it necessary to cook 30 minutes longer. To brown turkey, open foil during last 30 minutes of cooking time. To test for doneness, meat should read 170° when inserted into thickest part of the thigh. Close foil and let stand 15 – 60 minutes before carving. (If allowing to stand more than 30 minutes, remove from oven when temperature reaches 165° F.

Traditional Method

Place turkey, breast side up, in shallow baking pan. Brush with oil or butter. Bake at 325° until cooked through.

POUNDS	HOURS	REMOVE FROM OVEN
8-12	2¼ - 2¾	170°F (thigh)
12-16	2¾ - 3¼	170°F (thigh)
16-20	3¼ - 3¾	170°F (thigh)
20-24	3¾ - 4½	170°F (thigh)

PLEASE NOTE: For safety reasons, dressing should not be stuffed in the turkey, but baked separately. **However, if you do stuff your turkey, the dressing must reach an internal temperature of 165° F.**

Poultry

Probably the most important thing to remember when cooking roasts, turkey, or a whole chicken is to allow time for the meat to stand after roasting. Your meat will be juicier and easier to carve.

Poultry	Oven Temp.	Lbs.	Approx Total Cooking Hours	Remove when temp. reaches
Chicken	350° F	2½-3	1–1½	170° F (thigh)
Cornish Hens	350° F	1-2	1–1¼	170° F (thigh)
Turkey or Chicken Breast	325° F	5½-6	1½-2	160° F
Ground Chicken Or Turkey				160° F

*Juices should run clear when skin is pierced.

Cooking Tip

Today, when purchasing chicken breast halves, there are so many sizes to choose from that it really does affect the cooking time.

Chicken with bone-in takes longer than boneless pieces. Also, bear in mind that frozen boneless chicken breasts are usually considerably thinner than the fresh and may take very little time to cook. If your chicken is often dry and tough, this may be the reason.

Variation: *brush hens with a mixture of equal parts honey and apricot nectar; brush with additional sauce during baking.*

Roast Cornish Hens   Oven 425°F

4	Cornish hens
1	teaspoon seasoned salt
¼	teaspoon garlic powder
¼	teaspoon paprika

1. Wash and drain hens, but do not dry.

2. Combine last three ingredients; sprinkle evenly over hens. Place breast down in a sprayed shallow baking pan. Bake 30 minutes. If hens stick, add a little butter to the pan. Turn breast side up and bake 30 to 40 minutes longer or until golden brown and tender, basting occasionally with pan drippings. Makes 4 large servings.

Fried Chicken

When I was growing up in Missouri, fried chicken, the way my mother made it, was my favorite meal. This recipe is a lot like hers and very good.

1	chicken, cut up
1	large egg
½	cup milk
1	cup flour
	Salt and pepper
	Vegetable oil

1. Rinse chicken and pat dry.

2. Combine egg and milk in small dish. Combine flour, salt and pepper in small dish. Dip chicken in flour, then in milk mixture, then back in flour.

3. Heat 1-inch oil in large skillet. When hot, add chicken and brown on both sides. Reduce heat; continue cooking until chicken is tender, about 20 to 30 minutes (do not cover). Turn chicken several times . Drain on paper towels. Makes 4 servings.

Crunchy Fried Chicken

    1   chicken, cut up
    Salt and pepper
    1   to 1½ cups flour
    1   cup buttermilk
    Oil

1. Rinse chicken and pat dry. Sprinkle with salt and pepper. Coat with flour. Dip in buttermilk and again in flour.

2. Heat about 1¼-inches oil in a deep heavy skillet. Cook chicken in hot oil, about 20 to 30 minutes, turning once. Drain on paper towels. Makes 4 servings.

Oven Fried Chicken
Oven 400°F

    1   chicken, cut up
    ½   cup flour
    1½ teaspoons salt
    ¼   teaspoon pepper
    1   teaspoon paprika
    ¼   cup oil

1. Combine dry ingredients. Coat chicken pieces with flour mixture.

2. Pour oil into a 15 x 10 inch jellyroll pan. Add chicken, skin-side down. Bake 30 minutes. Turn and bake 30 minutes or until tender. If chicken pieces are small, bake 20 minutes on each side. Makes 4 servings.

Cooked Chicken

A lot of recipes call for cooked cubed or sliced chicken. On occasion you will use leftovers, but chances are most of the time you will need to cook the chicken. This is quick and easy and if desired, can be done ahead. I find the easiest chicken to use is the boneless skinless breasts or the chicken tenders.

Simply place the chicken in a large saucepan or skillet with enough water or broth to cover. Bring to a boil, reduce heat, cover and simmer until chicken reaches 160°F or until cooked through.

Chicken will be more moist if cooked with the skin on. If desired, remove after baking.

Note: *Do not double this recipe; it takes a much larger pan than you would think. Instead, make two individual recipes.*

Cooking Tip

Chicken and turkey purchased in stores have almost always been frozen first, then thawed at the store. If we take the chicken home and freeze it again, then it has been frozen twice. This is usually okay, but if the store refreezes chicken they haven't sold and then we buy it and freeze it again, we may be looking at one tough chicken. For best results, look for packages with the least amount of liquid in the bottom and cook chicken within a day or two of purchase.

Italian Chicken Casserole   Oven 350°F

> 4 chicken breast halves
> 1 cup uncooked long-grain rice
> 1 envelope (.65-ounce) Italian salad dressing mix
> 2½ cups boiling water
> 1 can (10¾-ounces) condensed cream of chicken soup
> Salt and pepper

1. Spread rice in a sprayed 13x9-inch baking dish. Combine salad dressing mix, water and soup; mix well. Pour over rice. Place chicken, skin-side up, on top of rice. Sprinkle with salt and pepper. Cover dish with foil, and bake 60 minutes.

2. Remove foil and bake 20 to 30 minutes or until liquid is absorbed and chicken is tender. Makes 4 servings.

Chicken & Coconut   Oven 350°F

> 4 whole chicken breasts, halved
> Salt and pepper
> Oil
> ⅓ cup fine dry breadcrumbs
> ⅓ cup Angel Flake coconut
> ¼ cup butter, melted

1. Sprinkle chicken with salt and pepper. Brush with oil.

2. Combine breadcrumbs and coconut. Roll chicken in mixture to coat. Place in sprayed shallow baking pan; drizzle with melted butter. Bake 40 minutes or until tender. Makes 4 servings.

Linda's Phyllo Chicken

Oven 350°F

6	chicken breast halves, cooked, cubed
2½	cups broccoli florettes
2	cups sour cream
10	sheets Phyllo
1	cup butter, melted
1	cup freshly grated Parmesan cheese

1. Steam the broccoli until it turns bright green and is not quite crisp tender. Rinse with cold water to stop the cooking process. Cut florettes into small pieces and set aside. Combine the chicken and sour cream and set aside.

2. Lay out one sheet of phyllo (keep remaining phyllo covered with wax paper and a slightly damp towel to prevent drying out). Brush with melted butter. Top with second sheet of phyllo and brush with butter. Repeat until you have 5 sheets. Spread phyllo with half the chicken mixture, leaving a 2-inch border all the way around. Sprinkle with half the broccoli and half the Parmesan cheese. Fold the 2-inch border over, covering outer edge of filling. Brush with butter. Starting with short end, roll up jelly-roll style. Place, seam-side down, on baking sheet. Brush with butter. Repeat with second half of ingredients.

3. Bake at 375° 20 to 25 minutes or until golden (may take longer if rolls have been refrigerated). Slice each roll into 4 to 6 slices. Makes 6 to 8 servings.

This is one of my daughter's favorite company recipes. She likes to prepare it the day before and bake just before serving. Very elegant and even good cold.

Menu

∾

Linda's Phyllo Chicken

Wild Rice

Baked Carrots

Sally Lunn Muffins

Cranberry-Nut Cake

This delightful dish features a combination of favorite ingredients made even better by the addition of a special tossed green salad and toasted French bread and muffins hot from the oven. It is a large recipe and should be baked in a deep 13x9-inch baking pan or dish. Some of the newer baking dishes are deeper than the older ones. For a nice change, omit the chicken and you have a delicious vegetable-rice dish.

Chicken Broccoli Casserole   Oven 350°F

1	package (20-ounces) frozen chopped broccoli
5	cups cooked long-grain rice
2½	cups cubed cooked chicken
2	cans (10¾-ounces each) condensed cream of chicken soup
1	cup mayonnaise
2	cups (8-ounces) Mozzarella cheese, shredded, divided

1. Place frozen broccoli in a colander and run under hot water; drain thoroughly. Spread on bottom of a sprayed 13x9-inch baking dish. Spoon rice over top.

2. Combine chicken, soup, mayonnaise and 1 cup of the cheese. Pour over rice. Sprinkle with remaining cheese. (Dish will be quite full.) Bake 30 to 35 minutes or until heated through. Watch carefully last few minutes. Cover with foil if cheese is browning too fast. Makes 8 servings.

Chicken Parmesan   Oven 350°F

4	chicken breast halves, skinned and boned
¼	cup freshly grated Parmesan cheese
¾	cup seasoned Italian breadcrumbs
¼	cup butter, melted

1. Combine Parmesan cheese and breadcrumbs. Dip chicken in butter and then in crumb mixture to coat. Place on sprayed shallow baking pan and bake 30 to 40 minutes or until lightly browned and cooked through. Brush with additional butter if coating appears dry. Makes 4 servings.

Oven Barbecued Chicken

Oven 350°F

1½ chickens, cut up
¾ cup honey
1 cup ketchup
¼ cup light corn syrup
2 tablespoons Worcestershire sauce
Juice of 1 lemon

1. Place chicken, skin-side down, in a sprayed 13x9-inch baking dish. Combine remaining ingredients and pour over top. Marinate at least one hour, basting occasionally.

2. Pour off marinade and reserve. Bake chicken 30 minutes. Turn chicken and baste with marinade. Continue baking 30 minutes longer or until chicken is tender and richly glazed, basting frequently. Makes 6 servings.

Cooking Tips

•Marinating adds flavor and makes for a more moist chicken.
•Cooking with skin on adds more flavor, but not fat. The fat does not transfer to the meat during cooking. Leaving the skin on helps to create a more tender and moist meat.
•For accurate doneness, use a good thermometer. Chicken or turkey breasts should be cooked to 160°. Don't overcook or it will be dry and tough. Watch closely the last few minutes of cooking time.
•Use tongs when turning chicken pieces. A fork will pierce the meat and allow too much of the juice to escape.

*C*hicken *P*ecan

Oven 450°F

The popular trend today is to serve a delicious sauce on the plate with the entrée placed on top. This is a wonderful dish and it tastes as good as it looks. **Note**: *This recipe doesn't re-heat well.*

4	chicken breast halves, skinned and boned
6	tablespoons butter, plus ¼ cup
½	cup Dijon mustard, divided
1¼	cups very finely chopped pecans
½	cup sour cream
½	cup heavy whipping cream

1. Place each chicken breast between plastic wrap and pound until the overall thickness is the same. Doing this will ensure that the chicken pieces will cook more evenly. Set aside.

2. Microwave 6 tablespoons of the butter until it is very soft, but before it starts to melt. Combine the butter with ¼ cup of the Dijon mustard. Brush both sides of the chicken generously with this mixture (it is somewhat messy) and coat with pecans until thoroughly covered.

3. Heat the ¼ cup butter in a large skillet. Add chicken and cook over medium heat until browned on both sides. Transfer chicken to a shallow baking dish, reserving pan juices, but removing all but a small amount of the nuts remaining in the pan. Bake chicken 10 to 12 minutes or until cooked through.

4. Meanwhile, add sour cream, heavy cream and the remaining ¼ cup Dijon mustard to skillet. Cook until heated through, but do not boil. Spread a small amount of sauce on each plate and top with chicken. Makes 4 servings.

Chicken Pecan Mounds

Oven 350°F

4 small whole chicken breasts, leave skin on
Salt and pepper
3 cups seasoned stuffing mix
½ cup butter, melted
½ cup finely chopped pecans

1. Sprinkle chicken with salt and pepper; set aside.

2. Combine remaining ingredients with ½ cup water. Divide into 4 equal portions. Shape into mounds in a shallow baking pan. Place chicken, skin-side up, over stuffing. Cover with foil; bake 30 minutes. Remove foil; bake 20 minutes or until chicken is lightly browned and tender. Makes 4 large servings.

Almost as good as turkey and dressing and a whole lot easier. Serve with mashed potatoes, Baked Acorn Squash or Minted Petite Peas, Strawberry Nut Salad and Key Lime Pie.

Sesame Chicken

Oven 350°F

4 chicken breast halves, skinned and boned
Flour
2 tablespoons olive oil
¼ cup light soy sauce
2 tablespoons sherry
2 tablespoons sugar

1. Rinse chicken and pat dry. Coat chicken with flour; shake off excess. Heat oil (it should be very hot) in large skillet and quickly brown chicken, turning once.

2. Place in a sprayed 11x7-inch baking dish. Bake 15 minutes. Baste with sauce and continue baking 15 minutes or until cooked through, basting every 5 minutes. Makes 4 servings.

This has always been a favorite recipe in our family. It is richly glazed, tender and delicious. If you want to make an impressive dish for company, you can sprinkle with sesame seeds before baking and then serve on an attractive dish garnished with parsley sprigs.

Menu

❧

Chicken Pineapple
Supreme

Almond Rice Pilaf

Sally Lunn
Muffins

Sweet-Sour Spinach
Salad

Cherry Parfaits

Chicken Pineapple Supreme

PER SERVING:

    1   chicken breast half, skinned and boned
    Salt and pepper
    1   pineapple ring
    1   broccoli spear, cooked crisp tender
    ½   slice Swiss cheese
    Paprika

1. Place chicken between two pieces of plastic wrap. Gently pound to about ¼-inch thickness. Place, rounded side down, in heated sprayed nonstick skillet. Cook, over medium heat, until browned and cooked through, turning once. Total cooking time shouldn't take more than 8 to 10 minutes. Sprinkle lightly with salt and pepper.

2. Place a pineapple ring on each chicken breast. Top with a broccoli spear. Place a cheese slice diagonally over the broccoli. Sprinkle cheese lightly with paprika. Cover skillet and cook just long enough to melt the cheese. Makes one serving.

Herb Chicken Bake   Oven 350°F

    1   chicken, cut up
    ⅓   cup butter
    1   can (10¾-ounces) cream of chicken soup with herbs

1. Place chicken pieces, skin-side down, in a 13x9-inch baking dish. Slice butter and arrange on chicken. Bake 20 minutes. Turn chicken and bake 20 minutes.

2. Stir soup and spoon over chicken. Bake 20 minutes or until chicken is cooked through. Makes 4 servings.

Chicken Cordon Bleu

Oven 400°F

- 4 large chicken breast halves, skinned and boned
- 4 thin slices boiled ham (about 3-inch squares)
- 4 small thin slices Swiss cheese
- ¾ cup fine dry breadcrumbs

Salt and pepper

- ⅓ cup butter, melted

1. Cut a deep pocket in the side of each chicken breast at its thickest part. Fold a ham slice around a cheese slice, tuck in pocket. Skewer with wooden toothpicks to secure.

2. Combine breadcrumbs, salt and pepper. Roll chicken in butter, then in breadcrumbs. Place in sprayed shallow baking pan. Bake 30 to 40 minutes or until lightly browned and tender. If chicken becomes dry, brush with butter. Makes 4 servings.

Chicken Dijon

- 4 chicken breast halves, skinned and boned
- 3 tablespoons oil
- 2 tablespoons flour
- ½ cup half and half
- 1 cup chicken broth
- 2 tablespoons Dijon mustard

1. Rinse chicken pieces and pat dry. Heat oil in a large skillet. Add chicken and cook 10 to 12 minutes or until cooked through, turning once. Remove chicken and keep warm.

2. Add flour to pan drippings; stir well to blend. Add half and half and chicken broth, stirring until smooth. Add mustard and cook over medium heat until thickened. Return chicken to the pan, coat with sauce and reheat, if necessary. Makes 4 servings.

Quick Chicken Recipes

⊠ ⊠ ⊠

- Brush chicken with mayonnaise or yogurt and roll in crushed cracker crumbs. Bake at 350° for 30 to 45 minutes.

- Brush chicken with Italian dressing; bake at 350° for 30 to 45 minutes. If cooking for a crowd, I like to do this ahead. Then place on grill over medium coals; brush with barbecue sauce and cook, basting frequently until heated through.

- Combine cooked pasta with pesto and cooked cubed chicken. Sprinkle with shredded Parmesan cheese.

211

Kabob Tips

Kabobs will cook more evenly if you leave a little space between the meat. Grilled vegetables make wonderful accompaniments, but because of the different cooking times, it is best if they are cooked on separate skewers.

Chicken Kabobs

Boneless Chicken pieces

Oil

Apricot preserves

Thread chicken pieces onto skewers. Brush lightly with oil. Cook over medium hot grill, turning to cook all sides. Brush with apricot preserves last few minutes of cooking time. Serve with sautéed apples and Almond Rice Pilaf.

Lemon Chicken

4	chicken breast halves, skinned and boned
⅓	cup flour
6	tablespoons butter, divided
2	tablespoons finely chopped onion
1	cup chicken broth
3	tablespoons fresh lemon juice

1. Slice chicken crosswise into narrow strips. Coat lightly with flour, shaking off excess. Sauté chicken in 3 tablespoons of butter, over medium high heat, until cooked through, stirring frequently. Remove and keep warm.

2. Remove all but 1 tablespoon butter from skillet; add onion and cook until soft, about 1 to 2 minutes. Add chicken broth and bring to a boil. Add lemon juice and continue to boil until mixture is reduced to about ⅓ cup, about 4 to 5 minutes. Remove from heat and add remaining 3 tablespoons butter. Return chicken to pan and heat through. Makes 4 servings.

Baked Chicken Curry   Oven 350°F

1	chicken, cut up
½	cup butter, melted
1	teaspoon lemon juice
2	cloves garlic, minced
1	teaspoon salt
2	teaspoons curry powder (or to taste)

1. Place chicken, skin-side down, in a sprayed 13x9-inch baking dish.

2. Combine remaining ingredients. Brush chicken with some of the sauce. Bake 30 minutes, basting once. Turn chicken, bake 20 minutes , or until chicken is tender, basting every 10 minutes. Makes 4 servings.

Chicken Almond

Oven 350°F

1   chicken, cut up
⅓   cup flour
1   teaspoon lemon pepper
2   tablespoons vegetable oil
1   can (10¾-ounces) condensed cream of chicken soup
⅓   cup slivered almonds

1. Rinse chicken and pat dry. Combine flour and pepper. Coat chicken with flour, shaking off excess.

2. Heat oil in a large skillet and brown chicken on both sides. Place, skin side up, in a sprayed 13x9-inch baking dish.

3. Stir soup, then spread over chicken pieces. Sprinkle with almonds. Bake 50 to 60 minutes or until chicken is cooked through and tender. Makes 4 servings.

Golden Chicken Bake

Oven 375°F

1   chicken, cut up
⅓   cup butter
1   can (10¾-ounces) condensed cream of chicken soup
1   teaspoon minced dried parsley

1. Arrange chicken, skin-side down, in a 13x9-inch baking dish. Place dabs of butter over chicken. Bake 20 minutes. Turn chicken and bake 20 minutes.

2. Stir soup and pour over chicken. Sprinkle with parsley. Bake 20 minutes more. Makes 4 to 6 servings.

SIX Ingredients or Less

Menu

Chicken Almond

Rice

Green Peas

Sourdough Rolls

Cookies &
Ice Cream

After just a short preparation time, you can relax while this bakes in the oven. Serve with rice to compliment the wonderful sauce and a favorite green vegetable.

213

Chicken Madeira

This makes a delicious mild flavored sauce that you will be tempted to eat with a spoon. Enjoy the chicken and sauce served over rice or pasta.

Tip: *Clarified butter is great for browning since it tends to burn less than regular butter. I try to keep some in the refrigerator at all times. Or you can use half oil and half butter.*

4	chicken breast halves, skinned and boned
	Lemon pepper
3	tablespoons butter
1¾	cups heavy cream, divided
¼	cup Madeira wine
2	cups sliced fresh mushrooms

1. Sprinkle both sides of chicken with lemon pepper. Melt butter in a 10-inch heavy skillet. Add chicken and brown lightly on both sides (do not overcook). Remove chicken from skillet. Add 1 cup of the cream and the Madeira; stir to blend.

2. Bring mixture to a simmer, return chicken to pan and cook 20 minutes over medium low heat. Add remaining ¾ cup cream and the mushrooms. Cook about 10 minutes or until chicken is cooked through.

3. If sauce is a little on the thin side, remove chicken and keep hot. Cook sauce over medium high heat until thickened, about 3 to 4 minutes. Serve sauce over chicken. Makes 4 servings.

"A lack of knowledge about basic cookery can be somewhat inconvenient."

James Beard

Chicken with Artichokes and Cream

4	chicken breast halves, skinned and boned
⅓	cup flour
¼	cup butter
1	cup white wine
1½	cups heavy cream
2	cups marinated artichoke hearts, drained and cut up

1. Wash chicken and pat dry. Place each chicken breast between plastic wrap and pound to ¼-inch thickness. Cut crosswise into 3 pieces. (If chicken pieces are small, cut into 2 pieces.) Coat lightly with flour.

2. Heat butter in a large heavy skillet over medium heat. Cook chicken, turning once, until lightly browned and cooked through, about 3 minutes each side.

3. Pour off butter, but leave any brown pieces in skillet. Add wine and bring to a boil. Reduce heat and simmer 2 to 3 minutes. Add cream and cook over medium heat until slightly thickened. Add artichokes and heat through. Makes 4 servings.

Chicken with Marmalade Sauce   Oven 350°F

1	chicken, cut up
¼	cup butter, melted
1	cup orange marmalade
¼	cup packed light brown sugar
½	teaspoon dry ginger

1. Place chicken, skin-side down, in a sprayed 13x9-inch baking dish. Brush with butter. Bake 15 minutes. Turn chicken, baste with butter and bake 15 minutes.

2. Combine remaining ingredients and brush on chicken. Bake 20 minutes or until tender and richly glazed, basting frequently. Makes 4 servings.

This is a very delicate flavored dish that calls for a more robust rice, vegetable and salad accompaniment.

Easy Chicken Stir-fry
⊞ ⊞ ⊞

Cook 1 pound cubed boneless chicken breast in 1 tablespoon oil until cooked through. Remove and set aside.

If necessary, add more oil, and cook 1 clove garlic, minced with 3 to 4 cups assorted fresh or frozen vegetables, cooking only until crisp-tender.

Return chicken to skillet and add about ⅓ cup teriyaki or stir-fry sauce. Cook only until heated through. Makes 4 servings.

Orange and honey team up to make a very flavorful chicken dish. Serve with Dinner Hash Browns, Broccoli Salad and Poppy Seed French Bread.

Orange Chicken Delight   Oven 350°F

1	chicken, cut up
1	tablespoon freshly grated orange peel
¼	cup honey
½	cup oil
2	teaspoons ground ginger

1. Place chicken, skin-side down, in a sprayed 13x9-inch baking dish. Combine remaining ingredients. Baste chicken with some of the mixture. Bake 30 minutes, turn and bake 30 minutes longer, basting frequently. Watch carefully during last 10 minutes of baking time. Makes 4 servings.

This delightful dish features a combination of popular ingredients. Serve with a tossed green salad, rolls and Strawberry Margarita Pie.

Chicken Enchiladas in Cream   Oven 350°F

3	cups cubed cooked chicken
1	cup green chili salsa (this is a red salsa)
1	can (4-ounces) chopped green chilis
10	(8-inch) flour tortillas
2½	cups whipping cream
2	cups (8-ounces) Monterey Jack cheese, shredded

1. Combine chicken, salsa and green chilies. Fill each tortilla with a portion of the chicken mixture. Roll up and place, seam-side down, in sprayed 13x9-inch baking dish. Pour cream over top. Sprinkle evenly with cheese. Bake 45 minutes or until golden and most of the cream is absorbed. Makes 6 servings.

Chicken & Celery Casserole

Oven 350°F

> 4 chicken breast halves, skinned and boned
> Salt and pepper (optional)
> 4 ounces cream cheese, softened
> 1 can (10¾-ounces) condensed cream of celery soup
> Parsley, freshly chopped or dried

1. Rinse chicken and pat dry; sprinkle with salt and pepper. Place, skin-side up, in a sprayed 11x7-inch baking dish. Place cream cheese in mixer bowl and beat until smooth. Gradually add the soup and beat until smooth. Spoon over chicken. Bake 35 to 40 minutes or until chicken is cooked through. Sprinkle lightly with parsley. Makes 4 servings.

You'll love how quickly this casserole goes together. The flavorful sauce reminds me a little bit of Stroganoff, only a lot easier to make. I'm not sure why, but this recipe just isn't as good with the lowfat celery soup.

Chicken Elegant

Oven 375°F

> 4 small whole chicken breasts, boned
> ⅓ cup, plus 3 tablespoons butter
> 1 cup chicken broth
> ¼ cup flour
> 1 cup half and half
> Salt and pepper

1. Chicken breasts should be left whole with bones removed (do not remove skin). Heat ⅓ cup butter in heavy skillet. Tuck chicken breast ends under, shaping into a nice round mound. Brown bottom side first, turn and brown top side. Place in a sprayed 13x9-inch baking dish. Add chicken broth. Cover with foil and bake 45 to 60 minutes or until cooked through. Remove chicken and keep warm (reserve broth).

2. Melt the 3 tablespoons butter in a small saucepan; stir in flour until blended. Remove from heat; stir in reserved broth and half and half. Cook, stirring frequently, until mixture boils and thickens. Season to taste with salt and pepper. Place chicken on serving plate; pour sauce over top. Makes 4 servings.

Menu

Chicken Elegant

Broccoli with Pecan Dressing

Garlic Mashed Potatoes

Almond Spinach Salad

Ice Cream Cake

217

Chicken Enchiladas   Oven 350°F

3   whole chicken breasts, cooked
2   cups sour cream
1   can (4-ounces) diced green chilies
3   cans (10¾-ounces each) condensed cream of chicken soup
4   cups (16-ounces) Cheddar cheese, shredded
10 (8-inch) flour tortillas

1. Cut chicken into bite-size pieces. Combine chicken with sour cream, chilies, 1 can soup and 1 cup cheese. Spoon a generous amount of filling down center of each tortilla. Roll up and place, seam-side down, in sprayed deep 13x9-inch baking dish.

2. Combine remaining 2 cans soup and stir to soften. Spread over tortillas. Sprinkle remaining cheese over top. Bake 45 to 60 minutes or until hot and cheese is golden. Makes 8 servings.

Gourmet Baked Chicken Bundles   Oven 325°F

10   chicken breast halves, skinned and boned
2   cups sour cream
1   tablespoon Worcestershire sauce
2   teaspoons salt
1¼   teaspoons paprika
1½   cups fine dry bread crumbs

1. Place chicken in a 13x9-inch baking dish. Combine sour cream, Worcestershire sauce, salt and paprika; pour over chicken. Turn chicken to coat. Cover and refrigerate overnight.

2. Drop chicken pieces, one at a time in breadcrumbs, turning to coat. Tuck ends under to make a nice round fillet. Place in sprayed shallow baking pan. Cover and chill at least 1½ hours.

3. Bake 45 to 60 minutes or until golden and cooked through. (If chicken looks dry, baste with a little melted butter.) Makes 10 servings.

Orange Glazed Chicken

Oven 350°F

1 chicken, cut up
Salt and pepper
¼ cup orange juice
1 tablespoon honey
¼ teaspoon Worcestershire sauce
¼ teaspoon dry mustard

1. Place chicken, skin-side up, in sprayed 13x9 baking dish. Sprinkle with salt and pepper. Bake 30 minutes.

2. Combine remaining ingredients and brush some of the sauce over the chicken. Continue baking, brushing occasionally with remaining sauce, 20 to 30 minutes or until cooked through. Makes 4 servings.

A great tasting family dish made even better served with Almond Rice Pilaf and fresh green beans. Add ice cream and sliced fruit for dessert.

Chicken Curry

6 chicken breast halves, skinned and boned
¼ cup butter
¼ cup flour
2 cups milk
½ teaspoon salt
1½ teaspoons curry powder or to taste

1. Cook chicken and cube as directed on page 203.

2. Melt butter in a 2-quart saucepan. Add flour and whisk until blended. Add milk gradually, stirring constantly. Bring mixture to a boil and continue cooking about 2 minutes. Reduce heat and cook, stirring frequently, until thickened. Stir in curry. Add cooked chicken and heat through. Makes 6 servings.

This is one of the easiest curries I have made and equally as delicious. Serve over rice with sides such as peanuts, raisins, pineapple, coconut, dried cranberries, and fruit salsas.

Chicken & Wine Dish

Oven 375°F

Even after twenty plus years, this is still a family favorite. The sauce is delicious served over rice.

4	chicken breast halves
⅓	cup butter, thinly sliced
¼	cup white wine
1	can (10¾-ounces) condensed cream of chicken soup
2	tablespoons sliced almonds
1	tablespoon chopped parsley

1. Place chicken, skin-side down, in a sprayed 13x9-inch baking dish. Arrange slices of butter over top. Bake 20 minutes. Turn chicken and bake 20 minutes.

2. Meanwhile, combine wine and soup; spoon over chicken. Sprinkle with almonds and parsley. Bake 10 to 20 minutes. Chicken should be golden and tender. Makes 4 servings.

Cooking Tip

When you are sautéing, browning or frying chicken (or meat), make sure that you don't crowd the pieces in the pan. You will end up steam cooking instead of browning. Ever wonder why you have all that liquid in the pan? This may be the reason.

Chinese Browned Chicken

Oven 350°F

4	chicken breast halves
2	tablespoons butter, melted
2	tablespoons Worcestershire sauce
1	tablespoon soy sauce

1. Line baking pan with foil for easier cleaning. Place chicken on foil, skin-side up.

2. Combine remaining ingredients. Brush chicken with mixture and bake 30 to 40 minutes, basting occasionally. Makes 4 servings.

Panko Chicken Dijon

Oven 375°F

4   chicken breast halves, skinned and boned
4   tablespoon melted butter, divided
1½ tablespoons Dijon mustard
3   tablespoons grated Parmesan cheese
½   cup Panko breading

1. Wash chicken and pat dry. Combine 3 tablespoons of the butter with the mustard in a small shallow dish. It may look curdled, but that's okay.

2. Combine Parmesan and Panko in a flat dish. Dip chicken in butter mixture, then in crumb mixture, coating both sides. Place on sprayed shallow baking pan. Brush with remaining tablespoon butter. Bake 30 to 40 minutes or until cooked through and golden. Makes 4 servings.

A lot of flavor is packed into this chicken dish. Serve with fresh asparagus and Angel hair pasta tossed with butter and lemon juice. Serve with Dijon Mustard Sauce on page 301.

Note: *Panko is a crunchy Japanese style breading found in the Asian department of most supermarkets.*

Chicken with Sour Cream Gravy

1   chicken, cut up
3   tablespoons butter
Seasoning salt
3   tablespoons flour
¼   cup sour cream

1. Heat butter in a large skillet. Brown chicken on both sides. Sprinkle with seasoning salt. Add ½ cup water; bring to a boil. Reduce heat and cook, covered, 20 minutes. Turn chicken; continue cooking 15 to 20 minutes or until cooked through. Remove chicken and keep warm.

2. In small jar, combine flour and ½ cup water; shake to mix well. Gradually add to liquid in skillet. Cook, stirring constantly, until mixture comes to a boil and thickens. Stir in sour cream, but do not boil. Taste for seasoning. Makes 4 servings.

Serve the gravy over the chicken and mashed potatoes or rice. Add hot buttered peas and rolls and you have a delicious meal without any fuss.

221

What would we do without boneless chicken breasts? You can do so many things with them. They are low in fat, delicious and can be used for almost any occasion.

Mozzarella Chicken Bake

4 large chicken breast halves, skinned and boned
⅓ cup flour
¼ cup butter
Salt and pepper
4 large mushrooms, sliced
4 slices Mozzarella cheese

1. Place chicken between waxed paper and pound to ¼-inch thickness, being careful not to tear the meat. Coat chicken with flour and shake off excess.

2. Heat butter in skillet; add chicken and cook until tender, about 4 to 5 minutes each side. Place chicken on broiler pan; sprinkle with salt and pepper.

3. Quickly sauté mushrooms in skillet; arrange slices on chicken. Top with a slice of cheese. Place under broiler just long enough to melt cheese. Makes 4 servings.

This recipe is delicious just as it is, but if want to elaborate just add any of the following: sliced mushrooms, slivered almonds, or water chestnuts.

Company Chicken and Rice   Oven 250°F

8 chicken breast halves
1½ cups uncooked long-grain rice
1 can (10¾-ounces) condensed cream of celery soup
1 can (10¾-ounces) condensed cream of mushroom soup
1 can (10¾-ounces) condensed cream of chicken soup
½ cup butter, melted

1. Place rice in bottom of large sprayed roasting pan (pan should be at least 2-inches deep). Combine soups in mixing bowl; gradually stir in 1½ soup cans of water, stirring to blend. Pour over rice.

2. Dip chicken in butter; place skin-side up on rice mixture. Bake, uncovered, at 250° for 2½ hours or at 350° for 1½ hours or until liquid is absorbed, and chicken is cooked through. Makes 8 servings.

Peachy Chicken

Oven 350°F

1   chicken, cut up
1   can (29-ounces) peach halves, save juice
¼   cup soy sauce

1. Arrange chicken, skin-side down, in a sprayed 13x9-inch baking dish. Combine peach syrup with soy sauce. Pour over chicken. Bake 30 minutes. Turn and bake 20 minutes or until cooked through, basting frequently. Serve with peaches. Makes 4 servings.

If desired, peach halves can be heated along with chicken the last 10 minutes of baking time.

Ritz Baked Chicken

Oven 325°F

4   chicken breast halves
½   cup sour cream
1   tablespoon Worcestershire sauce
1   tablespoon lemon juice
1   cup crushed Ritz® crackers

1. Combine sour cream, Worcestershire sauce and lemon juice. Dip chicken in mixture; roll in cracker crumbs. Place on baking sheet and bake 30 to 40 minutes or until cooked through. Makes 4 servings.

Tell your children they can't eat the rest of the box of Ritz® crackers. You're going to use them for dinner tonight. This is an easy recipe, so it is actually something they could do.

Teriyaki Chicken

Oven 350°F

1   chicken, cut up
2   tablespoons oil
½   cup soy sauce
1   teaspoon sugar
⅓   cup finely chopped onion
1   garlic clove, minced

1. Combine last 5 ingredients. Pour over chicken; marinate at least 2 hours. Place chicken in a sprayed 13x9-inch baking pan. Bake 45 to 60 minutes or until cooked through, basting occasionally. Makes 4 servings.

223

Roast Chicken

A roast chicken for dinner is one of the most delicious meals you can easily prepare. All you need to do is wash the whole chicken and pat dry. Place, breast side up, on a cooking rack set in a baking pan. Tuck wing tips under and toward the back. Insert meat thermometer in thigh area, taking care not to touch any bone. Brush with about 1 tablespoon vegetable oil and place in a 350° oven. Cook about 1½ hours according to the size of the chicken and how hot your oven bakes. The thermometer should read 175°. Cover with foil and let stand about 10 minutes. My favorite time saver is to cook two at a time; serve one for dinner and the other one for sandwiches or recipes calling for cubed cooked chicken. When doing this, place both chickens in large roasting pan (the one that comes with your oven is great) and follow the directions above.

Roquefort Chicken   Oven 350°F

6   chicken breast halves, skinned and boned
Salt and pepper
¼   cup butter
4   ounces Roquefort cheese
1   garlic clove, minced
1   cup sour cream.

1. Sprinkle chicken with salt and pepper. Heat butter in heavy skillet and lightly brown chicken; remove. Place in a sprayed 13x9-inch baking dish.

2. Add Roquefort, garlic and sour cream to skillet. Heat, but do not boil. Pour over chicken. Bake 30 to 40 minutes or until cooked through. Makes 6 servings.

Quick Chicken Divan   Oven 350°F

1   pound fresh broccoli, cooked
4   large slices cooked chicken or turkey
1   can (10¾-ounces) condensed cream of chicken soup
⅓   cup milk
½   cup (2-ounces) Cheddar cheese, shredded

1. Place broccoli in a sprayed 11x7-inch baking dish. Top with chicken.

2. Combine soup and milk until blended. Pour over chicken. Sprinkle with cheese. Bake 30 minutes or until heated through. Makes 4 servings.

Sweet-Sour Chicken

Oven 350°F

1   chicken, cut up
1   cup ketchup
¾   cup white vinegar
1½ teaspoons prepared mustard
1½ cups firmly packed light brown sugar

1. Combine last 4 ingredients in a small saucepan. Bring to a boil; reduce heat and simmer 30 minutes.

2. Place chicken, skin-side down, in a sprayed 13x9-inch baking dish. Brush generously with sauce. Bake 30 minutes; turn, bake 20 to 30 minutes, basting frequently with the sauce. Makes 4 servings.

A nice sweet-sour sauce flavors this easy chicken recipe. Serve with rice to absorb all the wonderful sauce.

Shopper's Chicken

Oven 350°F

6   chicken breast halves
1   cup sour cream
2   tablespoons lemon juice
1   teaspoon salt
1   teaspoon paprika
½   cup butter, melted

1. Place chicken, skin-side up, in a sprayed 13x9-inch baking dish.

2. Combine sour cream, lemon juice, salt, and paprika. Spread over chicken. Spoon butter over top. Bake 30 to 40 minutes or until cooked through. Makes 6 servings.

Chicken and Pasta Salad

❈ ❈ ❈

Chicken, pasta and greens combine to make a full-meal salad. Combine a 9 or 12-ounce package refrigerated cheese-filled tortellini, cooked and chilled, with one bag assorted greens. Add about 2 to 3 cups cubed cooked chicken, some croutons and then toss with Caesar dressing. Sprinkle with shredded Parmesan cheese. Makes 4 to 6 servings.

Topping Variations

Pineapple slices
Cooked broccoli spears
Monterey Jack cheese

Sliced tomatoes
Cooked broccoli spears
Mozzarella cheese

Sliced Ham
Cooked asparagus spears
Swiss cheese

Company Swiss Chicken

4   chicken breast halves, skinned and boned
2   tablespoons oil
1   jar (6½-ounces) marinated artichoke hearts, drained
4   slices Swiss cheese

1. Place each chicken breast between plastic wrap and pound to ¼-inch thickness. Heat oil in a large skillet. Add chicken and cook 6 to 8 minutes or until cooked through, turning once.

2. Arrange artichokes on top of chicken; top with a slice of cheese (trim if too large). Cover skillet and cook until cheese is melted. Makes 4 servings.

Chicken Stovetop Dinner

4   chicken breast halves, skinned and boned
1½ teaspoons oil
1   can (14½-ounces) chicken broth
2   cups fresh broccoli florettes
2   cups instant rice
½   cup (2-ounces) Cheddar cheese, shredded

1. Rinse chicken and pat dry. Heat oil in a large nonstick skillet. Cook chicken, about 4 minutes on each side, or until cooked through. Remove chicken from pan.

2. Add broth to skillet and bring to a boil. Add rice and broccoli. Arrange chicken over top. Cover skillet and cook, over low heat, about 5 minutes or until rice is tender and liquid is absorbed. Sprinkle with cheese. Cover and let stand 1 to 2 minutes to melt cheese. Makes 4 servings

Orange Almond Chicken
Oven 350°F

6 large chicken breast halves, skinned
Salt and pepper
¾ cup flour
3 oranges (you will need ¾ cup orange juice and 1½ teaspoons orange peel)
6 tablespoons butter
6 tablespoons sliced almonds

1. Sprinkle chicken with salt and pepper. Coat with flour. Place in 13x9-inch baking dish, skin-side up.

2. Combine juice and orange peel; pour over chicken. Dot chicken with butter. Sprinkle with almonds. Bake 45 to 60 minutes, basting 2 or 3 times. If using boneless chicken breasts, cooking time will be less. Makes 6 servings.

Savory Grilled Chicken
Grill

1 chicken, cut up
Seasoned salt
Butter, melted

1. Preheat grill.

2. Place chicken on a large piece of heavy-duty foil. Sprinkle generously with salt. Fold foil over and secure tightly. Place on grill and cook 45 minutes, turning frequently, to avoid burning. Remove chicken from foil and place directly on grill, turning to brown both sides. Baste with butter. Meat is so tender it will literally fall off the bone. Makes 4 servings.

Menu

✍

Orange Almond Chicken

Buttered Angel Hair Pasta

Lemon Broccoli

Hot Rolls

Almond Angel Food Cake

227

Butterflied Chicken on the Grill · Grill

1 (2-2½ pound) chicken
¼ cup butter, melted
1 tablespoon lemon juice
Salt and pepper

1. Rinse chicken, trim off excess fat and pat dry. Using a sharp knife or kitchen shears, split chicken open through the back. With two large skewers, skewer chicken diagonally to keep chicken flat.

2. Combine butter and lemon juice; brush over chicken. Sprinkle with salt and pepper.

3. Place, skin-side up, on grill over medium-low coals, cover and cook 30 to 45 minutes, turning and basting occasionally with the butter mixture.

As my family will tell you, "I love chicken!" And this recipe is no exception. It turns out very tasty, and has the added bonus of being low in fat. Cooking times can vary considerably with this recipe. Butterflying the chicken speeds up the cooking time, but it also depends on the size of the chicken and the heat of your grill. Allow plenty of time, and use a good thermometer. For a more smoky flavor, place chicken on grill opposite the coals, cover and cook over low heat until cooked through.

Chicken with Sun-Dried Tomatoes

4 chicken breast halves, skinned and boned
½ cup chopped oil-packed sun-dried tomatoes (with 2 tablespoons of the oil)
2 large garlic cloves, finely chopped
¼ cup finely chopped onion
1 cup heavy whipping cream

1. Heat 1 tablespoon of the oil from the tomatoes in a large skillet. Add chicken and cook 4 to 5 minutes per side until cooked through.

2. Remove and keep warm. Add remaining 1 tablespoon oil, garlic, onion and sun-dried tomatoes to skillet. Sauté until onions are tender, about 3 to 4 minutes. Add cream and simmer 4 to 5 minutes or until sauce has thickened. Spoon over chicken. Makes 4 servings.

Chinese Noodle Casserole

Oven 350°F

1½   cups diced cooked chicken or turkey
1   cup finely chopped celery
1   cup cashews, split
2   cans (10¾-ounces each) condensed cream of mushroom soup
1   cup chicken broth
1   can (5-ounces) Chow Mein Noodles

1. Combine chicken, celery, and cashews in a mixing bowl.

2. Combine soup and broth in a small mixing bowl. Pour over chicken mixture; stir to mix.

3. Layer in sprayed deep 2-quart casserole dish, starting with half of the chicken mixture, then half of the noodles. Repeat, ending with noodles. Bake 45 minutes or until heated through. Makes 6 servings.

*This is best served hot from the oven as Chow Mein Noodles tend to soften when reheated. **Variation**: add finely chopped onion or sliced mushrooms.*

Chicken and Noodles

3   cups chicken broth
4   ounces (or about 1½ cups) medium egg noodles
2   cups fresh broccoli florettes
2   cups cubed cooked chicken or turkey
¼   teaspoon lemon pepper
½   cup sour cream

1. Heat chicken broth in a 2 quart saucepan; bring to a boil. Add noodles and cook about 4 minutes; stirring occasionally. Add broccoli; cover and continue cooking 4 minutes. Add chicken and lemon pepper; cook about 4 minutes or until heated through and broccoli is just tender.

2. At this point you probably have very little liquid left in the pan, but this needs to be drained off. Stir in sour cream and cook, over low heat, until heated through. Makes 4 servings.

This recipe is very easy and very fast. If you already have some leftover chicken or turkey, it can be made in less than 15 minutes. The servings aren't overly generous, so add a nice large salad and dinner rolls. Brownies would be nice too.

Makes enough dressing for one large turkey. This recipe has a lot more flavor when cooked in the turkey rather than baked in a casserole. For safety reasons, internal temperature of stuffing, when cooked in the turkey, must reach at least 165°.

Apple Sausage Stuffing

1	pound seasoned bulk sausage
1	cup chopped onion
2	cups chopped apples, peeled
10	cup seasoned bread cubes for stuffing
1	large egg, lightly beaten
½	cup chicken broth

1. In a large skillet, brown sausage. Remove from skillet. Pour off all but 2 tablespoons fat. Add onion and apples. Cook until tender, about 5 minutes. Combine this mixture with the sausage, bread cubes, egg and broth. Stir until well mixed and bread cubes are coated.

Apricot Bread Stuffing

2	tablespoons butter
¼	cup finely chopped onion
¼	cup finely chopped dried apricots
⅓	cup rich chicken broth
¼	cup finely chopped walnuts
1½	cups dry bread cubes, for stuffing

1. Heat butter in a small skillet. Add remaining ingredients except bread cubes, and cook 3 to 4 minutes or until onion is soft. Pour over bread cubes; toss to coat.

Chicken and Pesto Fettuccine

4	Chicken breast halves, skinned, boned, cubed
½	cup heavy whipping cream
½	cup butter plus 2 tablespoons
⅓	cup freshly grated Parmesan cheese
1	tablespoon pesto, plus ¼ cup
12	ounces fettuccine

1. Cook pasta according to package directions. If pasta is ready before the rest of the ingredients, drain off the water, return to pan and add about 1 tablespoon butter, tossing to coat. Cover and keep warm.

2. Meanwhile, in small saucepan, heat the cream. Add ½ cup of the butter and heat until melted. Gradually add the Parmesan cheese, stirring after each addition, until melted. Keep warm until ready to use.

3. Heat skillet over medium-high heat. Toss chicken with remaining 2 tablespoons butter (melted). Add to skillet and cook, stirring frequently, until chicken is cooked through, being careful not to overcook. Remove chicken and toss with 1 tablespoon pesto.

4. Add cream sauce and ¼ cup pesto to the pasta, tossing to coat. Place on heated platter and top with the chicken. Makes 4 to 6 servings.

This pasta dish takes a little more time than some of the recipes, but it is well worth the effort. Serve with toasted bread or rolls, a nice green salad and Apple Raspberry Crisp or ice cream and sliced strawberries for dessert.

Hint: *Most pasta dishes should not be allowed to stand, but should be served immediately. Heated serving dishes will also help to keep the pasta hot as long as possible.*

Gorgonzola fans will treasure this recipe and those who aren't fans should give it a try. Gorgonzola isn't my favorite cheese, but I love this recipe.

Variation: *Add cooked chicken or ham for 4 main dish servings.*

Penne with Gorgonzola

8   ounces penne pasta
1   cup heavy whipping cream
2   ounces Gorgonzola cheese, crumbled
⅛   teaspoon freshly ground pepper
Parmesan cheese, freshly grated

1. Cook pasta according to directions on package.

2. Meanwhile, in medium saucepan, heat cream to boiling; reduce heat and simmer 2 minutes. Add Gorgonzola and stir until smooth. Add pepper.

3. Drain pasta and return to pan. Stir in sauce. Spoon onto a serving platter; sprinkle with desired amount of Parmesan. Makes 6 side dish servings.

Fettuccine Alfredo

16   ounces fettuccine
½   cup butter, melted
1   cup heavy whipping cream
1   cup freshly grated Parmesan cheese
Salt and Pepper to taste

1. Cook pasta as directed on package; drain. Return pasta to pan. Add butter, cream and cheese. Add salt and pepper. Toss over low heat until pasta is coated and mixture is heated through. Makes 4 servings.

Cheese Ravioli

2	packages (9-ounces each) cheese-filled ravioli
2	tablespoons butter
1	large garlic clove, minced
1	tablespoon chopped fresh parsley
1	cup heavy whipping cream
¼	cup grated Asiago or Parmesan cheese

1. In large pot, cook pasta according to directions on package.

2. Meanwhile, just before pasta is ready, melt butter in a small skillet. Add garlic and parsley and cook over medium-low heat about 45 seconds (you don't want the garlic to brown).

3. Drain pasta and rinse with cold water. Return to pot; add garlic mixture and cream. Cook on low heat until cream is reduced slightly, about 3 to 4 minutes. Place in a 11x7-inch baking dish and sprinkle with cheese. Place under broiler and broil until cheese is melted and lightly browned. Makes 6 side dishes or 4 main dishes.

Serve as a side dish with Chicken Parmesan on page 206.

Pasta & Shrimp

16	ounces fettuccine or linguine
1	cup butter, softened
½	cup freshly grated Parmesan cheese
¾	to 1 pound cooked shrimp
	Black pepper

1. Cook pasta as directed on package. Drain and return to pot; reduce heat. Add butter and stir until melted. Add Parmesan cheese and continue to heat until cheese is melted. Stir in the shrimp. Add pepper to taste. Serve with additional Parmesan cheese, if desired. Makes 4 very large servings or 6 average servings.

   Hint: If shrimp is precooked, heat through before adding to pasta. If you are having company, you might want to add some chopped parsley for additional color.

This is a very good pasta dish and can be prepared in less than 30 minutes. I have also made this recipe with spaghetti noodles with, no complaints.

Baked Fettuccine

Oven 350°F

8 ounces fettuccine
¼ cup butter
½ cup milk
2 large eggs, lightly beaten
6 tablespoons grated Parmesan cheese, divided
1 tablespoon seasoned breadcrumbs

1. Cook pasta according to directions on package; drain and return to pan. Stir in butter. Add milk, eggs and 5 tablespoons Parmesan. Pour into sprayed 8x8-inch baking dish. Combine remaining Parmesan and breadcrumbs. Sprinkle over top. Bake 20 to 25 minutes or until set. Makes 4 to 6 servings.

Quick Pasta Sauce

Cook heavy whipping cream until thickened. It should be thick enough to lightly coat the pasta. This works nicely as a side-dish pasta and for simple pasta dishes with a cream sauce.

Rigatoni Bake

Oven 350°F

8 ounces rigatoni
8 ounces of Cheddar cheese, cut into strips
1 jar (15.5-ounces) spaghetti sauce
3 tablespoons grated Parmesan cheese

1. Cook rigatoni as directed on package. Drain and rinse thoroughly. Cut cheese into strips 1¼-inches long by ¼-inch thick. Insert a strip of cheese in each cooked pasta and place in sprayed 1½ quart casserole dish. Pour sauce over top and sprinkle with Parmesan cheese. Bake, uncovered 25 to 30 minutes or until heated through. Makes 6 to 8 servings.

Note: If you must have meat with your meal, brown one pound lean ground beef and add to the sauce. Vary by substituting 1 cup (4-ounces) shredded Mozzarella cheese for the Parmesan.

Spinach Tortellini with Tomato Sauce

1 tablespoon olive oil
1 large garlic clove, minced
2 cans (14.5-ounces each) whole Italian style tomatoes, cut up
1 tablespoon sugar
1 package (8-ounces) spinach tortellini with cheese

1. Heat oil in a medium saucepan. Add garlic and cook about 2 minutes, but do not brown. Add tomatoes (do not drain); and sugar. Bring to a boil; reduce heat and simmer about 45 minutes or until thickened.

2. Meanwhile, cook tortellini according to directions on package. Drain and rinse thoroughly. Place tortellini on a large serving platter and top with some of the tomato sauce. Makes 4 servings.

Parmesan Cheese

In my Six Ingredients or Less® Pasta cookbook, I suggest using the real Parmesan cheese stamped "Parmigiano-Reggiano®", but I have since done some rethinking about that. Even though it is the "best", it has become too expensive for most of us. At $17 per pound and up, it isn't something all of us can use for everyday cooking.

I have recently started using Stella® Parmesan cheese for most of my recipes and it is wonderful. I haven't had any complaints yet. I suggest buying it in wedges for the best flavor. Grate as needed and the cheese will taste better and last longer. Wrap in plastic wrap and then in foil for a longer shelf life.

Cream

Whipping Cream
30-36% butter fat

Heavy Whipping Cream
36-40% butter fat

Half-and-Half
10-12% butter fat, equal parts of milk and cream

Ultrapasteurized Cream*
Processed to dramatically increase shelf-life. Doesn't whip well. Doesn't work in all recipes. Seen more and more in stores.

*I try to avoid this product.

Mostaccioli & Sun-Dried Tomatoes

8 ounces mostaccioli
¼ cup oil-packed sun-dried tomatoes
1 tablespoon oil from tomatoes
1 jar (6½-ounces) marinated artichoke hearts, coarsely chopped

1. Cook pasta according to directions on package; drain.

2. Meanwhile, chop tomatoes and place in a large serving bowl. Add the oil (if you don't have enough oil from the tomatoes, add olive oil to make up the difference). Add artichokes and pasta and toss to coat. Makes 6 side-dish servings.

Easy Noodles Parmesan

1 package (10-ounces) egg noodles
⅓ cup butter
½ Parmesan cheese

Cook noodles according to directions on package; drain. Melt butter in pot noodles were cooked in; return noodles to pot and toss. Add Parmesan cheese and toss to coat. Makes 6 servings.

Browned Butter and Myzithra Cheese

8 ounces spaghetti
⅓ cup butter
2 medium garlic cloves, minced
½ cup grated Myzithra cheese

1. Cook pasta according to directions on package; drain.

2. Meanwhile, in a small skillet, melt butter over medium-low heat. Add garlic and cook until butter turns a light brown. Watch carefully at this point. If it turns too dark, it will have to be discarded. Add to pasta and toss to coat. Place on individual serving dishes and sprinkle with about 2 tablespoons cheese. Makes 4 side-dish servings or 2 main dish servings.

Kid's Corner

Kid's Cooking Corner

Hi, my name is Paulina Hazen and I have been cooking with my Mom and Grandma Carlean since I was 2 years old. Learning to cook is so much fun and now that I have had lots of practice, my recipes turn out better and better. I enjoy cooking and my Mom really appreciates my help in the kitchen.

I don't know about your house, but at my house I always have to ask my Mom if I can cook and then I have to clean up my mess. That way I get to cook more often. I get lots of contented smiles and thank yous when my recipes turn out good. If they don't turn out the way I want them to, my family is really nice about it and gives me lots of encouragement. Sometimes my Dad teases me, but that's okay. I hope you will enjoy learning to cook too.

I have some hints that will help you be more successful right from the start:

- Make sure there is a grown up helping you.
- "Always" read through the recipe first, before you begin.
- Make sure you have all the ingredients.
- Always wash your hands before cooking
- Have all the ingredients out on the counter and measured before assembling the recipe.
- Ask a grown up if you don't understand the recipe.

Happy cooking and happy eating,

Paulina

239

Apple Peanut Butter Discs

These apple slices and a glass of milk make a great after school snack.

1   apple, such as Gala, Fuji or Golden Delicious
2   tablespoons peanut butter

1. Wash apple and pat dry with a paper towel. Core the apple (you may need Mom for this part). Fill center with peanut butter. Wrap in plastic wrap or foil and chill about 30 minutes. When ready to eat, cut crosswise into ½-inch slices.

My brothers don't enjoy cooking as much as I do, but they sure enjoy being the taste testers!

Benjamin

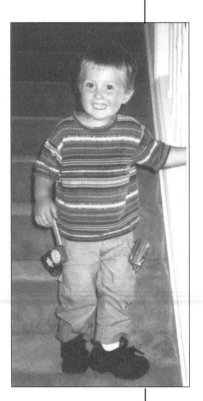

Patrick

240

Children's Bird Seed

    2   cups Corn Pops® cereal
    ½   cup raisins
    ½   cup peanuts
    ½   cup M&M® candies

1. Combine ingredients in large bowl. Makes 3½ cups.

Pumpkin Seed Snacks

Oven 350°F

    2   cups fresh pumpkin seeds
    1   tablespoon vegetable oil
    1   tablespoon butter, melted
    Salt

1. Preheat oven to 350°.

2. Wipe fibers from pumpkin seeds, but do not wash. Place in a medium-size bowl.

3. Combine oil and melted butter. Pour over seeds and toss to coat. Spread out on a large baking sheet. Sprinkle lightly with salt.

4. Place baking sheet in oven and bake 30 minutes or until golden in color and crisp. Remove from oven and let cool. Store in covered container. Makes 2 cups.

A great school snack when it's your turn to provide the treat.

When you carve your pumpkins for Halloween, have Mom or Dad save the seeds. They make a very tasty snack, but you must bake them first.

Memories

The favorite meals we prepare today will be fond memories when our children look back on their childhood.

241

Lemonade

1 cup lemon juice
1 cup sugar
6 cups club soda, chilled

Combine lemon juice and sugar; stir until well mixed. Add club soda and chill until ready to serve.

Peppermint Fizz

2 tablespoons chocolate syrup
4 scoops peppermint ice cream
1 cup lemon-lime soda pop

Place ingredients in blender and process until smooth. Makes 2 cups.

Pink Punch

⅓ cup Kool-Aid® cherry flavor sugar sweetened soft drink mix
3 cups water
1 cup vanilla ice cream, softened
4 cups lemon-lime soda pop, or to taste

1. In large bowl or container, combine Kool-Aid® and water. Add ice cream and stir until melted. Cover and refrigerate until ready to serve.

2. Just before serving, add soda pop to mixture and stir until blended. Makes 8 cups.

Raspberry Smoothie

1 package (10-ounces) frozen sweetened raspberries, thawed
2 cups orange juice
½ cup milk
6 ice cubes

1. Place ingredients in blender and process until smooth. Makes 4½ cups.

Lemon Julius Smoothie

1 can (6-ounces) frozen lemonade concentrate
1 can (6-ounces) frozen orange juice concentrate
2 cups vanilla ice cream

1. Combine ingredients in blender along wtih 4 cups water; blend on medium speed until mixed and foamy. If blender is too small to hold all the ingredients, make half the recipe at a time and combine the two mixes. Makes 7½ cups.

Red and White Popcorn Crunch   Oven 250°F

4	quarts popped popcorn
½	cup butter
¼	cup light corn syrup
1	stick (5-ounces) peppermint candy, coarsely chopped
1	to 2 drops of food coloring

1. Preheat oven to 250°F.

2. Place popcorn in a very large baking dish or roasting pan. Large enough that you will be able to stir the mixture.

3. Place butter, corn syrup and chopped candy in a small saucepan. Bring to a boil over medium heat, stirring constantly. Boil 5 minutes, stirring frequently. Add 1 to 2 drops of food coloring (if desired).

4. Quickly pour over popcorn and toss, using two large spoons or spatulas. Do this carefully because the mixture is very hot and sticky. The popcorn will not be entirely coated.

5. Place in oven and bake 60 minutes, stirring mixture every 15 minutes. Remove from oven and stir occasionally as it cools. If you do not stir it while cooling, it will form one big clump.

You can serve this to your family and friends on any special occasion. It would also be great for school parties. Just change the color to fit the occasion. :

Red-Valentine's Day
Green-St. Patrick's Day
Blue-4th of July
Red-Christmas Day

Easy Popcorn Balls

¼	cup butter
½	teaspoon vanilla extract
1	package (10½-ounces) marshmallows
6	quarts popped popcorn

1. Combine butter, vanilla, and marshmallows in top of a double boiler. Stir until melted and smooth.

2. Pour over popcorn. Butter hands and form into balls, but be careful, mixture may be hot. Makes 12 to 15 balls.

Great Idea

Mold popcorn balls around the straight end of a candy can. Wrap with plastic wrap, tie with a ribbon and hang on your Christman tree. Give to your friends and family on Christmas day.

Easy Kid's Cookies

Oven 350°F

1 cup butter
1 cup firmly packed light brown sugar
1 cup flour
1 teaspoon baking soda
2 cups quick-cooking oats

1. Preheat oven to 350°F.

2. Cream butter and sugar in mixer bowl. Add flour and baking soda and beat until mixed. Stir in oats. Roll into 1-inch balls. Place on an ungreased baking sheet and press slightly. Bake 8 to 10 minutes. Makes 4 dozen.

Butterscotch Crunchies

1 cup butterscotch chips
½ cup peanut butter
2 cups (3-ounce can) Chow Mein Noodles
1 cup miniature marshmallows

1. Melt butterscotch chips and peanut butter in top of double boiler; stir to blend. Remove from heat.

2. Gently stir in noodles and marshmallows. Drop by teaspoon onto waxed paper-lined cookie sheets. Chill until set. Makes 3 dozen.

Rice Krispie® Treats

Instead of a 13x9-inch pan, it's fun to use a 12-inch pizza pan. Then drizzle with just a little bit of unsweetened melted chocolate. Then hide them from the adults or there won't be any for the you. Better yet, make two pans.

¼ cup butter
40 large marshmallows
5 cups Rice Krispies® cereal

Melt butter and marshmallows in a heavy 3-quart saucepan, over very low heat. Remove from heat and quickly add cereal. Press into a sprayed 13x9-inch pan. Let cool. Makes about 25 bars.

Quick Chocolate Coconut Cookies   Oven 350°F

- 1   package (18.25-ounces) white cake mix
- ⅓   cup oil
- 2   large eggs
- ½   cup dried cranberries
- 1   cup Angel Flake coconut

1. Preheat oven to 350°F.

2. In mixer bowl, combine first 3 ingredients; mix until blended. Add remaining ingredients and beat just until mixed through.

3. Drop into mounds, about the size of a walnut, onto a cookie sheet. Bake 10 to 12 minutes or until slightly soft in center and light golden brown. Cool on rack. Makes 36 to 42 cookies.

Keep the ingredients on hand and kids can make these for snacks or treats.

Peanut Butter Bars

- 1   cup semi-sweet chocolate chips
- ⅓   cup peanut butter
- 4   cups Cocoa Krispies®

1. Melt chocolate chips in top of double boiler. Stir in peanut butter. Remove from heat. Gently stir in Cocoa Krispies®.

2. Press mixture into a sprayed 8x8-inch baking dish. Let cool and then cut into bars. Makes 3 dozen.

*Some of my first toys...
measuring cups!*

245

These are quite rich and are equally as good with or without frosting. Have fun and try a different flavor of cake mix.

Peanut Butter Cupcakes

Oven 350°F

1	package (18.25-ounces) yellow cake mix
1	cup creamy peanut butter
1⅓	cups water
3	large eggs
½	cup mini semi-sweet chocolate chips
1	can (16-ounces) chocolate frosting

1. Preheat oven to 350°F.

2. In large mixer bowl, combine first 4 ingredients following mixing directions on package. Stir in chocolate chips.

3. Pour batter into sprayed muffin tins, filling ⅔ full. Let cool, then spread with frosting. Makes 12 to 18 cupcakes, depending on the size of the muffin tins.

You'll be impressed by how tall this cake is and how easy it is to make.

Pretty in Pink Angel Food Cake

1	package (16-ounces) angel food cake mix
¼	cup Kool-Aid® cherry flavored sugar sweetened drink mix

1. In mixer bowl, place cake mix and Kool-Aid®. Prepare cake as directed on package using a 10-inch Angel food cake tube pan. Follow directions very carefully. The only other ingredient you have to add is water, as directed on the package.

2. Pour into ungreased pan and bake as directed on package. Makes 12 servings.

   To Serve: You can serve the cake by itself or with a serving of fruit or ice cream. A dollop of whipped cream sprinkled with coconut is very good, too.

Miniature Cherry Cheesecakes
Oven 400°F

1 package (10-ounces) frozen puff pastry shells
2 packages (3-ounces each) cream cheese, room temperature
¼ cup powdered sugar
½ teaspoon lemon or almond extract
1 can (21-ounces) cherry pie filling
Frozen whipped topping, thawed

1. Preheat oven to 400°F.

2. Place frozen pastry shells on baking sheet with topside up.

3. Bake 18 to 20 minutes or until golden brown. Remove from oven and place on baking rack. Using a fork, carefully remove the center top (lid) from the pastry shell. Then remove any soft filling underneath.

4. In mixer bowl, beat cream cheese until soft. Add sugar and extract and beat until fluffy, 4 to 5 minutes.

5. Spoon equal amounts of cream cheese mixture into each pastry shell. Place back on baking sheet. Return to oven and bake 5 minutes. Remove from oven and place on rack to cool.

6. Top each cheesecake with about 1 tablespoon of the cherry pie filling. Top with a dollop of whipped topping. Makes 6 servings.

My family ate these up fast, and then wanted more.

Note: You will have quite a bit of pie filling leftover. You can use this for a topping on ice cream or cheesecake slices.

Just taking a break from a hard day of cooking.

You'll enjoy building all the layers, crushing the cookies and eating this recipe. This is even better the next day when the cookies have softened a bit.

Lowfat Banana Pudding

1	package (3.4-ounces) sugar free instant vanilla pudding mix
1½	cups 2% milk
¼	cup sour cream
1	container (8-ounces) fat free frozen whipped topping, thawed
42	vanilla wafer cookies
3	large bananas

1. Place pudding mix and milk in a large bowl. Whisk or stir until mixture thickens. Stir in sour cream. Lightly stir in the whipped topping.

2. Place 20 vanilla wafers in bottom of a 2-quart bowl. Cover cookies with half of the sliced bananas. Spoon half of the pudding mixture over bananas.

3. Repeat the layering of step #2 using the remaining ingredients.

4. Take the 2 remaining cookies, put them in a baggie and crush. Sprinkle the crumbs over the top of the pudding.

5. Cover bowl with plastic wrap and place in refrigerator and chill at least 3 hours. The longer you chill the pudding the softer the cookies will become. Makes 6 servings.

Frozen Fudgesicles

Believe it or not, these are much better than store bought. My Grandma made these for me when I was growing up. She still makes them, but now I can make them, too. Always make more than you think you need. The gown ups like them almost as much as the kids do.

1	package (3.9-ounces) instant chocolate pudding mix
2	cups milk
¼	cup sugar
1	cup canned evaporated milk

1. In large mixer bowl, combine pudding and the 2 cups milk. Beat 2 minutes with a mixer and watch carefully, it might splatter on you.

2. Stir in sugar and canned milk. Pour immediately into popsicle molds (I use Tupperware® molds). Freeze. Makes about 12 to 14 Fudgesicles.

Popsicles

1 package (0.17-ounces) unsweetened Kool-Aid®, any flavor
1 cup sugar
4 cups water

1. Combine all the ingredients in a large pitcher. Stir until the sugar is dissolved. Pour into popsicle molds and freeze. Makes about 18 popsicles, depending on the size of the molds.

Cherry Almond Ice Cream Dessert

1 pint nonfat frozen vanilla yogurt
1⅓ cups light cherry pie filling
1 teaspoon almond extract

1. Spoon frozen yogurt into four dessert dishes. Combine pie filling with almond extract and spoon over top. Makes 4 servings.

We like...

Something Yummy

A delightfully easy fruit dip can be made by combining ¼ cup Nutella® (a chocolate hazelnut spread) with ½ cup sour cream.

...Something Easy

Helping Grandma sell Cookbooks at a trade show

Holiday Sausage Pizza
Oven 425°F

1	package (12-ounces) sausage
¾	cup chopped onion
1	12-inch pizza crust (I like Boboli®)
½	cup pizza sauce
12	ounces Mozzarella cheese, shredded

Sweet peppers, 1 red, 1 yellow and 1 green

1. Preheat oven to 425°F.

2. Place sausage in a large skillet and break up with spoon or spatula. Add onion and cook over medium heat, stirring often, until sausage is cooked through. Drain off all the fat and set aside.

3. While sausage is browning, place pizza crust on a baking pan and spread with pizza sauce. Spoon sausage and onion over sauce and sprinkle with cheese.

4. From the top, cut each pepper into fourths. Remove seeds. Place peppers on cutting board and with small star shaped cookie cutter, cut stars out of the peppers. Place stars over the cheese. Bake 10 to 12 minutes or until cheese is melted and just lightly browned. Makes 6 to 8 servings.

Vegie Pesto Pizza
Oven 425°F

1	purchased 12-inch baked pizza crust
½	cup pesto
1½	cups (6-ounces) Mozzarella cheese, shredded
¾	cup broccoli florettes, broken into small pieces
¼	cup sliced black olives
1	plum tomato, thinly sliced crosswise

1. Preheat oven to 425°.

2. Place pizza crust on large baking sheet. Spread pesto to within 1-inch of edge. Sprinkle with cheese. Sprinkle broccoli and olives over the cheese. Arrange tomato slices in a circle around outer edge of pizza.

3. Place baking sheet on lower rack in oven and bake 12 to 15 minutes, or until heated through and cheese has melted. Makes 6 servings.

Hotdogs & Breadsticks   Oven 350°F

    1   package (11-ounces) refrigerated breadstick dough
    12 hotdogs

1. Preheat oven to 350°F.

2. Open package and unroll dough. Separate into 12 strips.

3. Wrap one strip around each hotdog, stretching a little if necessary to wrap around three times with both ends tucked under bottom of the hot dog. Place on a baking sheet.

4. Bake 12 to 15 minutes or until lightly browned.

Lemon Dill Sole   Oven 425°F

    1   to 1¼ pounds filet of sole
    2   green onions
    1   lemon
    2   tablespoons Dijon mustard
    ¼   cup olive oil
    ½   teaspoon dried dill weed

1. Preheat oven to 425°.

2. Place fish in a sprayed 11x7-inch baking dish.

3. Slice both green and white part of onions and sprinkle over fish.

4. Squeeze juice from lemon and place in a small bowl. Add mustard, olive oil and dill weed. Beat with a whisk until ingredients are blended and smooth. Pour over fish.

5. Cover dish and marinate in refrigerator at least one hour before baking.

6. Place baking dish in oven. Bake 8 to 10 minutes or until fish flakes easily and a wooden toothpick inserted in center looks dry when removed. Makes 4 to 5 servings.

Have your friends over and impress them with lunch. Serve with Macaroni and Cheese and sliced fresh fruit.

Tip: If desired, use as many hot dogs as needed. If you don't need 12 hotdogs, twist remaining breadstick dough and place on baking sheet. Sprinkle with poppy seeds or garlic salt and bake along with the hotdogs.

Today, you can make the main dish and Mom can make the salad and set the table.

251

Barbecue Chicken Pizza   Oven 425°F

4 chicken breast halves, skinned and boned
2 large garlic cloves, finely chopped
1 tablespoon vegetable oil
1 package (10-ounces) refrigerated pizza crust
¾ cup your favorite barbecue sauce
1 package (8-ounces) pizza cheese blend

1. Preheat oven to 425°.

2. Wash chicken and pat dry. Cut into small cube-size pieces. Heat oil in a large skillet. Add garlic and about ⅓ of the chicken. Cook over medium-high heat, stirring frequently, until cooked through. Remove and set aside. Cook remaining chicken, adding additional oil, if necessary.

3. Unroll pizza dough. Press into a 15x10-inch jelly roll pan that has been sprayed with cooking spray, building up the edges slightly.

4. Spread barbecue sauce evenly over pizza dough.

5. Spoon chicken over sauce. Sprinkle with cheese.

6. Bake 12 to 15 minutes or until crust is lightly browned.

Tip: For a crisper crust, pre-bake dough for 6 minutes before adding topping.

Even easier: Use a large purchased pizza crust and pre-cooked chicken.

Kid Convincing soup

1 package (12-ounces) low-fat sausage
1 cup chopped onion
1 can (14½-ounces) stewed tomatoes with basil
1 can (15-ounces) garbanzo beans, drained
1 can (14½-ounces) beef broth
1 medium zucchini

1. Cook sausage and onion in a 3-quart pot or saucepan; drain off liquid.

2. Add tomatoes, beans and broth.

3. Cut zucchini into ¼-inch slices. Cut each slice into quarters. Add to soup mixture. Add 1½ cups water.

4. Bring mixture to a boil. Reduce heat and simmer 3 to 5 minutes or until zucchini is just tender. Makes 8 cups.

Quick Ham-Broccoli Dish

1½ cups fresh broccoli florettes, chopped
8 ounces process cheese spread, cubed
3 cups cooked small-size penne pasta
¾ cup small cubed ham

1. In medium saucepan, cook broccoli in a small amount of water, until just tender; drain. Add cheese cubes, pasta and ham and heat until cheese is melted. Makes 4 to 6 servings.

I enjoy making soups and pasta almost as much as I enjoy making cookies and desserts. Both of these recipes are fairly easy if you already have some cooking experience. If you want to, you can make the soup ahead and the reheat it for dinner.

253

Quick Lunch Meal

1 can (15-ounces) baked beans
1 can (11-ounces) Mexicorn, drained
¼ cup ketchup
6 hot dogs, sliced

1. In small saucepan, combine all the ingredients and heat through. Makes 4 to 6 servings.

Surprise Mom and tell her you will fix lunch.

Yummy Hot Dogs   Oven 375°F

1 package (8-ounces) refrigerated Crescent rolls
4 teaspoons melted butter
4 teaspoons prepared mustard
8 hot dog

1. Preheat oven to 375°F.

2. Separate crescents into 8 rolls. Brush each with melted butter and spread with mustard. Place hot dog on wide end and roll toward narrow end.

3. Place on ungreased baking sheet. Brush with melted butter and bake 12 to 14 minutes or until rolls are lightly browned. Makes 8.

Simple and delicious. For variety, add ¼ cup pineapple juice. An adult may need to help you with this recipe.

Kid's Favorite Flank Steak   Broil

1 flank steak
¼ cup soy sauce

1. Pour enough soy sauce in a shallow dish to cover bottom. Add flank steak and marinate 60 minutes, turning steak frequently.

2. Remove from marinade and broil or grill. Do not overcook, as this tends to toughen the meat. Slice crosswise to serve. Makes 4 servings.

Candied Chicken
Oven 425°F

4 to 6 chicken breast halves, skinned and boned
1 cup maple syrup
½ cup ketchup
¼ cup white vinegar
Salt and pepper

1. Wash chicken and pat dry. Sprinkle with salt and pepper. Place rounded-side up in a sprayed 13x9-inch baking dish.

2. Combine remaining ingredients and pour over chicken. Bake 20 minutes. Carefully remove from oven and baste with sauce. Bake 10 minutes and baste again. Bake 10 minutes or until cooked through. Makes 6 servings.

Easy Parmesan Knots
Oven 375°F

1 package (11-ounces) refrigerated breadsticks
3 tablespoons butter
1 tablespoon grated Parmesan cheese
¼ teaspoon garlic salt
½ teaspoon dried parsley

1. Preheat oven to 375°.

2. Unroll breadsticks and separate. Tie each breadstick into a loose knot (remember the bread will get bigger when it bakes) and place on a baking sheet. Bake 10 to 12 minutes or until golden.

3. While rolls are baking, place butter in a small microwave safe bowl and microwave until melted. Stir in the Parmesan cheese, garlic salt and parsley. Brush butter mixture over each baked roll.

4. Put rolls in a pretty basket or dish and serve hot. Makes 12 rolls.

Tip: Do not use chicken breasts that are too thin; they will cook too fast and will be tough and dry. If using just 4 chicken breasts, go ahead and bake in a 13x9-inch dish. If a smaller dish is used, the sauce will not have a chance to thicken before the chicken is done.

Menu

Candied Chicken

Rice

Buttered Peas

Easy Parmesan Knots

Banana Pudding

or

Ice Cream

The recipe can be easily adjusted for a smaller number of servings. If you have the larger size muffin cups, use those. If not, use small size eggs, to prevent the egg white from running over onto the tins.

Egg Nests

Oven 350°F

12 slices bread
12 large eggs
   Salt and pepper
6 teaspoons butter

1. Preheat oven to 350°F.

2. Grease a 12-cup muffin tin. Remove crust from bread. Place one bread slice in each muffin cup; push down gently so it looks like a cup with four corners.

3. Carefully drop a raw egg into each cup. Sprinkle with salt and pepper. Top each egg with ½ teaspoon butter. Bake 15 minutes or until eggs are cooked and bread is toasted. Makes 6 servings.

Beef & Cheese Macaroni

1 pound lean ground beef
2 cups chunky salsa
2 cups elbow macaroni, uncooked
8 ounces process cheese spread

1. Brown meat in a large skillet; drain.

2. Add salsa and 1¾ cups water. Bring to a boil and then add macaroni. Reduce heat to a simmer, cover and cook 8 minutes or until pasta is just tender.

3. Cut cheese into small cubes. Add to skillet and cook, stirring frequently, until melted. Makes 6 servings.

Slow Cooking

Beef & Salsa Dip

1 pound lean ground beef
16 ounces process cheese spread, cubed
1 can (15-ounces) creamed corn
1½ cups salsa

This is so good I doubt you'll have leftovers, but if you do, serve over baked potatoes for a quick and easy lunch or dinner.

1. Brown ground beef; drain and add to slow cooker. Add cheese along with remaining ingredients. Cook on High 1 to 1½ hours or until cheese is melted and mixture is hot. Turn heat to Low, until ready to serve, stirring occasionally. Serve with chips. Makes 5½ cups.

Chili con Queso

1 pound lean ground beef
1 cup chopped onion
1 can (4-ounces) chopped green chilies
1 cup chunky salsa
2 pounds process cheese spread, cubed

1. In medium skillet, brown ground beef and onion; drain. Place in slow cooker. Add remaining ingredients. Cover and cook on Low 2 to 3 hours, stirring to blend when cheese is partially melted. Serve with chips. Makes about 6 cups.

I don't know anyone who will turn down ribs. They are moist, tender and delicious cooked in a slow cooker. You may want to brush additional sauce on the ribs just before serving or pass extra sauce at the table

This recipe is very similar to the above recipe, except the sauce is added at the table.

If you can find it in your area, my favorite brand of chili for this recipe is Cattle Drive®. It is a little bit sweet and a little bit spicy and packs a lot of flavor.

Barbecue Ribs

1½   racks baby back ribs, about 20 ribs
     Choice of barbecue sauce

1.   Wash and trim ribs of excess fat. Cut into 2-rib sections. Brush both sides of ribs with barbecue sauce. Place as many ribs, meaty side out, as you can, around the pot. Place remaining ribs on the bottom, meaty side up. Cover and cook on Low 6 to 7 hours or until tender. Makes 4 to 5 servings.

Easy Tender Ribs

1   rack baby back ribs
   Salt and pepper
   Choice of barbecue sauce

1.   Cut ribs in half crosswise. Sprinkle both sides with salt and pepper and place in slow cooker, meaty side up. Add ½ cup water. Cover and cook on Low 6 to 7 hours or until tender. Cut into individual ribs and serve with your favorite sauce. Makes 2 to 3 servings.

Chili Beef Dish

1½   pounds lean ground beef
1½   cups chopped onion
 3   large plum tomatoes, diced
 2   cans (15-ounces each) chili with beans

1.   In a large skillet, brown ground beef and onion. Place in slow cooker. Add tomatoes and chili. Cover and cook on Low 4 to 5 hours.   Makes about 8 servings.

Family Pot Roast

1	5 pound rump roast
12	small new potatoes
6	carrots
1	large onion
1	teaspoon seasoning salt

1. Place half the potatoes in slow cooker. Cut carrots into 2-inch pieces and onion into wedges; place half over potatoes. Add roast and arrange remaining vegetables around meat. Add 1 cup water. Sprinkle with salt. Cover and cook on Low 10 to 12 hours. If you happen to be at home, half way through cooking time, push the vegetables down into the broth. Makes 6 to 8 servings.

When I know I'm going to have a busy day or I'm going to be gone all day, I love to use my slow cooker. Plan ahead and you can have a meal on the table in minutes.

Lemon Pepper Roast

1	2½ to 3 pound chuck roast
½	teaspoon seasoned salt
½	teaspoon lemon pepper
¼	teaspoon paprika
1	cup beef broth

1. Sprinkle meat with the combined mixture of salt, pepper and paprika. Place in slow cooker. Add beef broth. Cover and cook on High about 4 ½ to 5 hours or until meat is tender. Makes 4 servings.

Note: Beef or chicken bouillon cubes are excellent substitutes for canned broth. They are economical to use and often even more flavorful than some of the canned brands we find today.

If gravy is desired, thicken liquid with a mixture of about ¼ cup flour dissolved in ½ cup water. Add enough flour mixture to thicken gravy to desired consistency. To quickly dissolve flour: place water in a small jar, add flour and cover. Shake jar until flour and water are well mixed.

This recipe is only as good as the meatballs you use. There are very good ones you can purchase fresh or frozen and then there are those that aren't so good. Of course, you can always make your own. See Basic Meatballs page 160.

Stroganoff Meatballs

1	can (14½-ounces) beef broth
¼	cup flour
1	cup chopped onion
2	tablespoons butter, melted
30	precooked meatballs, fresh or frozen
1	cup sour cream

1. Combine beef broth and flour in slow cooker, whisking until smooth. Add onion, butter and meatballs. Cover and cook on Low 4 to 5 hours.

2. Add sour cream and stir until blended. Cook on High 30 minutes. Serve on rice over noodles. Makes 4 to 6 servings.

Ground Beef and Beans

1½	pounds lean ground beef
1½	cups chopped onion
1	can (1-pound,15-ounces) pork and beans
1	can (14-ounces) whole tomatoes, drained
½	cup firmly packed light brown sugar
½	cup ketchup

1. In a large skillet, brown ground beef and onion; drain. Place in slow cooker.

2. Cut tomatoes into small pieces and add to pot. Stir in remaining ingredients. Cover and cook on Low 6 to 7 hours. Makes about 10 servings.

Beef and Rice Casserole

1½ pounds lean ground beef
1½ cups chopped onion
1½ cups uncooked long-grain rice
 1 can (10¾-ounces) condensed cream of celery soup
 1 can (10¾-ounces) condensed cream of mushroom soup
 1 teaspoon salt

1. In medium skillet, brown ground beef and onion; drain. Place in slow cooker. Add remaining ingredients along with 2 soup cans of water. Cover and cook on Low 6 to 7 hours, or until liquid is absorbed and rice is tender, but not overcooked. Makes 8 servings.

Meat Loaf Dijon

1½ pounds lean ground beef
 ⅓ cup crushed crackers
 ½ cup finely chopped onion
 ⅓ cup ketchup
 1 tablespoon Dijon mustard
 1 large egg

1. In a large bowl, combine all ingredients until well mixed. Place in slow cooker and form into a round about the size of the bottom of the pot. Cook on Low 5 to 6 hours. Temperature should reach no less than 160° F. Makes 6 servings.

Process Cheese Spread

What is it? My generation knows what it is, but not all the younger generation does. Process cheese spread is most often found under the name Velveeta or American process cheese spread. It can usually be found in the refrigerated cheese department or on the shelf with the jars of cheese spread. It comes in one and three pound boxes, although you will find it in five pound boxes at the discount warehouses. This cheese was quite popular in the 50's and 60's, but seems to have lost some of its appeal in recent years. In fact, I started using it again when doing this section of the cookbook and you will be amazed at how good the recipes are. Process cheese is often used in slow cooking and some soups because it is less likely to curdle from the high heat or extended cooking.

Stuffed Green Peppers

1½	pounds lean ground beef
1¼	cups chopped onion
1	teaspoon salt
½	cup cooked long-grain rice
4	medium green peppers
1	can (8-ounces) tomato sauce

1. In large skillet, brown ground beef and onion; drain. Add salt and rice and mix well.

2. Meanwhile, cut top off the green peppers and remove seeds. Place in slow cooker. Fill with ground beef mixture, spooning remaining meat around the peppers. Pour tomato sauce over top. Cover and cook on Low 4 to 5 hours or until peppers are tender when pierced with a fork. Makes 4 to 6 servings.

Broccoli Ham Casserole

I have to tell you, this taste a lot better than it looks. But it is a tasty way to use up that last bit of ham and broccoli you may have in the refrigerator.

1	can (10¾-ounces) condensed cream of mushroom soup
1	cup milk
1	cup diced ham
2	cups broccoli florettes
1	cup uncooked instant rice
8	ounces process cheese spread, cubed

1. Place soup in slow cooker and gradually whisk in the milk until smooth. Add remaining ingredients. Cover and cook on Low 3½ to 4 hours. If possible, stir mixture half way through the cooking time. Makes 4 servings.

Slow Cooked Ham

    1   5 to 6 pound cooked ham
    ½   cup apricot preserves

1.   Place ham, cut side down in slow cooker. Cover and cook on Low 4 to 5 hours or until meat thermometer reaches 120°F. Brush with apricot preserves, cover and cook on High 20 to 30 minutes or until meat thermometer reaches 140°.

Pork Chops in Orange Sauce

    4   thick loin cut pork chops
    Lemon pepper
    1   teaspoon oil
    1   large orange
    ¼   cup orange marmalade
    ½   cup ketchup

1.   Sprinkle pork chops lightly with lemon pepper. Brown in oil and place in slow cooker.

2.   From the orange you will need ½ cup orange juice and 1 teaspoon orange peel. Then combine with marmalade and ketchup and pour over pork chops. Cover and cook on Low 6 to 8 hours or until meat is tender. Makes 4 servings.

A slow cooker is a great way to cook a ham. On Easter, I had a ham that was too large for the slow cooker. It would fit inside, but the lid wouldn't go on. I covered the top of the ham with heavy-duty foil, and pressed tightly around the rim of the slow cooker. It worked beautifully. Plus it freed up my oven space for other dishes.

Sausage and rice makes a nice combination for lunch or a light dinner.

Sausage Pilaf

1	package (12-ounces) pork sausage
¾	cup thinly sliced celery
¼	cup slivered almonds
1	package (6-ounces) long-grain and wild rice mix
3	cups chicken broth

1. In large skillet brown sausage; drain. Add to slow cooker along with remaining ingredients. Cover and cook on Low 5 to 5½ hours or until liquid is absorbed and rice is tender. Makes 4 servings.

   Note: If rice tests done, drain any remaining liquid in the pot, as further cooking will produce a soft mushy rice.

Variations of this recipe have been around for as long as I can remember. Making it in the slow cooker will free you to do other things.

Sausage Rice Casserole

1½	pounds sausage
2	cups chopped celery
1	cup chopped onion
¼	cup slivered almonds
2	packages (4.2-ounces) chicken noodle soup mix
1	cup uncooked long-grain rice

1. In large skillet, brown sausage until almost cooked through. Add celery and onion and cook until almost soft; drain. Place in slow cooker.

2. Add remaining ingredients along with 4 cups of water. Cover and cook on Low 4 to 4½ hours or until liquid is absorbed and rice is tender. Makes 8 to 10 servings.

Chicken Fettuccine

½ cup butter, plus 3 tablespoons
1 cup heavy whipping cream
1 cup freshly grated Parmesan cheese
¼ teaspoon pepper
3 chicken breast halves, skinned and boned
8 ounces fettuccine

1. Place ½ cup butter, cream, Parmesan and pepper in slow cooker. Cover and cook on Low about 45 minutes. All you really need to do here is melt and blend the ingredients together.

2. Meanwhile, cut chicken into bite-size pieces and cook in remaining butter in large skillet, until cooked through. Drain and set aside.

3. Meanwhile, bring water to a boil and cook pasta according to directions on package. Drain and add to slow cooker along with the chicken. Serve immediately, or cover and keep hot until ready to serve. Makes 4 servings.

I can't think of an easier way to make Fettuccine. The slow cooker also solves the problem of how to keep it hot while you get everything else on the table. This recipe would work well for a buffet.

Lemon Pepper Chicken

1 3 to 4 pound chicken
1 medium onion
Lemon pepper

1. Trim chicken, rinse and pat dry.

2. Cut onion into quarters and separate. Place ¼ of the slices in chicken cavity. Scatter remaining in bottom of slow cooker. Place chicken over onions and add ¼ cup water. Sprinkle chicken with lemon pepper. Cover and cook on Low about 7 to 8 hours or until chicken is tender. Watch carefully after 6 hours. To be sure, insert thigh with thermometer; chicken is done when temperature reaches 170°. Makes 4 to 6 servings.

Of course, slow cooked chicken makes an excellent dinner meal, but it's also a convenient way to cook chicken for sandwiches, salads and casseroles.

I prepare this recipe so often in the oven that I decided to try it in the slow cooker. How convenient on days when I am out of the house for just a few hours.

D on't omit the coconut. It is that extra touch that really makes the difference.

Chicken Italian with Rice

4	large chicken breast halves, skinned and boned
1	cup uncooked long-grain rice
1	package (.65-ounces) Italian dressing mix
1	can (10¾-ounces) condensed cream of chicken soup

1. Place rice in slow cooker. Combine dressing mix and soup. Gradually stir in 1¾ cup water ; pour over rice. Place chicken over top. Cover and cook on Low 3½ to 4 hours or until rice is tender. Makes 4 servings.

Cranberry Chicken

4	to 6 chicken breast halves, skinned and boned
1	can (16-ounces) whole-berry cranberry sauce
1	Golden Delicious apple, chopped
1	teaspoon curry powder
⅓	cup chopped pecans or walnuts
⅓	cup Angel Flake coconut

1. Place chicken in slow cooker. Combine cranberry sauce, apple and curry; pour over chicken. Cover and cook on Low 3½ to 4 hours. Add nuts. Pass coconut at table. Makes 4 to 6 servings.

Sherried Chicken

10	chicken legs
1	medium onion, sliced
4	ounces fresh mushrooms, sliced
½	cup dry sherry
1	teaspoon Italian seasoning

1. Place onion and mushrooms in slow cooker. Top with chicken legs; add sherry and sprinkle with seasoning. Cover and cook on Low 7 to 8 hours or until chicken is tender. Makes 4 servings.

Cooked Chicken

Chicken breasts or parts, with skin
Salt and pepper
2   stalks celery, cut up
½   cup chopped onion
2   carrots, cut up

1. Place chicken in slow cooker. Sprinkle with salt and pepper. Add remaining ingredients. Add 2 to 4 cups of water to cover the chicken. Cover and cook on Low 4 to 5 hours or until cooked through.

When you need a lot of cooked chicken for casseroles, salad and soups, it is so easy to just cook it in your slow cooker.

Garlic Chicken & Potatoes

1   chicken, cut up
4   medium potatoes, peeled and quartered
8   large garlic cloves
¼   cup butter, melted
¼   cup honey
½   teaspoon lemon pepper

1. Rinse chicken and pat dry.

2. Place potatoes in slow cooker. Arrange chicken over top. Add garlic. Drizzle butter and honey over chicken. Sprinkle with lemon pepper. Cover and cook on Low 5 to 5½ hours or until chicken is tender and potatoes are cooked through. Makes 4 servings.

The aroma of this dish cooking will entice everyone into the kitchen.

Note: *Remove thin, paper-like skin from garlic cloves, but do not peel.*

269

To Serve: Curries cry out for an accompaniment of something sweet such as a chutney, coconut, peanuts, green onion, raisins, orange pieces, etc. Serve over rice with accompaniments on the side.

Curried Chicken

4	chicken breast halves, skinned and boned
¼	cup butter, melted
¼	cup honey
2	tablespoons prepared mustard
½	teaspoon curry powder
½	teaspoon salt

1. Place chicken in slow cooker. Combine remaining ingredients and pour over chicken. Cover and cook on Low 3 to 4 hours or until chicken is cooked through. Makes 4 servings.

Rosemary Chicken

1	3 to 4 pound chicken
4	medium potatoes
1	teaspoon olive oil
1	teaspoon dried rosemary

1. Cut potatoes into 1½-inch chunks, and place in slow cooker. Add ½ cup water. Place chicken over potatoes. Brush with oil and sprinkle with rosemary. Cover and cook on Low 7 to 8 hours or until chicken is cooked through. Watch carefully after 6 hours. Makes 4 servings.

Chili

2	pounds lean ground beef
1½	teaspoons salt
2½	teaspoons chili powder
1	teaspoon ground cumin
2	cans (15-ounces each) diced tomatoes, do not drain
2	cans (15-ounces each) kidney beans, drained

1. In large skillet, brown ground beef; drain. Add seasonings and cook 3 to 4 minutes. Add to slow cooker along with remaining ingredients. Add ¾ cup water. Cover and cook on Low 7 to 8 hours. Makes 8 cups.

Ground Beef and Cheese Soup

1	pound ground beef
⅔	cup chopped onion
2	cups cubed potatoes
1	cup peas
1	cup corn
16	ounces process cheese spread, cubed

1. Brown ground beef and onion in a large skillet; drain. Place in slow cooker. Add potatoes and 2 cups water. Cook on Low 8 to 10 hours.

2. Add corn and peas and cook about 20 minutes, or until heated through.

3. Add cheese cubes, and cook 5 to 10 minutes or until melted. Stir to blend. Makes 7 cups.

Everyone in my family was amazed by this delicious soup. They didn't think they liked process cheese, but they loved this recipe.

Note: *The soup may be quite thick when reheated. You can thin with milk or broth.*

Potatoes take a long time to cook in a slow cooker. To shorten the cooking time, you can partially cook the potatoes before adding to the slow cooker.

Navy Bean Soup

1	pound dried small white beans
1	cup finely chopped onion
1	cup finely chopped celery
2	cups diced cooked ham
	Salt and pepper to taste

1. Clean beans as directed on package. Place in a 3-quart saucepan or stock pot. Add 8 cups water. Bring to a boil and cook about 3 minutes. Remove from heat and let stand one hour.

2. Place beans (and liquid) in slow cooker along with the onion, celery and ham. Cover and cook on Low 13 to 14 hours (I know, that's a long time isn't it?). Season with salt and pepper. Makes 10 cups.

Variation*: To serve beans as a side dish, cook 12 hours (they will be a bit firmer than for soup; drain off most of the liquid.)*

Hint*: Beans take a long time to cook in the slow cooker. I would suggest making the soup one day and reheating it when ready to serve.*

Potato-Corn Chowder

1	pound frozen O'Brien hash browns, thawed
¼	cup chopped onion
1	can (15-ounces) whole corn, undrained
1	can (15-ounces) creamed corn
1	can (12-ounces) evaporated milk
½	teaspoon salt

1. Combine ingredients in slow cooker, cover and cook on Low 7 to 8 hours. Makes 7 cups.

A nice blend of vegetables and cheese. Very good reheated.

Veggie Cheese Soup

1	can (15-ounces) creamed corn
4	cups potatoes, cubed
1½	cups carrots, cubed
¾	cup finely chopped onion
2	cans (14-5ounces each) chicken broth
16	ounces process cheese spread, cubed

1. Place first 5 ingredients in slow cooker. Cover and cook on Low 8 to 10 hours or until vegetables are tender. Add cheese, cover and cook until melted. Makes about 12 cups.

I really should cook barley more often. This recipe is easy to prepare, quite delicious and inexpensive. You can serve it with just about anything in place of rice or potatoes.

Easy Barley Casserole

1	cup pearl barley
2	tablespoons butter
¾	cup chopped onion
⅓	cup slivered almonds
3	cups chicken broth

1. Rinse barley and drain. Melt butter in medium skillet. Add barley, onion and almonds. Cook until lightly browned. Place in slow cooker, add chicken broth, cover and cook on Low 4½ to 5 hours or until barley is tender and most of the liquid is absorbed. Makes 6 servings.

Wild Rice and Cheese Casserole

2	packages (6-ounces each) white and wild rice with seasoning packet
1½	cups chopped onion
1	cup chopped celery
½	cup butter, melted
8	ounces process cheese spread, cubed
1	can (10¾-ounces) condensed cream of mushroom soup

1. Place first 5 ingredients in slow cooker.

2. Place soup in a medium mixing bowl and gradually add 1 cup water, whisking until smooth. Add to rice mixture along with 2 cups water. Cover and cook on Low 4 to 5 hours or until onion is soft and liquid is absorbed. Mixture will still be quite moist. If rice starts to brown around the edges, stir once or twice during cooking time. Makes 8 to 10 servings.

A lot of flavor is packed into these six ingredients. It can also be turned into a main dish with the addition of cooked cubed chicken or ground beef.

Acorn Squash

2	small acorn squash
	Salt and pepper
	Butter

1. Cut squash in half lengthwise; remove seeds. Rinse with water (don't dry) and place, cut side up in slow cooker. Sprinkle lightly with salt and pepper. Cover and cook on Low 2 to 3 hours, depending on size. Remove and place a thin slice of butter in each center. Makes 4 servings.

   Additions after cooking:

   • Dot with butter and brown sugar and cook until melted.

   • Fill with cooked apples and pears. Sprinkle lightly with nutmeg.

   • Fill with hot buttered peas.

This is what I do if acorn squash is hard to cut: with a strong knife, pierce squash deeply in 2 or 3 places. Place in microwave and heat for 1 minute. The squash should feel slightly warm. Then cut in half. It works every time.

Baked Beans & Bacon

2   cans (31-ounces each) pork and beans
½   cup packed light brown sugar
2   teaspoons dry mustard
½   cup ketchup
8   slices bacon, cooked and crumbled

1. Drain off most of the liquid from the top of the beans. Place in slow cooker along with the next three ingredients. Cover and cook on Low 5 to 6 hours. If beans are more liquid than you like, cook on High for an additional hour. Add bacon the last 30 minutes of cooking time. Makes 8 to 10 servings.

I think Baked Beans were made to be cooked in a slow cooker. It is ideal for cooking in quantities and for keeping the beans warm.

Company Carrots

3   pounds carrots, sliced diagonally into ½-inch slices
¼   cup packed light brown sugar
1   teaspoon salt
½   teaspoon cracked black pepper
½   cup butter

1. Place carrots in slow cooker. Sprinkle with brown sugar, salt and pepper. Distribute butter slices over top. Cover and cook on High 4 to 5 hours. Stir carrots half way through cooking time. Makes about 12 servings. Watch carefully the last hour of cooking time to ensure that the carrots aren't overcooked. Makes 8 servings.

The slow cooker is a great way to cook carrots for a crowd. It frees up your oven, stove and warming tray. Just make sure you allow enough time for them to cook.

Baked Potatoes

> 4 medium baking potatoes
> Choice of toppings

1. Wash potatoes, but do not dry. Place in slow cooker in one layer. (If using more potatoes, stand them on end, so each one is touching the bottom.) Cover and cook on Low 7 to 8 hours or until cooked through.

Au Gratin Potatoes

> 8 medium potatoes, peeled (8 cups sliced)
> 1 can (10¾-ounces) condensed cream of chicken soup
> ⅓ cup milk
> 1 teaspoon salt
> ¼ teaspoon pepper
> 1 cup (4-ounces) Cheddar cheese, shredded

1. Place potato slices in slow cooker. Combine soup, milk, salt and pepper. Pour over potatoes. Add cheese and stir until mixed. Cover and cook on Low, 9 to 10 hours or until potatoes are tender. Stir, if possible, about half way through cooking time. Makes 6 servings.

If you layer and cook more than 4 potatoes, you will need to rotate them once or twice as the bottom layer will cook faster than the top layer.

Potatoes take a long time to cook in a slow cooker. You may want to cook on High for the last few hours. If desired, add cooked cubed chicken or ham and serve as a main dish.

I haven't had a lot of success cooking sliced potatoes on Low in a slow cooker. They tend to take so long to cook that by the time they are tender, they often turn an ugly brown. If you have the same problem, cook your recipes on High, but watch carefully the last hour of cooking time.

275

Cooking time can vary according to the types of apples used. If you are ready for the applesauce, but it isn't ready for you, you can speed things up by cooking on High or place in a large stock pot and continue cooking until soft.

Chunky Applesauce

5	large Golden Delicious apples
5	large Rome apples
¾	cup sugar
½	teaspoon cinnamon
¼	teaspoon ground ginger
5	large strips of fresh orange peel

1. Peel, slice and core apples. Cut into ¼ to ½-inch slices. You should have about 12 cups. Place in slow cooker along with remaining ingredients and ¼ cup water. Cover and cook on Low 8 to 10 hours, stirring about every 2 hours. When done, apples should be soft, but not mushy. Remove orange peel and discard. Makes 5 to 6 cups.

You can use other baking apples than Golden Delicious, but I have found some take a little longer to bake, such as the Granny Smiths.

Baked Apples

4	Golden Delicious apples
1	cup apple cider
¼	cup butter
1	can (14-ounces) sweetened condensed milk
⅓	cup chopped pecans
1	teaspoon rum extract

1. Core apples (do not peel) and place in slow cooker. Add apple cider. Cook on Low 3½ to 4 hours or until apples are tender. Test for doneness with the thin blade of a sharp knife.

2. Meanwhile, melt butter in a small saucepan. Add remaining ingredients and cook over medium heat, stirring constantly, until mixture is smooth and creamy, about 8 to 10 minutes. Sauce will thicken as it cools. Reheat the sauce when ready to serve with the apples. Makes 1½ cups sauce.

Salads, Dressings & Sauces

Mini Chef Salad

FOR EACH SALAD:

Assorted greens, chilled
Four bean salad, drained
Chopped fresh mushrooms
Tiny squares thinly sliced ham or turkey
Shredded Cheddar cheese
Choice of dressing

1. Place salad greens on an 8-inch salad plate. Top with remaining ingredients, in order given, and drizzle with your choice of dressing.

Makes a delicious and filling luncheon dish; serve with honey rye bread or rolls. The Thousand Island recipe on page 300 goes especially well with this salad.

Italian Salad

1 to 2 heads romaine, torn into bite-size pieces
1 jar (6-ounces) marinated artichoke hearts, drained, cut if too large
¾ cup olive oil
¼ cup red wine vinegar
¼ cup grated Parmesan cheese
Salt and pepper to taste

1. Place romaine in salad bowl. Add artichoke hearts.

2. Combine remaining ingredients. Add to salad and toss with just enough dressing to lightly coat. Sprinkle with additional Parmesan cheese, if desired. Makes 4 to 6 servings.

Always have washed and chilled greens ready in the refrigerator and you have the makings of a salad at a moments notice.

279

You can't beat a really good Caesar salad. You can use purchased dressing, but if you have the time, make my Caesar Salad Dressing recipe. It can be made a day ahead and is well worth the small effort involved.

This is a great way to use leftover breads and is so easy I don't know why we don't make them more often. You can make them ahead and they can also be frozen.

Caesar Salad

2 bunches romaine lettuce, torn into bite-size pieces, chilled
Croutons, desired amount
Purchased Caesar salad dressing or see dressing on page 295.
Freshly grated or shredded Parmesan cheese.

1. Combine romaine and croutons in a large salad bowl. Toss with just enough dressing to lightly coat. Sprinkle with Parmesan. Makes 6 large servings.

Croutons   Oven 400°F

2 cups (½ to 1-inch cubes) French bread
1½ tablespoons olive oil
3 tablespoons freshly grated Parmesan cheese

1. Place bread cubes in a mixing bowl. Add olive oil as needed to lightly coat the bread - it may take more or less oil according to the type of bread used. Spread in a single layer on a baking sheet and bake 8 to 10 minutes or until crisp and lighty browned. Remove from oven and place in a mixing bowl. Toss with Parmesan cheese. Makes 2 cups.

Crisp Green Salad

4 cups assorted salad greens
1 cup cherry tomatoes
1 cup cauliflower pieces
½ green pepper, sliced
½ small cucumber, sliced
Choice of dressing

1. Combine first 5 ingredients in salad bowl. Toss with your favorite salad dressing. Makes 6 servings.

Sweet-Sour Spinach Salad

  1   bunch fresh spinach
  1   tablespoon white vinegar
  1   tablespoon sugar
 ¼   cup mayonnaise
  1   very small red onion, thinly sliced, separated into rings
  8   slices bacon, cooked, crumbled

1. Wash spinach thoroughly and dry. Remove long stems and tear into bite-size pieces; chill.

2. Combine vinegar, sugar and mayonnaise; chill.

3. When ready to serve, combine spinach, onion and bacon. Toss with just enough dressing to lightly coat. Serve immediately; greens have a tendency to get limp if allowed to sit very long. Makes 3 to 4 servings.

You may not be able to entice your children to eat cooked spinach, but you can serve them a salad. Just don't tell them it is spinach and they'll never know.

Almond Spinach Salad

  1   pound spinach
 ⅓   cup sliced or slivered almonds, toasted
  6   slices cooked bacon, crumbled
  1   small onion, thinly sliced and separated into rings
     Vinaigrette dressing

1. Combine first 4 ingredients in large salad bowl. Toss with just enough dressing to lightly coat. Makes 4 to 6 servings.

Jicama is a delightful vegetable. It is crisp, slightly sweet and tastes wonderful in a salad or as a vegetable with dips. It's also great when dieting.

You will love the crunch of the sliced almonds. They add that extra special touch to a salad. If you prefer a mild vinegar taste, make dressing ahead to blend flavors and to mellow somewhat.

Spinach Salad with Jicama

1   large bunch spinach
2   medium oranges
½   cup jicama, julienned
⅓   cup toasted sliced almonds or pecan halves
   Red onion, thinly sliced (desired amount)
   Poppy seed dressing

1. Wash spinach, remove stems and let dry. Peel oranges, slice and cut into small segments. Place in large salad bowl along with the jicama, almonds and onion. Toss with just enough dressing to lightly coat. Makes 4 to 6 servings.

Spinach Salad with Sugared Almonds

½   cup sliced almonds
3   tablespoons sugar
½   cup olive oil
3   tablespoons balsamic vinegar
1   can (11-ounces) mandarin oranges, well drained; save juice
1   package (10-ounces) fresh spinach; remove stems

1. Place almonds and sugar in small nonstick skillet over medium-low heat. Cook, stirring frequently, until sugar has melted and almonds are glazed. Watch carefully the last few minutes to prevent burning.

2. Combine the oil and balsamic vinegar with 2 tablespoons of the mandarin orange juice. Place oranges and spinach in a large salad bowl. Toss with dressing to lightly coat. Top with almonds. Makes 4 to 6 servings.

Salad Suggestions

Do you ever get tired of making the same old salads? These suggestions should give you a good start and provide an assortment of delicious salads. Omit or add ingredients according to what you and your family enjoy. Use your favorite prepared or purchased dressing.

10 ounces spinach
½ cup shredded purple cabbage
⅓ cup raisins
¼ cup sliced almonds

1 large head romaine
2 kiwis, peeled, sliced
½ cup croutons
⅓ cup pecan halves

10 ounces spinach
2 small fresh nectarines
2 fresh plums, sliced
½ English cucumber

6 cups assorted salad greens
4 ounces Swiss cheese, cubed
1 cup red seedless grapes, halves
8 slices bacon, cooked

1 large head romaine
8 slices bacon, cooked
2 ounces feta or blue cheese
⅓ cup coarsely chopped walnuts
1 apple, thinly sliced or cubed

10 ounces spinach
1 pint fresh strawberries
⅓ cup slivered almonds

10 ounces spinach
1 red onion, thinly sliced
1 can mandarin oranges
⅓ cup pecan halves

6 cups assorted salad
4 ounces mushrooms, sliced
8 slices bacon, cooked
4 green onions, sliced

6 cups assorted salad greens
Carrot strips
Cherry tomatoes, halved
Red onion, thinly sliced
Whole black olives

1 large head romaine
1 cup cubed cooked chicken
⅓ cup dried cranberries
⅓ cup sliced almonds

1 large head romaine
¼ cup dried cranberries
Mushrooms, sliced
Red onion, thinly sliced

Ice Cold Salad Greens

A nice cold crisp salad is hard to beat, but sometimes hard to achieve. My favorite method for chilling salad greens works every time, but you do have to allow some chilling time in the refrigerator. Line a large bowl with several layers of paper towels. Place clean dry greens in bowl. Cover greens with 3 to 4 layers of paper towels. Cover paper towels with one layer of ice cubes. Chill at least 8 hours or overnight. Before serving, if paper towels get too wet, replace with new ones and add additional ice cube.s

Stuffed Tomatoes

Small to medium-size firm tomatoes
Desired stuffing
Lettuce leaves

1. Remove tops from tomatoes; carefully scoop out seeds and meat; drain. Fill with any one of the following fillings or if using small to-matoes make a double tomato salad using two different fillings:

Chicken salad garnished with green grapes
Shrimp salad
Crab salad
Tuna salad
Rice salad garnished with pineapple
Cooked peas
Chopped cucumbers with dressing
Potato salad

Waldorf Coleslaw

5 to 6 cups shredded cabbage
½ cup dried cranberries or raisins
⅓ cup pecans
1 Golden Delicious apple, cubed
¾ cup mayonnaise
2 tablespoons sugar

1. Combine first 4 ingredients in a large mixing bowl.

2. Combine mayonnaise and sugar until well mixed. Add to cabbage mixture and toss to coat. Cover and chill at least 30 minutes before serving. Makes 6 to 8 servings.

Needless to say, there are many versions of coleslaw. Everyone has their own idea of what a coleslaw should be, but the one constant is that you must use raw cabbage. You can then add your favorite combination of ingredients and your choice of dressings.

Easy Family Cole Slaw

4 cups shredded cabbage
½ cup raisins
½ cup mayonnaise
1 tablespoon milk
1 tablespoon sugar
Salt and pepper to taste

1. Combine cabbage and raisins. In small mixing bowl, combine remaining ingredients and pour over cabbage; mix well. Cover and chill at least 30 minutes before serving. Makes 4 to 6 servings.

We could make a different salad everyday and still not exhaust the possibilities. Unfortunately, it is easy to get into a rut and make the same tossed green salad with perhaps a few assorted vegetables thrown in. We are also purchasing a lot of salad dressings at the store.

Commit yourself to making one new salad and one new salad dressing recipe a week. Then choose your favorites that you'll want to make again and again.

Honey Mustard Salad

- ¼ cup mild-flavored honey
- ¼ cup oil
- 1 tablespoon red wine vinegar
- ¼ teaspoon dry mustard
- ⅓ cup coarsely chopped walnuts
- 6 cups assorted greens

1. Combine first 4 ingredients. Cover and chill.

2. When ready to serve, combine walnuts and salad greens. Drizzle with just enough dressing to lightly coat. Makes 4 servings.

Pear & Gorgonzola Cheese Salad

- 8 cups assorted salad greens
- 1 small red onion, thinly sliced
- ½ cup pecan halves
  Purchased dressing or Raspberry Vinaigrette on page 296
- 1 pear, thinly sliced
- 6 tablespoons crumbled Gorgonzola cheese

1. Combine salad greens, onion and pecans in a large mixing bowl. Toss with just enough dressing to lightly coat. Spoon onto plates. Arrange 2 to 3 pear slices on each salad, then sprinkle with 1 tablespoon Gorgonzola cheese. Makes 6 servings.

Ham Salad

2 cups (8-ounces) cooked ham, ground
1 teaspoon prepared mustard
3 tablespoons sweet pickle relish
½ cup diced Cheddar cheese
½ cup mayonnaise (approximately)

1. In a small mixing bowl, combine first 4 ingredients. Add enough of the mayonnaise to moisten. Makes about 2 cups.

Serve on a bed of lettuce as a salad or on toasted bread for a sandwich. To make the salad go a little further, add 1 to 2 hard-boiled eggs, chopped.

Broccoli Bean Salad

4 cups broccoli florettes
4 plum tomatoes, chopped
1 can (8¾-ounces) garbanzo beans, drained
1 small red onion, sliced
1 cup (4-ounces) Monterey Jack cheese, cubed
¾ cup Italian style dressing

1. Combine first five ingredients in a large bowl. Toss with just enough dressing to lightly coat. Cover and chill at least 2 hours. Makes 6 to 8 servings.

The dressing makes the salad, so choose a brand you really enjoy, or better yet, make your own.

Broccoli Pasta Salad

2 cups small shell macaroni, cooked, cooled
2½ cups fresh broccoli, cooked until just tender
1 cup cherry tomatoes, halved
½ cup (2-ounces) Swiss cheese, cubed
½ cup Italian dressing

1. Combine ingredients in a large bowl, using just enough dressing to lightly coat. Cover and chill. Makes 8 servings.

For a main course salad, add leftover cooked roast beef, ham or chicken.

Broccoli Salad

1	large bunch broccoli (about 5 cups florettes)
1	cup (4-ounces) Monterey Jack cheese, cubed
½	cup sugar
1	cup mayonnaise
2	tablespoons white vinegar
8	slices bacon, cooked and crumbled

1. Place broccoli and cheese in a large bowl.

2. Combine sugar, mayonnaise and vinegar, stirring until smooth. Pour over broccoli and mix well. Cover and chill at least 2 hours before serving, stirring occasionally. When ready to serve, add bacon and toss. Makes 6 servings.

There are so many variations of this colorful, delicious and nutritious salad.

Any of the following are delicious additions: sliced red onion, raisins, sunflower seeds, Cheddar cheese, sliced water chestnuts, almonds, dried cranberries, etc.

My Favorite Potato Salad

6	medium red potatoes (about 5 cups diced)
	Salt and pepper
2	tablespoons chopped green onion
3	hard-boiled eggs, chopped
¼	cup finely chopped celery
1¼	cups mayonnaise (approximately)

1. Cook potatoes in boiling water just until tender. Cool slightly; peel. While still warm, dice potatoes and sprinkle with salt and pepper. Add remaining ingredients; toss gently to mix. Cover and chill several hours or overnight. Makes 8 servings.

For additional color, add 2 tablespoons finely chopped pimiento. If desired, decorate top of salad with egg slices and tomato wedges; sprinkle with cracked pepper.

Waldorf Salad

2   Golden Delicious apples, cut into cubes
1   cup sliced celery
⅓   cup coarsely chopped walnuts
½   cup raisins
2   tablespoons lemon juice
¾   cup mayonnaise

1. Combine first 5 ingredients in mixing bowl. Add mayonnaise and gently toss to coat. Chill until ready to serve. Makes 4 servings.

Still a favorite salad with almost everyone. For a main course salad add 2 cups cooked cubed chicken.

Taco Salad

1   pound lean ground beef
1   package (1¼-ounces) Taco seasoning mix
Shredded lettuce
Shredded Cheddar cheese
Chopped tomatoes
Salsa (or Thousand Island Dressing)

1. Brown ground beef; drain. Add seasoning mix and amount of water called for on package. Bring to a boil; reduce heat and simmer uncovered, 15 to 20 minutes, stirring occasionally, until liquid is absorbed.

2. Place shredded lettuce in salad bowl; top with ground beef, cheese, tomatoes and sauce. Toss lightly and serve. Makes 4 servings.

Variation: *Substitute 1 cup thick and chunky salsa for the seasoning mix.*

Pecan Chicken Salad

2　cups cubed cooked chicken
½　cup pecan halves, broken in half
⅓　cup chopped celery
½　cup mayonnaise

1. Combine ingredients, adding just enough mayonnaise to moisten. Cover and chill until ready to serve. Makes 2 large or 3 small servings.

This recipe works wonderfully as a salad, a sandwich or to fill cream puffs, croissants and cantaloupe halves.
Variation: *Add ⅓ cup dried cranberries.*

Hawaiian Chicken Salad

4　cups diced cooked chicken
½　cup thinly sliced celery
¾　cup crushed pineapple, drained
⅓　cup Angel Flake coconut
¼　teaspoon curry powder (or to taste)
1　cup mayonnaise

1. In large mixing bowl, combine first 4 ingredients. Combine curry powder and mayonnaise. Add enough mayonnaise to chicken mixture to lightly coat. Cover and chill. Makes 4 servings.

I have found that men enjoy chicken salad as much as women do and this recipe is quite popular. One of our local deli's uses cooked rice as an extender, and it is quite good paired with the taste of curry.

Pasta Herb Chicken Salad

1½　cups cubed cooked chicken
2½　cups cooked rotini pasta
1　head lettuce, torn into bite-size pieces
¼　cup grated carrots
½　cup sliced almonds
　　Bernstein's® Creamy Herb & Garlic Italian Dressing

1. Combine first 5 ingredients in a large mixing bowl. Toss with just enough dressing to lightly coat. Makes 4 to 6 servings.

One of our local restaurants serves a delicious pasta salad with chicken. This recipe comes very close to the one they make.

Variation: *Use tri-colored rotini and add artichoke hearts. Also, try tossing with Honey Mustard Dressing on Page 297.*

Strawberry Jello Salad

1　package (3-ounces) strawberry gelatin
1　cup boiling water
1　cup sour cream, room temperature
1　package (10-ounces) frozen strawberries, thawed

1.　Combine gelatin and water; stir to dissolve. Stir in sour cream until blended. Add strawberries. Pour into serving dish or mold and chill until set. Makes 6 servings.

Strawberry Nut Salad

1　package (3-ounces) strawberry gelatin
½　cup boiling water
1　package (10-ounces) frozen strawberries, thawed
1　can (13-ounces) crushed pineapple (and juice)
2　medium bananas, mashed
½　cup chopped walnuts

1.　Combine gelatin and water, stirring to dissolve. Add remaining ingredients. Pour into a 5 cup mold or 11 x7-inch glass dish. Chill until set. Makes 8 servings.

If you have a little difficulty blending in the sour cream, use a rotary beater or a mixer at low speed.

Look in most of the cookbooks in your bookstore and you won't find a "Jello" salad recipe on any of their pages. But look in a Junior League cookbook or a Church or Club cookbook and you will find page after page of contributors' favorite recipes. Rarely will you go to a picnic or potluck where you won't find 2 or 3 salads beautifully presented as someone's favorite dish. So forget about what some cookbook authors say and enjoy your Jello salads. Try some of the recipes on these pages and you might just add a new one to your list of family favorites.

All Seasons Fruit Bowl

6	canned pear halves, chilled
3	medium bananas, sliced
2	small apples, cut into cubes
2	cans (11-ounces each) mandarin oranges, chilled
1½	cups sliced strawberries
1	container (4-ounces) frozen whipped topping, thawed

1. When ready to serve, drain fruit. Slice pears. Combine with remaining ingredients and toss gently to coat. Makes 6 servings.

Honeydew Slices

Honeydew melon, chilled, sliced crosswise into 1-inch slices
Cantaloupe balls
Watermelon balls
Fresh mint leaves (optional)

1. Place a honeydew slice on individual salad plates. Fill each with cantaloupe and watermelon balls. Garnish with mint leaves.

If honeydew melon is too large to make attractive slices, you could use a cantaloupe and make honeydew melon balls. Tuck in a few blueberries or sliced strawberries if you have them.

Peachy Fruit Salad

1	package (6-ounces) strawberry gelatin
4	cups boiling water, divided
1	cup thinly sliced peaches
½	cup thinly sliced bananas
½	cup thinly sliced strawberries

1. Combine gelatin and 2 cups water. Stir until dissolved. Add remaining 2 cups water. Chill until consistency of unbeaten egg white. Gently fold in fruit. Pour into 13x9-inch glass dish; chill until firm. Makes 6 to 8 servings.

Orange Sherbet Salad

1   package (6-ounces) orange gelatin
2   cups liquid (part water and part juice)
1   pint orange sherbet, softened
2   cans (11-ounces each) mandarin oranges, save juice
1   can (8-ounces) crushed pineapple, save juice
1   cup whipping cream, whipped

1. Pour juice in measuring cup; add water to make 2 cups. Heat to boiling in saucepan. Remove from heat; add gelatin and stir until dissolved. Add sherbet; stir until melted. Chill until just slightly thickened.

2. Add mandarin oranges and pineapple; fold in whipped cream. Pour into a ring mold or 11x7-inch flat dish. Chill until set. Makes 8 servings.

If desired, garnish each serving with a combination of fresh fruits such as raspberries, blueberries and/or peaches and garnish with a mint leaf.

Pudding & Fruit Salad

1   package (3.4-ounces) instant vanilla pudding mix
2   cups milk
1   container (4-ounces) frozen whipped topping, thawed
1   can (11-ounces) mandarin oranges, drained
1   can (16-ounces) fruit cocktail, drained
3   bananas, sliced

1. Prepare pudding mix with milk as directed on package. Stir in whipped topping. Add the remaining ingredients. Pour into a 11x7-inch glass dish. Cover and freeze. Remove from freezer 1 hour before serving. Or, instead of freezing, place in refrigerator and chill at least 2 hours before serving. Makes about 8 servings.

This fruit salad is a hit with children (adults too). If you choose not to freeze the salad, it is best served same day made.

293

This is an old recipe and I almost left it out of this edition, but so many people enjoy it I decided it would be a shame not to include it. If you love nuts as much as our family does, you can add ½ cup chopped pecans.

Pistachio Fruit Salad

1 container (12-ounces) frozen whipped topping, thawed
1 package (3.4-ounces) pistachio instant pudding mix
1 can (11-ounces) mandarin oranges, save 3 tablespoons juice
1 can (17-ounces) chunky mixed fruits, drained
2 cups miniature marshmallows

1. In large bowl, combine whipped topping and pudding mix with the reserved juice. Gently fold in remaining ingredients. Cover and chill. Makes 6 to 8 servings.

Pineapple-Strawberry Salad

1 cup fresh pineapple chunks
1 pint strawberries
Lettuce leaves
2 tablespoons oil
2 tablespoons lime juice
1 tablespoon honey

1. Combine pineapple and strawberries; place on lettuce leaves on salad plate. Combine remaining ingredients and drizzle over fruit. Makes 4 servings.

Caesar Salad Dressing

2 large garlic cloves
1 tablespoon stone ground or Dijon mustard
1 teaspoon Worcestershire sauce
¼ cup fresh lemon juice
½ cup olive oil
½ cup freshly grated Parmesan cheese

1. Combine first 4 ingredients in a blender or small food processor and mix until smooth. Slowly add olive oil until blended. Add cheese and blend 2 to 3 seconds. Chill, covered, at least two hours to blend flavors. Makes 1¼ cups.

Creamy Caesar Dressing

1 medium garlic clove
¼ cup fresh lemon juice
1 tablespoon Dijon mustard
1 teaspoon Worcestershire sauce
½ cup freshly grated Parmesan cheese
1 cup mayonnaise

1. Combine first 4 ingredients in a blender or small food processor and process until mixed. (You can do this by hand if you mince the garlic first.) Add cheese and mayonnaise and process just until blended. Cover and chill at least one hour to allow flavors to blend. Makes about 1½ cups.

This is my favorite Caesar salad dressing, the next recipe is a close second. Can make several hours ahead. If desired, add anchovies to taste or toss anchovies with the salad.

Caesar Salads

Although not exactly traditional, you can enhance these wonderful salads by adding your choice of the following items: chicken, turkey, salmon, shrimp, fried oysters, bacon, sun dried tomatoes or rotini pasta.

Betty and I go way back. She is a dear friend and co-worker who has sold almost as many of my cookbooks as I have. Over the years, we have enjoyed exchanging recipes and this one is quite unique, very good, and easy to prepare.

Betty's Parmesan Cheese Dressing

1	cup vegetable oil
½	cup rice wine vinegar
¼	cup egg substitute
6	tablespoons sugar
½	teaspoon pepper
1	cup freshly grated Parmesan cheese

1. Place all the ingredients in a blender or food processor and process until blended and light in color. Chill and store in refrigerator. Makes 2¼ cups.

This dressing is convenient to make ahead and have on hand when you need it.

Dijon Vinaigrette

1¼	cups vegetable oil
⅓	cup Dijon mustard
⅓	cup garlic red wine vinegar
¼	teaspoon freshly ground black pepper

1. Place ingredients in a 2-cup jar or plastic container. Whisk slightly to mix. Cover tightly and shake until blended. Will keep about one week in the refrigerator. Makes about 1¾ cups.

A sweet-tart type of dressing. Can be made in just minutes and chilled until ready to use

Raspberry Vinaigrette

2	tablespoons sugar
¼	teaspoon salt
1	teaspoon Dijon mustard
3	tablespoons raspberry wine vinegar
⅓	cup olive oil

1. Combine all ingredients and mix thoroughly. Makes ½ cup.

Red Wine Garlic Dressing

¼ cup sugar
1 garlic clove, thinly sliced
⅓ cup red wine vinegar
⅓ cup vegetable oil

1. Combine ingredients and chill at least two hours to blend flavors. Remove garlic slices before tossing dressing with the salad. Makes about ¾ cup.

A sweet-sour type dressing that is delicious mixed with Romaine, sliced onion, mandarin oranges and toasted walnuts or pecans. This is the salad dressing I use most often for company. The Poppy Seed Dressing is a close second.

Oriental Dressing

¼ cup sugar
1 teaspoon salt
½ teaspoon freshly ground black pepper
6 tablespoons rice wine vinegar
½ cup vegetable oil

1. Combine ingredients in a jar and shake to mix thoroughly. Let stand to dissolve the sugar. Makes 1 cup.

My favorite dressing to serve on a salad of shredded lettuce, cooked cubed chicken or bacon, and toasted almonds.

Honey Mustard Dressing

1 cup mayonnaise
1 tablespoon sugar
1 tablespoon prepared mustard
1 tablespoon mild-flavored honey
1 teaspoon fresh lemon juice
Dash salt and pepper or to taste

1. Combine all ingredients and beat with a whisk until well mixed. Cover and chill until ready to serve. Makes 1 cup.

This dressing is very good on a tossed salad or a salad with pasta, chicken, lettuce and artichoke hearts. When ready to serve, if dressing is a little too thick, add 1 to 2 teaspoons milk to thin.

This popular recipe seems to be a hit with children as well as adults. The flavor is wonderful teamed with a spinach or romaine salad combined with some fruit, toasted almonds or pecans and pomegranate seeds.

Poppy Seed Dressing

1	tablespoon finely chopped onion
6	tablespoons sugar
½	teaspoon dry mustard
3	tablespoons white vinegar
½	cup vegetable oil
1½	teaspoons poppy seeds

1. Combine ingredients in a small bowl or jar and mix thoroughly using a fork or small whisk. Cover and chill at least an hour to blend flavors. Let stand at room temperature 30 minutes before using. Makes 1 cup.

French Dressing

⅓	cup vegetable oil
2	tablespoons red wine vinegar
2	tablespoons ketchup
¼	cup sugar
¼	teaspoon salt

1. Combine ingredients in a jar or small container with a tight fitting lid. Shake well to blend and dissolve sugar. Makes about ¾ cup.

Quick Roquefort Dressing

❈ ❈ ❈

Combine equal amounts of a purchased Roquefort dressing such as Aunt Marie's® with sour cream. Cover and chill until ready to use.

Roquefort Dressing

8 ounces Roquefort cheese
1 can (12-ounces) evaporated milk
1 quart mayonnaise
2 small garlic cloves, minced

1. Combine Roquefort and milk in top of double boiler. Cook over low heat until cheese is melted, stirring until blended and smooth. Add mayonnaise and garlic. Cover and chill overnight to blend flavors. Makes about 1 quart.

This is a large recipe, but will keep several weeks in the refrigerator. May also be used as a dip with fresh vegetables or chips.

Creamy Italian Dressing

¾ cup sour cream
⅓ cup mayonnaise
¼ cup milk
1 package (0.6-ounce) Italian dressing mix
2 tablespoons sugar
⅛ teaspoon salt (optional)

1. Combine ingredients until well mixed. Chill to blend flavors. Serve over salads or use as a dip with fresh vegetables. Makes about 1¼ cups.

Prepared Thousand Island Dressing is so much better than any of the purchased dressings I have tried. This one is very good on the Mini Chef Salad on page 279.

Thousand Island Dressing

½   cup mayonnaise
¼   cup whipping cream, whipped
2   tablespoons finely chopped pimiento
¼   cup chopped sweet pickles or pickle relish
1   tablespoon finely chopped onion
⅓   cup chili sauce

1. Combine ingredients and chill to blend flavors. Makes about ¾ cup.

Spinach Salad Dressing

A delicious dressing when combined with 1 bunch fresh spinach, thinly sliced red onion rings and cooked crumbled bacon or sliced mushrooms. If using spinach, add to salad and serve immediately.

1   tablespoon sugar
1   tablespoon white vinegar
¼   cup mayonnaise

1. Combine ingredients and mix well. Chill to mix flavors and dissolve sugar. Add dressing to salad just before serving. Makes about ⅓ cup.

Dijon Mustard Sauce

¼ cup Dijon mustard
¼ cup mayonnaise

1. Combine ingredients and mix to blend. Cover and chill until ready to serve. Makes ½ cup.

Serve with the delicious Panko Chicken Dijon recipe on page 221.

Easy Bordelaise Sauce

4 tablespoons minced shallots (or onion)
4 tablespoons butter, divided
2 bay leaves, finely crumbled
1 cup Burgundy wine
5 teaspoons cornstarch
1½ cups canned condensed beef broth or bouillon (undiluted)

1. In saucepan, sauté shallots in 2 tablespoons of the butter until tender but not browned. Add crumbled bay leaves and wine; simmer over medium heat until reduced to about one-third its original volume.

2. Combine cornstarch and about ¼ cup beef broth, mixing to form a smooth paste. Stir into wine mixture along with remaining beef broth. Cook, stirring frequently, until sauce thickens. Add remaining 2 tablespoons butter. Makes about 2 cups.

Excellent served with steaks or beef fondue. Especially nice with beef tenderloin.

Mock Hollandaise Sauce

½ cup sour cream
½ cup mayonnaise
2 teaspoons fresh lemon juice
1 teaspoon prepared mustard

1. In small saucepan, combine all the ingredients and cook over very low heat until heated through. Makes 1 cup.

So easy. Serve warm over cooked asparagus, broccoli, or green beans. Can be made ahead and reheated.

301

This is just one of several ways that you can prepare portobello mushrooms. They take on an almost meaty texture and can be purchased in your local supermarkets. Serve this recipe over flank steak, grilled steaks or ground beef patties.

Variation*: Substitute a variety of mushrooms for the portobellos.*

This sauce is absolutely delicious served over baked potatoes. Pass the sauce and let everyone pour their own.

Portobello Steak Sauce

2	tablespoons vegetable oil or butter
2	large portobello mushrooms
1	bunch green onions
½	cup beef broth
2	tablespoons Sherry

1. Heat oil in a large skillet.

2. Meanwhile, cut portobellos in half, then in slices. Cut green onions into 1-inch slices. Cook mushrooms and onions in oil, over medium heat, until just tender, 5 to 6 minutes. Add broth and Sherry and bring to a boil. Makes 4 servings.

Cheese Sauce

3	tablespoons butter
3	tablespoons flour
1	cup milk or half and half
½	cup (2-ounces) Cheddar cheese, shredded
½	cup (2-ounces) American cheese, shredded
1	to 2 tablespoons Sherry

1. Melt butter in saucepan; stir in flour and cook 2 minutes, but do not allow to brown. Remove from heat and add milk; stir until smooth. Cook over low heat, stirring constantly, until thickened.

2. Add cheese and sherry; stir until cheese is melted and sauce is hot, but do not allow to boil. Makes 1½ to 2 cups.

Mustard Sauce

    1   cup whipping cream, whipped
    ½   cup mayonnaise
    ¼   cup prepared mustard

1. Combine ingredients; cover and chill at least 2 hours to blend flavors. Makes about 1¼ cups.

Serve with ham. Can make day ahead and store in refrigerator until ready to use.

Snappy Horseradish Sauce

    ½   cup sour cream
    ¼   cup mayonnaise
    1½ teaspoons prepared horseradish
    ¼   teaspoon onion salt
    ¼   teaspoon garlic salt

1. Combine ingredients and mix thoroughly. Cover and chill at least 1 hour to blend flavors. Makes ¾ cup.

For that special dinner, fill large mushroom caps with sauce; garnish with finely chopped chives or green onions and bake at 325° for 10 to 15 minutes. Serve on dinner plate with prime rib, roast beef, etc.

Tartar Sauce

    ¾   cup mayonnaise
    1   teaspoon finely chopped or grated onion
    1   tablespoon finely chopped fresh parsley
    1   tablespoon finely chopped sweet pickle

1. Combine ingredients; cover and chill at least 1 hour to blend flavors. Makes 1 cup.

Cream Fraiche is good served over fresh fruit, especially strawberries, and over fruit desserts and molded salads. It can be sweetened and flavored with vanilla. In some recipes, it can also be substituted for sour cream, and will not curdle if brought to a boil

Clarified butter will not burn as easily as plain butter. Use to sauté fish, chicken, chops, French toast, etc.

This is an easy sauce to prepare and has a delightful touch of onion flavor. Start the sauce when you put the water on for the pasta. They should be ready about the same time.

Cream Fraîche

> 1 cup heavy whipping cream
> 1 cup sour cream

1. Combine heavy cream and sour cream in a small bowl. Cover loosely with plastic wrap and let stand at room temperature, overnight or until thickened. Bowl should be placed in a warm area of the kitchen.

2. Cover and refrigerate until well-chilled before serving. Makes 2 cups.

Clarified Butter

> 1 pound butter

1. Melt butter in a small saucepan. Pour melted butter into a glass measuring cup; let stand. Skim off foam. Carefully pour off butter and discard the milky sediment that accumulates on the bottom. Refrigerate and use as needed. Makes about 1½ cups.

Alfredo Sauce

> 1 tablespoon butter
> ½ small onion, thinly sliced
> 2 cups heavy whipping cream
> 2 tablespoons freshly grated Parmesan cheese
> Salt and freshly ground pepper to taste

1. Melt butter in a medium saucepan. Add onion and cook until tender. Add cream and bring to a boil. Add Parmesan cheese, salt and pepper. Reduce heat and simmer about 20 minutes or until sauce has thickened. Makes about 1½ cups sauce. Makes enough sauce to coat 10 to 12 ounces of fettuccine or linguine.

White Sauce

Sauce	Butter	Flour	Salt	Pepper	Milk
Thin	2 tbsp.	2 tbsp.	1 tsp.	$1/4$ tsp.	2 cups
Medium	4 tbsp.	4 tbsp.	1 tsp.	$1/4$ tsp.	2 cups
Thick	8 tbsp.	8 tbsp.	1 tsp.	$1/4$ tsp.	2 cups

Melt butter in a heavy saucepan over low heat. Stir in flour, salt, and pepper until well blended. Remove from heat. Add milk all at once and stir until blended. Return to heat and cook, stirring constantly, until thickened and smooth. Makes 2 cups.

Family Favorite Barbecue Sauce

½   cup firmly packed brown sugar
1   cup ketchup
2   tablespoons Worcestershire sauce
3   teaspoons prepared mustard
¼   cup fresh lemon juice

1. Combine ingredients and let stand at least an hour to blend flavors. Makes 1¾ cup.

Sauces

❧

A good sauce recipe can add moisture to, baste and enhance the flavor of the food it accompanies. Some of us wouldn't think of "barbecuing" without using a sauce to baste the meat or chicken. A tender cut of meat cooked to perfection can stand alone, but the right sauce can make it memorable. The Mustard Caper Sauce on page 171 is so good I have had guests ask for, not seconds on the meat, but seconds on the sauce.

Serve with Chicken Nuggets, Chicken Wings, Egg Rolls, etc.

Sweet and Sour Sauce

1   can (6-ounces) pineapple juice
¼   cup apple cider vinegar
¼   cup finely packed light brown sugar
1   tablespoon cornstarch

1. Combine ingredients in a small pan. Mix well to dissolve the sugar and cornstarch.

2. Cook over medium heat until mixture thickens, stirring frequently with a whisk. Makes ¾ cup.

Stir-Fry Sauce

1   teaspoon cornstarch
¾   teaspoon sugar
1½   teaspoons wine vinegar
2   teaspoons water
2½   tablespoons soy sauce
      Dash Tabasco

1. Combine ingredients and mix well. Use as a stir-fry sauce for: beef, pork, chicken, vegetables, etc.

Pizza Sauce

¼   teaspoon garlic powder
¼   teaspoon oregano
½   teaspoon basil
½   cup grated Parmesan cheese
1   can (8-ounces) tomato sauce

1. In small mixing bowl, combine all the ingredients and mix well. Makes about 1 cup.

Chinese Beef Marinade

    1   teaspoon cornstarch
    2   teaspoons soy sauce
    1   teaspoon sugar

1. Combine cornstarch and soy sauce, mixing until smooth. Stir in sugar.

Easy Steak Marinade

    ¼   cup soy sauce
    ¼   cup vegetable oil
    2   tablespoons fresh lemon juice
    1   tablespoon light brown sugar
    ¼   teaspoon garlic salt
    ⅛   teaspoon oregano

1. Combine ingredients in a small mixing bowl, stirring to blend. Use to marinate sirloin, chuck and flank steaks. Cover and marinate in refrigerator several hours, turning occasionally.

I first learned about this recipe in a Chinese cooking class I took years ago. Use this marinade to tenderize beef for some of your favorite stir-fry recipes. This is more of a meat tenderizer than an actual marinade. It works especially well on less tender cuts of meat such as round steak, but also works with other cuts as well. This is a small recipe but sufficient for about 1 pound of meat. The meat should be thinly sliced across the grain, then tossed with the marinade. Allow to marinate 2 to 3 hours in the refrigerator.

Never use a sauce, in which raw meat, poultry or fish has been marinated. If you plan to use some of the marinade as a table sauce, remove the amount neeeded first, then marinate the meat in the remaining sauce.

As for basting cooked foods, always bring the liquid used for marinating to a full boil in order to kill any harmful bacteria lurking in the sauce, then you can safely baste.

To be absolutely safe, I prefer to remove enough marinade for the table and basting sauce before marinating the meat in the remaining sauce.

Make your own salsa from garden fresh vegetables. Serve as a dip or as a topping for meats, salads and hamburgers.

First we had tomato based salsas. Then we started adding corn, black beans and olives. Now we have fruit based salsas which are wonderful served with flank steak, chicken, turkey, ham or tortillas.

Salsa

3	cups chopped Rome tomatoes
¼	cup chopped onion
1	can (4-ounces) chopped green chilis
1	tablespoon oil
1	tablespoon apple cider vinegar
¾	teaspoon salt

1. In medium mixing bowl, combine ingredients and mix well. Cover and chill several hours to blend flavors. Makes 3½ cups.

Pineapple-Strawberry Fruit Salsa

1	can (8-ounces) pineapple tidbits or ¾ cup
¾	cup chopped fresh strawberries
2	tablespoons finely chopped green pepper
1	tablespoon fresh lime juice
1	tablespoon apricot preserves

1. Combine ingredients; cover and chill until ready to serve. Makes 1¾ cups.

Corn-Tomato Salsa

1	cup fresh or frozen corn
1	cup chopped tomatoes (seeds removed)
¼	cup sliced green onions
1	small fresh jalapeño pepper, seeded and finely chopped
1	tablespoon chopped cilantro
1	tablespoon white wine vinegar

1. In a medium bowl, combine all the ingredients. Cover and chill until ready to serve. Makes 2¼ cups.

Orange Cream Cheese

    1   package (8-ounces) cream cheese, softened
    ¾   cup sifted powdered sugar
    1   tablespoon frozen orange juice concentrate
    1   tablespoon grated orange peel
    1   tablespoon Grand Marnier Liqueur

1. In mixer bowl, beat the cream cheese until smooth. Add remaining ingredients and mix until blended. Cover and chill. Makes 1¼ cups.

Serve with sweet-type crackers or muffins, French toast and pancakes.

Honey Butter

    ½   cup butter
    ¼   cup honey
    2   teaspoons freshly grated orange peel

1. Whip butter until fluffy. Gradually add honey and orange peel; mix until blended. Makes about ¾ cup.

To substitute, use fresh lemon peel for the orange peel. Serve on breads and French toast.

Chunky Applesauce

    5   large Golden Delicious apples, about 12 cups
    5   large Rome apples
    ¾   cup sugar
    ½   teaspoon cinnamon
    Dash ginger
    5   large strips orange peel

1. Peel, core and slice apples into ¼ to ½-inch slices. Put apples and remaining ingredients in a large heavy stockpot. Add ½ cup water. Cover and simmer 45 to 60 minutes or until apples are just tender. Don't let the apples get too soft, unless you prefer them that way. Remove from heat and discard orange peel. Let cool. Store in refrigerator. Makes about 5 cups.

You'll never want to buy applesauce again. See Slow Cooking section to make it in your slow cooker.

309

Orange-Raisin Ham Sauce

⅔ cup orange juice
2 tablespoons cornstarch
⅛ teaspoon ground allspice
½ cup orange marmalade
1 cup raisins

1. In small saucepan, combine first 3 ingredients along with 1 cup water. Heat, stirring constantly, until mixture thickens. Stir in marmalade and raisins and heat through. Makes 2 cups.

A delicious relish-jam recipe to serve on breads or with pork or ham. When in season, freeze fresh cranberries and you can prepare the relish year 'round.

Orange-Cranberry Relish

1¾ cups (6-ounces) fresh cranberries, coarsely chopped
1 jar (18-ounces) orange marmalade
2 tablespoons Grand Marnier

1. Combine ingredients in a medium saucepan. Cook on medium heat, stirring occasionally until cranberries are soft, about 10 to 15 minutes. Makes about 2 cups.

This relish makes a wonderful gift during the holidays. Spoon into small decorative jars and tie with raffia or ribbon.

Whole Berry Cranberry Sauce

1 pound fresh whole cranberries
2 cups sugar
½ cup apricot jam or preserves
¼ cup fresh lemon juice

1. Wash cranberries; discard the not so good ones. In large saucepan, combine sugar and ¾ cup water. Bring to a boil and cook 3 to 4 minutes. Add cranberries and cook 6 to 8 minutes. Cranberries will burst, cause a popping sound and will become transparent.

2. Remove from heat and stir in apricot jam and lemon juice. Cover and chill before serving. Mixture will be a little thin but will thicken as it cools. Makes about 4 cups.

Serve with turkey dinner or hot or cold turkey sandwiches.

Caramel Sauce

½   cup butter
¾   cup light corn syrup
1   can (14-ounces) sweetened condensed milk
1½ cups packed light brown sugar

1. Combine ingredients in a heavy medium saucepan. Cook over medium heat, stirring frequently, until sugar is dissolved. This should take about 8 to 10 minutes. Makes 3¼ cups.

Delicious! The best description I know for this easy versatile sauce. You can use the sauce over ice cream, cake and some cookie recipes. How about over baked apples or as a dip for fresh fruit.

Chocolate Sauce

½   cup butter
4   squares (1-ounce each) unsweetened chocolate
3   cups sugar
1   teaspoon vanilla extract
1   can (12-ounces) evaporated milk

1. Melt butter in top of double boiler. Add chocolate squares and heat until melted, stirring to blend. Add sugar, ¼ cup at a time, stirring until sugar is moistened (it will become quite thick and dry at this point). Stir in vanilla.

2. Add milk a little at a time, stirring to mix. Pour into a jar and store in refrigerator; sauce will thicken as it sets. Serve hot or cold. Makes 4 cups.

This sauce is somewhat less expensive to make than the one on page 312. It is a very good sauce and makes a lot, which still doesn't last very long in my house.

Chocolate Sauce Supreme

2   cups heavy cream
2   cups semisweet chocolate chips

1. Pour cream into a heavy medium saucepan. Over medium heat, bring to a boil. Remove from heat; add chocolate chips and stir quickly until chocolate is melted and sauce is smooth.

2. Pour into a container; cover and store in refrigerator. Makes 2½ cups.

    Hot Chocolate: Spoon about 4 tablespoons chocolate sauce (or to taste) in a 12-ounce mug. Fill with milk and microwave about 1½ minutes or until desired temperature.

Keep this sauce on hand during the cold winter months when hot chocolate and snow are a match made in heaven. You can also use this recipe for delicious chocolate milk and of course as an ice cream topping.

Tip: *For best results use a good brand of chocolate chips. Do not use ultrapasteurized cream or milk chocolate chips.*

Maple Flavored Syrup

½   cup firmly packed light brown sugar
1   cup light corn syrup
1   tablespoon butter
¼   teaspoon maple flavoring (Mapleine)

1. Combine ingredients in a small saucepan along with ½ cup water. Cook over low heat to dissolve sugar; simmer 5 minutes. Serve or cool and store in refrigerator until ready to use. Makes 1¾ cups.

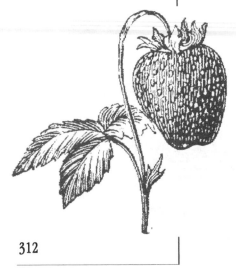

Brown Gravy

2 tablespoons butter
½ teaspoon sugar (for browning)
2 tablespoons flour
1 cup beef broth
 Salt and pepper

1. Melt butter in saucepan over low heat. Add sugar; cook 2 minutes, stirring occasionally. Add flour; cook about 3 minutes or until flour is lightly browned. Add broth, stirring until smooth. Add salt and pepper to taste. Cook over low heat 5 minutes, stirring frequently until thickened. Makes 1 cup.

Use this recipe to make a gravy to serve with left-overs. Additional seasonings such as minced onion, garlic powder, celery salt, etc. can be added. If a darker gravy is desired, stir in a few drops of Kitchen Bouquet.

Cream Gravy

4 tablespoons fat, from frying chicken (or other meats)
4 tablespoons flour
2 cups milk
 Salt and pepper

1. Leave 4 tablespoons fat in pan along with the crusty bits that stick to the bottom. Heat until hot. Stir in flour and cook until brown and bubbly, stirring constantly.

2. Add milk and continue cooking, stirring frequently, until gravy is thickened, about 5 minutes. Add salt and pepper to taste. Makes 2 cups.

Tip: If gravy is too thick, stir in a little milk. If too thin, add a little flour mixed with a small amount of water.

If you don't have 4 cups turkey stock, add water to make up the difference. If too thin, stir in additional flour mixed with a small amount of water or stock.

Add diced cooked turkey to leftover gravy. Reheat and serve over mashed potatoes, rice or noodles.

Turkey Gravy

½   cup fat drippings
½   cup flour
4   cups turkey stock (from turkey or from cooking giblets)
Salt and pepper

1. Remove turkey from oven and pour meat juices into a large measuring cup. Fat will rise to the top. Pour off ½ cup fat into a medium saucepan. Discard remaining fat, but save the turkey stock.

2. Reheat the drippings over meduim heat. Stir in flour and cook until lightly browned. Add 4 cups turkey stock. Cook over medium heat, stirring frequently, until thickened and smooth. Season with salt and pepper. Makes 4 cups.

Roast Pan Gravy

¼   cup fat from roast
¼   cup flour
2   cups liquid (meat juices plus water or broth)
Salt and pepper

1. Remove roast and keep warm. Pour meat juices into a large measuring cup, leaving crusty bits in pan. Skim off fat, reserving 4 tablespoons. Return reserved fat to pan and heat until bubbly. Stir in flour. Cook over low heat, stirring frequently, until mixture is thickened.

2. Remove pan from heat. Add 2 cups liquid all at once; stir to mix well. Return to heat and bring to a boil. Reduce heat and simmer 3 to 4 minutes, stirring frequently until thickened. Add salt and pepper to taste. Makes 2 cups.

Vegetables

Stir Fry Asparagus

1 pound fresh asparagus
2 tablespoons oil
⅛ inch slice fresh ginger
2 teaspoons soy sauce
¼ cup chicken broth or bouillon
½ teaspoon cornstarch

1. Wash asparagus and break end off where it snaps easily. Cut diagonally into 1-inch pieces. Place in rapidly boiling water; remove from heat and let stand 4 minutes. Drain.

2. Heat oil in a large skillet or wok. Add ginger and sauté about 1 minute; remove. Add asparagus to skillet and heat through.

3. Meanwhile, combine remaining ingredients in a small bowl, stirring to dissolve the cornstarch. Add to asparagus and simmer 2 to 3 minutes or until asparagus is just crisp tender. Makes 3 to 4 servings.

Variation: *Use fresh broccoli rather than asparagus. If desired, add sliced water chestnuts.*

Asparagus & Bacon

1 pound asparagus, using thin stalks
Italian Dressing
4 slices bacon, cooked, crumbled

1. Wash asparagus; break off where it snaps easily. Place in skillet with hot water to cover. Cook over medium heat until crisp tender – do not overcook. Remove immediately and drain thoroughly.

2. Toss with just enough dressing to lightly coat. Cover and chill until ready to serve. Place on serving dish and sprinkle with bacon. Makes 4 servings.

You will hear rave reviews every time you serve this dish and it couldn't be easier to make. Only three ingredients, and you could even omit the bacon and use just two ingredients. It can be easily doubled and can be made a day ahead. Serve as a side dish or as a salad. Use your favorite dressing.

A colorful green vegetable is the perfect side dish for your favorite family or company meal.

Asparagus with Butter Sauce

1 pound fresh asparagus
1 cup chicken broth
3 tablespoons butter
3 tablespoons sliced almonds

1. Wash asparagus; break off where it snaps easily. Place in medium skillet. Add chicken broth and bring to a boil. Reduce heat, cover and cook 6 to 8 minutes or until just crisp tender.

2. Meanwhile, lightly toast almonds in butter. Remove asparagus from skillet and drain. Place in serving dish and cover with butter sauce. Makes 4 servings.

This is a colorful dish to serve for the holidays, but equally as good year 'round.

Asparagus & Red Peppers

1¼ pounds fresh asparagus
½ small red pepper, cut into narrow strips
1 tablespoon butter
Dash of freshly ground black pepper
1 teaspoon freshly grated
Parmesan cheese

1. Wash asparagus; snap off ends where they break easily. Place asparagus and pepper strips in steamer basket. Cover; steam over hot water, 5 to 7 minutes or until just crisp tender.

2. Place in serving dish. Gently toss with butter. Sprinkle with pepper and Parmesan. Makes 4 servings.

Green Beans with Almonds

1   pound cooked green beans or 1 can (14.5 ounces)
⅓   cup thinly sliced celery
¼   cup slivered almonds
2   tablespoons butter
Salt and pepper

1. In medium skillet, sauté celery and almonds in butter until celery is tender and almonds are toasted. Add beans and heat through. Add salt and pepper to taste. Makes 4 servings.

Deviled Green Beans

1   pound cooked green beans or 1 can (14.5-ounces)
⅓   cup chopped onion
3   tablespoons butter
1   tablespoon prepared horseradish
1   tablespoon prepared mustard

1. In medium skillet, cook onion in butter until soft. Add horseradish and mustard. Add green beans and toss to coat. Cook until heated through. Makes 4 servings.

Variation: Add sliced mushrooms or water chestnuts.

Fresh Green Beans

Rinse green beans and trim the ends. Steam 10 to 15 minutes or until tender. Or drop into a large pot of boiling water and cook 4 to 8 minutes or until tender.

Unless you grow your own, "fresh" green beans are hard to find. Don't purchase them unless they feel firm and crisp to the touch. Limp beans are already too old and will not be satisfactory in most recipes.

Fresh green beans are usually preferred over canned, that is, if you can find some that are fresh. Unfortunately, by the time most of us find them at the supermarket, they may be several days old. Check out your local farmer's market and produce stands.

An addition of an 8-ounce can of crushed pineapple, is good. If you have the time, cook and crumble bacon ahead and add to the beans.

German Style Green Beans

4	slices bacon
1	tablespoon finely chopped onion
2	tablespoons red wine vinegar
1	tablespoon sugar
1	pound cooked green beans or 1 can (14.5-ounces)

1. In a small skillet, cook bacon until crisp. Drain, leaving 1 tablespoon of drippings in pan. Add onion and cook until tender.

2. Stir in vinegar and sugar. Crumble bacon and add along with the green beans. Cook until heated through. Makes 3 to 4 servings.

Easy Baked Beans   Oven 325°F

2	cans (16-ounces each) pork and beans
½	cup firmly packed light brown sugar
1	teaspoon dry mustard
½	cup ketchup
6	slices bacon, diced

1. Combine beans, brown sugar, mustard and ketchup. Pour into a sprayed 1½-quart casserole. Top with bacon. Bake 1 to 1½ hours. Makes 6 servings.

Broccoli Stir-Fry

4	cups cut broccoli, florettes and stems
1	tablespoon oil
6	thin slices fresh ginger
1	garlic clove, minced
1	teaspoon sugar
½	teaspoon salt

1. Steam broccoli until tender.

2. Heat oil in a large skillet or wok. Add ginger and garlic. Cook, stirring frequently, about a minute. Add broccoli, sugar, salt and one tablespoon water. Cook, stirring frequently, until heated through. Makes 4 servings.

During the Christmas holidays, add one tablespoon chopped pimiento.

Broccoli with Pecan Dressing   Oven 400°F

7	cups broccoli florettes
½	cup, plus ⅓ cup butter
¼	cup flour
2	cups milk
¾	cup pecans
3	cups herb bread stuffing mix

1. Steam broccoli until it starts to turn a bright green (do not cook until tender). Place in a sprayed 11x7-inch baking dish.

2. Heat the ½ cup butter in medium saucepan. Add flour and mix well. Cook about one minute. Add milk and stir to blend. Cook over low heat, stirring frequently, until thickened. Pour over broccoli.

3. Melt remaining ⅓ cup butter. Combine butter with ⅔ cup water, pecans and stuffing mix; spoon over broccoli. Bake 30 minutes or until heated through and top is golden. Makes 6 to 8 servings.

I love to serve this recipe with ham, mashed potatoes, a favorite jello salad and homemade rolls. A real company pleaser.

Just a touch of lemon gives broccoli that extra flavor it needs to please most appetites.

Note*: Broccoli spears can be cut so they are 4 to 5 inches in length or, for company I like to cut them so the spears are about 2½ inches long.*

Asparagus, broccoli or brussel sprouts can be substituted for the carrots.

Lemon Broccoli

¾   **pound fresh broccoli spears**
1½   **tablespoons butter**
1   **tablespoon fresh lemon juice**
¼   **teaspoon salt**
   Freshly ground black pepper

1. Place broccoli in a sprayed 11x7-inch baking dish. Add about ¼ cup water. Cover dish and microwave 4 to 6 minutes or until broccoli is bright green and just crisp tender. Drain off water.

2. Combine remaining ingredients and microwave until butter is melted. Stir to blend ingredients; pour over broccoli. Makes 4 servings.

Basil Carrots

1   **pound carrots, cut diagonally into ½-inch slices**
2   **tablespoons butter, melted**
2   **tablespoons sliced almonds**
¼   **teaspoon salt**
⅛   **teaspoon pepper**
½   **teaspoon basil**

1. Steam carrots until tender, but still crisp.

2. Combine remaining ingredients. Pour over carrots, tossing to coat. Makes 4 servings.

Company Baked Carrots

Oven 350°F

1   pound carrots, sliced into ½-inch slices
3   tablespoons butter, sliced thin
1   tablespoon packed light brown sugar
½   teaspoon salt
¼   teaspoon cracked pepper

1. Place carrots in a sprayed 1½-quart casserole. Distribute butter pieces over top. Sprinkle with brown sugar, salt and cracked pepper. Cover and bake 45 to 60 minutes or until carrots are tender. Makes 4 servings.

My favorite carrot recipe. For such a simple recipe, it packs a lot of flavor.

Corn Pudding

Oven 350°F

¼   cup sugar
3   tablespoons butter, softened
3   large eggs, lightly beaten
3½   cups cut fresh corn or frozen corn, thawed
1½   cup half and half
½   teaspoon salt

1. In mixer bowl, cream the butter and sugar. Add eggs and mix until blended. Stir in the corn, half and half and salt. Pour into a sprayed 1½-quart casserole. Bake 40 to 45 minutes or until firm. Makes 6 to 8 servings.

A great quick and easy side dish with just a touch of sweetness.

If desired, sprinkle with salt, pepper and Parmesan cheese. An even easier method is to dust slices with flour, brown on both sides; season with salt and pepper.

Fried Eggplant

1   eggplant, cut in ½ to 1-inch slices
2   tablespoons flour
½   teaspoon baking powder
2   large eggs, beaten
3   tablespoon water
    Oil or half oil and half butter

1. Combine flour, baking powder, eggs and water; mix thoroughly. Dip eggplant in batter; fry slowly in hot oil until nicely browned. Turn and brown other side. Cook a few slices at a time, adding more oil when necessary. Do not crowd pan. Makes 4 to 6 servings.

These delicious little gems look attractive served on a plate with grilled chicken, steaks or fish. They look rather unattractive in the pan, but look nice on a dinner plate.

Baked Onion Blossoms   Oven 350°F

4   small sweet onions
2   tablespoons butter, melted
2   teaspoons Dijon mustard
2   tablespoons packed brown sugar
    Coarsely ground black pepper
1   tablespoon chopped parsley

1. Peel onions and trim, but don't cut off the root end, as this is the only thing that will hold the onion together. Cut onion almost to the root, cutting into 8 wedges. Place in a sprayed 8x8-inch baking dish.

2. Combine butter, mustard, and brown sugar. Pour over onions. Sprinkle lightly with pepper. Cover dish with foil and bake 30 minutes. Remove foil; baste onions with liquid. Bake 10 to 15 minutes or until tender. Remove from oven and sprinkle with parsley. Carefully lift a blossom and place on each serving plate. Makes 4 servings.

Onions and Peppers Sauté

    1½   tablespoons oil
    ¼   teaspoon paprika
    ½   red pepper, cut into narrow strips
    ½   green pepper, cut into narrow strips
    2   onions, thinly sliced, separated into rings
         Salt and pepper to taste

1. Heat oil in large skillet. Stir in paprika. Add peppers and onions. Cook, stirring frequently, until vegetables are crisp tender. Depending on how they are used, makes about 4 servings.

Serve with steak and baked potatoes, or with beef or chicken fajitas.

Carmelized Onions

    3   large onions (about 48-ounces)
    1   tablespoon vegetable oil
    1   tablespoon butter

1. Thinly slice the onions and separate into rings. In large skillet or Dutch oven, heat oil and butter and cook onions over medium heat 30 to 45 minutes, stirring frequently, especially the last 10 minutes. Makes about 2 cups.

Note: *I have found that the cooking time can vary considerably, depending on intensity of heat, size and thickness of pan used and the amount and thickness of onion slices. Some recipes say to cook 25 minutes and others say 1½ hours. I prefer a medium golden color, but some prefer a dark brown color. You be the judge as to how long you want to cook them.*

Sautéed Mushrooms

    8   ounces fresh mushrooms, whole or sliced
    1   medium onion, coarsely chopped
    1   garlic clove, minced
    2   tablespoons butter
    1   tablespoon oil

1. Heat butter and oil in a medium skillet until hot (watch carefully so it doesn't burn). Add mushrooms, onions and garlic; cook, stirring frequently, 4 to 5 minutes or until lightly browned. Makes 4 servings.

Bacon Wrapped Baked Potato   Oven 350°F

If desired, split potato open like you normally would, and top with (ahem!) butter, sour cream and chives. Delicious!

EACH POTATO:

1   medium baking potato
Thinly sliced onion slices
Salt and pepper
2   slices bacon

1. Wash potatoes thoroughly. Cut in half lengthwise. Top one half with 4 to 6 onion slices. Sprinkle generously with salt and pepper. Top with remaining potato half.

2. Wrap with bacon slices, making sure all ends are tucked under. Place on baking sheet and bake 60 to 75 minutes or until potato is cooked through. Makes 1 serving.

Au Gratin Potatoes   Oven 350°F

This is one of those stand-by recipes you'll want to make often. It's quick and easy to make and looks beautiful — a nice golden color.

4   to 5 large russet potatoes (8 cups sliced)
¼   cup butter
¼   cup flour
2   cups milk
1   cup (4-ounces) Cheddar cheese, shredded
½   cup grated Parmesan cheese, divided

1. In a medium saucepan, melt the butter; stir in flour with a whisk. Add milk and stir until smooth. Bring to a boil over medium heat and cook, stirring frequently, until thickened. This should be about the consistency of a medium white sauce or gravy. Remove from heat. Add Cheddar cheese and ¼ cup Parmesan cheese. Stir until cheese is melted.

2. Layer half the potatoes and half the sauce in a sprayed 11x7-inch baking dish. Repeat with remaining potatoes and sauce. Sprinkle remaining ¼ cup Parmesan cheese over the top. Cover with foil and bake 1 hour. Remove foil and bake 30 to 40 minutes or until potatoes are tender. Makes 6 servings.

Party Baked Potatoes   Oven 400°F

4   large potatoes, baked
Butter
Salt and pepper
½   cup sour cream
⅓   cup cooked crumbled bacon
¼   cup finely chopped green onion

1. Cut baked potatoes in half lengthwise. Carefully remove potato pulp, leaving ¼-inch thick shell.

2. Whip potatoes with desired amount of butter; season with salt and pepper. Fold in sour cream and bacon. Fill potato shells; sprinkle top with green onion. If necessary, return to oven to reheat. Makes 8 servings.

Grilled Potatoes   Grill

3   large potatoes, peeled
Salt and pepper
1   onion, sliced
2   cups (8-ounces) Cheddar cheese, shredded
½   cup butter, sliced

1. Slice potatoes into ¼-inch slices. Divide potatoes and place in center of 4 large pieces of heavy-duty foil. Sprinkle with salt and pepper. Top with onion , cheese and butter .

2. Make a butcher fold with foil; tightly seal ends. Place on grill and cook 45 to 60 minutes, turning packages several times. Serve in foil. Makes 4 servings.

New Potatoes with Butter Sauce

2 pounds small new potatoes, peeled
¼ cup butter
1½ teaspoons lemon juice
   Salt and pepper
1 teaspoon dried parsley

1. Cook whole potatoes in boiling salted water until tender, about 25 to 30 minutes.

2. Meanwhile, melt butter with remaining ingredients. Drain potatoes; place in serving bowl. Pour butter mixture over top. Makes 4 servings.

Oven French Fries
Oven 475°F

2 large baking potatoes
1 tablespoon oil
¼ teaspoon paprika
   Salt

1. Scrub potatoes, but do not peel. Remove any bruises or green flesh. Cut in half lengthwise; cut each half into 6 to 8 wedges.

2. Place potatoes in a small bowl; sprinkle with oil and paprika. Toss to coat evenly. Arrange potatoes in single layer in a sprayed 11x7-inch baking dish. Bake about 20 minutes, stirring or turning to brown evenly. Cook until tender and lightly browned. Makes 4 servings.

Scalloped Potatoes Deluxe

Oven 450°F

7   medium potatoes, about 8 cups sliced
2   cups whipping cream
Salt and Pepper
¼   cup freshly grated Parmesan cheese, divided

1. Peel and slice potatoes about ¼-inch thick. Place half the potatoes in a sprayed 13x9-inch baking dish. Pour half the cream over the potatoes. Sprinkle with salt, pepper and 2 tablespoons Parmesan cheese. Layer with remaining potatoes, cream, salt, pepper and cheese. Bake about 45 minutes or until golden and potatoes are tender. Watch closely the last 15 minutes and if too brown, cover with foil. Makes 6 servings.

Dinner Hash Browns

Oven 325°F

1   package (24-ounces) frozen hash browns, partially thawed
2   cups half and half
¼   cup butter
¾   teaspoon salt
⅛   teaspoon white pepper
½   cup grated Asiago cheese

1. Arrange potatoes in a sprayed 13x9-inch baking dish. Combine half and half, butter, salt and pepper; heat in microwave or on top of the stove until hot. Pour over potatoes. Sprinkle with the cheese. Bake 40 to 50 minutes or until golden brown. Makes 8 servings.

This recipe is almost too easy to be so good, but it does come at a price. It is quite expensive to make and high in fat. I usually save it for special occasions.

This is also an easy recipe to make for any number of servings. Just layer the dish with the desired amount of potatoes and seasonings. Add cream to almost cover. You shouldn't fill the dish too full or you will have quite a mess in your oven. If desired, you can layer the potatoes with sliced onion, separated into rings. Increase or decrease the cooking time as needed.

Garlic Mashed Potatoes

3   pounds potatoes (about 5 medium-large)
3   large garlic cloves, peeled
¼   cup butter
½   cup milk
     Salt and pepper to taste

Unless you want a stronger garlic flavor, 1 large garlic clove per pound of potatoes is just about right.

1. Peel potatoes; slice each into about 4 pieces. Place in a large pot and cover with water. Add garlic cloves and about a teaspoon salt. Bring to a boil and cook 20 to 30 minutes or until potatoes are tender; drain.

2. Meanwhile, combine butter and milk and heat until butter is melted (this can be done in the microwave oven).

3. Mash potatoes and garlic; add milk mixture, adding just enough to make desired consistency for mashed potatoes (you may not need all of it, depending on the moisture content of the potatoes). Add salt and pepper to taste. Makes about 6 servings.

Criss-Cross Potatoes   Oven 450°F

2   large baking potatoes, halved lengthwise
¼   cup butter, melted
     Salt and pepper
     Paprika

1. Score potatoes in crisscross pattern, making cuts about 1-inch deep, without cutting through skins.

2. Brush with butter. Sprinkle with salt, pepper and paprika. Place on baking sheet and bake 35 minutes or until done, basting occasionally with butter. Makes 4 servings.

Yam and Apple Casserole

Oven 350°F

- 6 yams or sweet potatoes, cooked and peeled (or use canned)
- 6 tart apples, peeled (such as Rome)
- ½ cup butter
- 1 cup sugar
- 3 tablespoons cornstarch

1. Cut yams and apples into ½-inch slices. Layer in a sprayed 3-quart casserole dish, starting with apples and ending with yams.

2. Meanwhile, combine butter and 2 cups water in a medium saucepan and bring to a boil. Mix sugar with cornstarch; add just enough cold water to make a paste. Add to boiling water mixture, stirring constantly. Return to a boil and remove from heat. Pour over yams and bake 50 to 60 minutes or until apples are tender. Makes 12 servings.

This is a large recipe, and is delicious served with turkey or ham.

Candied Sweet Potatoes

Oven 350°F

Canned sweet potatoes, drained
Butter
Brown sugar
Large marshmallows

1. Place desired number of sweet potatoes in a shallow baking dish. Top generously with slices of butter. Sprinkle generously with brown sugar and bake for 1 hour.

2. Remove from oven and top with marshmallows spaced 1-inch apart. Return to oven; bake until marshmallows are puffy and lightly browned.

Some "snob" cookbook writers turn their nose up at this type of recipe (what, marshmallows!), but our family has enjoyed it every Thanksgiving for three generations. If desired, you can cook fresh sweet potatoes and use in place of the canned.

331

This is a great dish for using leftovers such as diced pork, ham or sausage. For variety, add 1 cup bean sprouts and/ or 1 can sliced water chestnuts.

Fried Rice

1	cup uncooked long-grain rice, cooked and chilled
5	slices bacon, cut into ½-inch pieces
1	small onion, chopped
¼	cup soy sauce
1	large egg, beaten
2	green onions, sliced

1. Heat large skillet or wok; add bacon and cook until partially browned. Add onion and cook, stirring occasionally, until tender but not browned. Stir in soy sauce and rice.

2. Push the rice to the sides; pour the egg into the middle. Cook until egg is cooked through, stirring to scramble. Stir egg into the rice along with the green onions. Cook until heated through. Makes 6 servings.

Almond Rice Pilaf

For such a simple recipe, this version of Rice Pilaf using instant rice has become one of my favorite and most often used recipes.

2	tablespoons butter
½	cup finely chopped onion
⅓	cup sliced almonds
2	cups chicken broth
1	tablespoon chopped fresh parsley or 1 teaspoon dried
2	cups uncooked instant rice

1. Melt butter in a medium saucepan; add onion and almonds and cook until onion is soft and almonds are just lightly browned. Add broth and parsley and bring to a boil. Stir in rice. Cover; remove from heat and let stand 6 to 7 minutes or until liquid is absorbed. Makes 6 servings.

Company Rice Casserole

Oven 350°F

3   tablespoons butter
3   ounces Angel Hair pasta, broken into 1-inch pieces
1   cup uncooked long-grain rice
1   can (10¾-ounces) condensed French onion soup
1   teaspoon light soy sauce
1   can (8-ounces) sliced water chestnuts, drained, halved

1. Melt butter in a medium skillet. Add pasta, and stirring frequently, cook until lightly browned. Remove from heat. Stir in remaining ingredients along with 2 cups of water. Pour into a sprayed 1½-quart casserole dish. Bake, uncovered 40 to 50 minutes or until liquid is absorbed and rice is tender. Stir once during last 15 minutes of baking time. Makes 6 servings.

This recipe doubles nicely, but you will need to thoroughly stir ingredients a couple of times during baking. If stirred only once, the rice settles to the bottom and the noodles to the top. It may also be necessary to increase cooking time. Can reheat.

Family Favorite Rice Dish

Oven 350°F

1   tablespoon vegetable oil
2   cups instant rice (do not substitute)
1   can (2-ounces) sliced mushrooms
1   can (10¾-ounces) condensed French onion soup
    Dash of salt and pepper

1. Heat oil in a small skillet. Add rice and cook until lightly browned, stirring frequently.

2. Place rice in a sprayed 1½-quart casserole dish. Add remaining ingredients along with ½ soup can of water. Bake, covered, 45 to 60 minutes or until liquid is absorbed and rice is tender. Makes 6 servings.

Whether being served to family or friends, this flavorful rice dish never fails to please. Our family has enjoyed it for almost forty years. My daughter likes to add pecans or water chestnuts, and for a main dish she adds 12 ounces of cooked sausage.

Minted Petite Peas

1 package (10-ounces) frozen baby peas in butter sauce
¼ cup apple-mint jelly

1. Cook peas according to directions. Add jelly and stir until melted. Makes 4 servings.

When in season, use fresh cooked peas and add a small amount of butter along with the apple-mint jelly.

Snow Peas

8 ounces fresh snow peas
1 can (8-ounces) water chestnuts, drained and sliced
2 tablespoons butter
Dash garlic salt

1. Melt butter in skillet or wok. Add remaining ingredients. Cook until tender, but still crisp. Makes 4 servings.

Snow peas must not be over-cooked or they lose that nice crunch we so enjoy.

Zucchini Tomato Casserole   Oven 350°F

2 medium zucchini, sliced
Salt and pepper
1 medium onion, thinly sliced
1 green pepper, thinly sliced
2 tomatoes, sliced
1 ½ cups (6-ounces) Cheddar cheese, shredded

1. Preheat oven to 350°F.

2. Place zucchini slices in a sprayed 2-quart deep casserole dish; sprinkle with salt and pepper. Separate onion slices into rings and spread on top of zucchini. Top with green pepper rings and tomato slices. Sprinkle with cheese. Bake, uncovered 60 minutes. Makes 6 servings.

Tip: This is an attractive dish to serve with almost anything. If you want the vegetables crisp tender, watch baking time carefully; if you prefer the vegetables soft and juicy, cook a few minutes longer.

Baked Acorn Squash

Oven 375°F

Acorn squash
Butter
Light brown sugar
Nutmeg

1. Cut squash in half; remove seeds. Place a generous dab of butter in each cavity. Sprinkle with brown sugar and nutmeg. Place in shallow baking dish; bake 45 minutes or until tender. Makes 2 servings.

Vegetable Stir-Fry

3   tablespoons butter
1   medium onion, cut into wedges, separated
1   cup sliced carrots
1½ cups fresh broccoli pieces
1½ cups sliced fresh mushrooms
3   tablespoons sherry

1. Heat butter in large skillet or wok. Add onion and carrots. Cook until crisp tender. Add remaining ingredients and cook, stirring occasionally, until broccoli is crisp tender. Serve immediately. Makes 4 servings.

See the Slow Cooking section for a convenient way to cook squash.

Stir-fry vegetables are nice because you can use your favorite vegetables or use whatever you happen to have on hand.

Baked Tomato Halves

Oven 350°F

Use the best tomatoes you can find. They must be ripe, but a little on the firm side.

3   large tomatoes
1   cup soft breadcrumbs
2   tablespoons butter
¼   teaspoon dried basil, crushed
Sour cream (optional)

1. Cut tomatoes in half crosswise; place cut-side up in a shallow baking dish.

2. Combine breadcrumbs, butter and basil; sprinkle evenly on tomatoes. Bake 20 minutes or until tomatoes are heated through, but still firm. Top with a dollop of sour cream just before serving. Makes 6 servings.

Sherried Vegetables

An excellent accompaniment to a steak and baked potato dinner.

2   cups onion, cut into thin wedges
3   tablespoons butter
½   pound fresh mushrooms, sliced
1   small green pepper, diced
3   tablespoons sherry
¾   teaspoon salt

1. In medium skillet, cook onion in butter until crisp tender. Add remaining ingredients; cook until green pepper is tender but still crisp. Makes 4 to 6 servings.

Index

A

B

C

CAKES,

Great Meals Begin With Six Ingredients Or Less

Six Ingredients or Less Cookbook - New revised and expanded edition. Over 600 recipes and 352 pages. Quick and easy recipes from everyday cooking to delicious company entertaining. Sections include: Appetizers, Breads, Cookies, Desserts, Beef, Poultry, Vegetables and many more.

Six Ingredients or Less Light & Healthy - There are 224 pages devoted to great cooking your family will love, and they'll never know the recipes are good for them. Recipes include nutritional analysis for calories, fat grams, cholesterol, sodium, etc.

Six Ingredients or Less Pasta and Casserole - A 224 page cookbook of today's busy lifestyles. The original and lowfat version is given for each recipe.

Six Ingredients or Less Slow Cooker - 224 Pages of Quick and Easy stress free meals by letting the Slow Cooker do the work for you.

If you cannot find our cookbooks at your local store, you can order direct. Copy or fill out the order blank below and return, with your check, money order, VISA or MC number to:

SIX INGREDIENTS OR LESS
PO BOX 922
Gig Harbor, WA 98335
1-800-423-7184

Remember, Cookbooks Make Great Gifts!

Six Ingredients or Less	(___) # of copies	$16.95 each	$ _____
Six Ingredients or Less Light & Healthy	(___) # of copies	$12.95 each	$ _____
Six Ingredients or Less Pasta & Casseroles	(___) # of copies	$14.95 each	$ _____
Six Ingredients or Less Slow Cooker	(___) # of copies	$14.95 each	$ _____
Plus Postage & Handling (First book $3.25, each add't book, add $1.50)			$ _____
Washington residents add 8.5% sales tax or current tax rate			$ _____
Total			$ _____

Please Print or Type
(Please double-check addition, differences will be billed)

Name _____ Phone ( ) _____

Address _____

City _____ State _____ Zip _____

MC or Visa _____ Exp _____

Signature _____

Check out our web site www.sixingredientsorless.com

About the Author

✒

Carlean Johnson, mother of four, resides in scenic Gig Harbor in the Puget Sound area of Washington state. For as long as she can remember, cooking and experimenting with recipes has been her hobby.

Six Ingredients or Less was first written 20 years ago and has stood the test of time. This is now the second revision and it has been expanded and updated to reflect today's cooking needs.